EXPLAINING AND ARGUING

The Social Organization of Accounts

CHARLES ANTAKI

SAGE Publications

London · Thousand Oaks · New Delhi

First published 1994

 SAGE Publications Ltd
6 Bonhill Street
London EC2A 4PU

SAGE Publications Inc
2455 Teller Road
Thousand Oaks, California 91320

SAGE Publications India Pvt Ltd
32, M-Block Market
Greater Kailash - I
New Delhi 110 048

British Library Cataloguing in Publication data

Antaki, Charles
  Explaining and Arguing: Social Organization of Accounts
  I. Title
  302.224

ISBN 0–8039–8605–X
ISBN 0–8039–8606–8 Pbk

Library of Congress catalog card number 94–66632

Typeset by Type Study, Scarborough
Printed in Great Britain by the Cromwell Press Ltd,
Broughton Gifford, Melksham, Wiltshire

For my parents

Contents

Acknowledgements

I should like to thank Félix Díaz, Alan Collins and, especially, Ivan Leudar for friendly advice and support as I was preparing this book. The final version benefited from close reading by Derek Edwards, John Rae and Richard Buttny; I owe them a debt of thanks for their improvements, and acknowledge responsibility for the faults that remain.

Notation Conventions

The conversational examples in the book come from a number of sources, not all of which transcribe the talk to the same degree, nor use the same notation conventions. Where the data are first-hand they come from the London–Lund corpus of conversational English (for the provenance of which see the note on p. 42), and there I have left out much of the original tagging. Examples taken from published sources require more respectful handling, and there I have tried more consciously not to distort the data when simplifying the original notation. The following set of conventions captures most of the transcriptions and re-transcriptions in the book. Occasionally, I have kept more specialized transcriptions where they are analytically important (e.g. laughter tokens or intonation contours); they are described when they appear.

(0.2)	timed pause in seconds
(.) *or* . .	untimed short pause
. . . *or* —	untimed longer pause
[	two or more speakers speaking at the same time, e.g.
	A: how was the ⌈movie
	B: ⌊great
=	speech continuing with no discernible break, e.g.
	A: Paul de Wald. Guy out of =
	B: = De Wa:ld yeah I know'm
but–	word cut off abruptly
:	extended sound, e.g.
	A: oh n::::o
italics	emphasis
CAPITALS	greater emphasis
[*door opens*]	transcriber's description/explanation
(but?) *or* ((but))	transcriber's guess
(. . .)	extract begins or ends in mid-speech

1

Introduction

This book is about the kind of talk that can be understood as 'explanatory' in any of its generous variety of senses, stretching up to and over the boundary that explanation shares with reasoning and argument. Explanatory talk in this broad landscape attracts visits from social scientists with very different motivations and expectations. Some believe that in ordinary reasoning they will find the clue to the internal mental representations by which individuals predict and control their worlds. Others expect to come and chart explanations in their visible and necessarily social role of excusing and justifying. Still others believe more grandly that they will be cataloguing the way in which people use explanations and arguments as tools for the construction of social reality itself. Whichever of these views one endorses, the common thread among them is that explanations offer up to the analyst what is, in other stretches of talk, less graspable and obvious: the social reasoning that people go through to make sense of their worlds, and (perhaps) impose that sense on other people.

Nothing in the book is new. I have tried to collect together, in one place, descriptions of the principal ways of studying explanation and its near neighbours so as to make available to students and researchers a handy catalogue of theory and usable technique. I should say that the catalogue is partial, and, even among the approaches I have surveyed, I have leant towards those that are appropriate to the study of explanations as they actually appear in the exchange of talk. That betrays a sympathy with a certain style of theory but does not, I hope, too badly compromise the appreciation of others.

In this brief chapter I shall say something about explanation in a general way, moving towards a sense of explanation as a joint accomplishment rather than a single act. (Argument will be rather a subordinate theme in this introductory section, but I shall have more to say about it in Chapters 8 and 9.) To review explanation so crudely is, of course, brutally to crop an extensive and philosophically ancient debate, but in a book like this that is inevitable: and here in the introductory chapter I shall stick to a manageable précis of only those parts of the story that are most relevant to the book's empirical concerns. The brief sketch of explanation immediately below will bring me on to a description of the chapters in the book, and the particular sort of joint accomplishment each takes as its key.

Explanatory relations

As a preliminary to the sketch of explanation, I should perhaps make the obvious observation that 'an explanation' can't be defined without reference to the thing it's meant to be explaining: it would be absurd to say that the utterance *there are six people for dinner* is an 'explanation' in its own right. It only becomes an explanation when it is prefaced by some other utterance like *why did you cook so much food?* The question is not 'what is an explanation?' but, rather, 'what relation does one utterance have to have to another to qualify as an explanation?' The explanatory relations we shall be seeing much of in this book are of three kinds: those that propose some kind of *cause* for the state of affairs referred to in the question that solicits the explanation; those that *make it plain*; and, most closely related to argument and reasoning, those that *warrant* it.

Explanation as a causal relation

If we look at the classic debate on the explanatory relation we see that it proceeds from the premiss that the explanation should show, in some sense or other, what it was that 'brought about' the thing to be explained. The argument is then over the propriety of causes and reasons as agents which 'bring about' things; and, thereafter, what the best way is of discriminating among subtypes of each (and, indeed, whether they are themselves assimilable to some more overarching concept).

This argument maps onto the debate in that corner of the explanation literature that models ordinary explanation as a description of cause, principally as a manifestation of individuals' beliefs and the way they mentally work out the answer to puzzles about causal candidates. As we shall see in Chapter 2, some social psychologists take a strong line on the answer (and a very full range of the kinds of positions in their debate can be found in Hilton, 1988). But it is better, I think, not to enter the debate on that footing. To think of explanations only as causes and reasons would be to foreclose too early on the issue, and would make this book too narrow in its application. Instead, we should keep the options open and ask what explanations do to 'make plain' more broadly speaking.

Explanation as 'making plain' and warranting

If we pursue this agnostic line and follow Draper (1988), we quickly see that a request to explain can intelligibly be put in front not only of 'why' but of any 'wh-' word (who, what, when, how) – or, indeed, in front of any state of affairs (as in the injunction to *explain unemployment*, say) – without explicitly specifying which of its aspects needs explaining. The list of requests below shows the range. (I should, by the by, warn that the utterances in the list are idealized and stripped of any context, two features we shall have reason to worry about later; but the list will do us for the moment, as it shows the variability of the word 'explain' in reasonably familiar usages.)

Explain why you were late
Explain where you went
Explain how you got there
Explain who you went to see
Explain who Ms Williams is
Explain what you were doing there
Explain the job you've applied for
Explain when the decision will be made
Explain why it is a good job
(after Draper, 1988: 16)

Of that variety of uses of 'explain', only the first request looks as if it would solicit an answer over which the classic dispute between reasons and causes might rage. (Is the explanation *I felt like it* as proper as *fate decreed that it should be so* or *we had an accident*?) But its conclusion would not transfer well to the question of what constituted a sensible answer to the other examples. The answer to the question *explain who you went to see*, for example, might be the simple specification *the employment agency*, or *Ms Williams*; the answer to *explain how you went* might be the description of some mechanism like *I took the bus to the station and then walked the rest of the way*; and so on. None of the explanations to these questions involves 'bringing about'.

If there is anything in common between all of these question and answer pairs, it might be that they all shelter under the dictionary definition of explaining as 'making plain' or 'making intelligible'. If we take explaining in this, rather non-committal, sense, we see that Draper is right to say that, in proper context, just about any utterance can be made to qualify as an explanation. As a quick demonstration, there would be nothing odd about taking a blank phrase (*it's four o'clock*, for example) and forcing it to do explanatory work, either by putting it as a reply to a question which clearly wants something 'making plain', or by simply shortcutting the exercise and putting it into reported speech (*'it's four o'clock', she explained*). Moreover, we should see nothing odd in a question which is apparently orientated to one kind of explanation being satisfactorily answered by a different one: as Rimmershaw (1992) observes after reviewing a range of explanatory exchanges in ordinary talk, explainers take enormous liberties with their replies to even the narrowest and apparently most directive of questions. Thus, for example, the plea *how do you stop a neighbour's cat scratching up your garden?* printed in a newspaper can attract the following replies: *concrete one or the other*; *I am trying short pieces of holly in the ground* and *get a cat of your own* (Rimmershaw, 1992: 247).

The important thing to recall is that this 'making clear' is a relational matter: what makes something a making-plain rather than (or as well as) a mere report of information is its force as a response to some puzzle. But this puzzle has to be something more substantial than a mere lack of information, otherwise we should be extending 'explanation' too widely, allowing *it's half past four* to count as an 'explanation' when it is more simply a flat response to a simple request for the time. Puzzles which require 'making clear' lean towards the 'accountable': social or interpersonal thorns on which something in the moral order has snagged, however temporarily, until it is unhooked and proceedings can continue. I shall be saying more about this in Chapter 4.

A specialized sense of making plain is the warranting that something is the case, or is as the speaker claims it is. To say *it's late, because it's four o'clock* is to explain how it is that it is late: one is showing that something is the case *by virtue of* some evidence. The explanation is some brisk or laborious chain of reasoning that leads (or so the explainer hopes) inevitably to the conclusion that so and so is indeed the case. The explanation has the burden not only of revealing the sense of something, but also of convincing the listener that it warrants some proposition or course of action. This sense of explanation is closest to argument, and, as we shall see in Chapters 8 and 9, is illuminated by logic, rhetoric and argumentation theory.

Context

If we are anxious about what will cover reports of cause, makings-plain and warranting, perhaps the safest thing is to take no strict line on what will count as an explanation beyond the very general principle that it be *some stretch of talk hearable as being a resolution of some problematic state of affairs*. The prototypical case is, of course, the answer to a question that explicitly casts something as problematic and demands its resolution; but the hinterland sweeps away in all directions from the prototype. Thus the question may be implicit, or may be posed by the explainers themselves; the puzzle it signals may be a matter of causality, warrantability, or interested description; the solution offered may be a causal linkage, a reason for action, an excuse, an account or a narrative; and the ensemble may all be bound together by very carefully fitted joints or by the glue of the cooperative principles that hold together any human dealings.

To keep all options open I have used the turn of phrase 'hearable as', rather than the balder 'is', under the influence of the maxim that it is less profitable for the analyst to track down the (given) meaning of an utterance than it is to watch for how it is responded to by those to whom it is addressed or, more generally, to read its significance from its surrounding context taken at some grain of fineness. It would be a mistake, for example, to rely on straightforward lexical markers because explanations can happily be given and understood without being specially or identifiably marked (*I couldn't get through to her, the line was engaged*). Nor do explicit markers discriminate between different kinds of explanation: where they do appear (and the most common one in English is *because*: see Altenberg, 1984) they sometimes mark a causal explanation (*I was late because the car broke down*), and sometimes mark the backing of a claim (*I'm Christian because I was baptized*).

Moreover, we shall often need to know what the explainer has done to trim what he or she says so as to be cooperative: not to say too much or too little, not to say an untruth, not to be irrelevant, and not to be unintelligible (these are references to the cooperative principles outlined by Grice, 1975, of which we shall see much more later). To abide by all these strictures, the explainer has to make a guess at what the person asking for the explanation might already know, or be expected to need to know. So rather than fix on saying that some utterance pair *is* an explanation-giving one, we pull back until we have more of the context in shot so that we can judge whether it would have been reasonable for its audience to have considered it to be so.

The organization of the book

I have organized the book by tracking through the intellectual landscape of the various schools of research which claim expertise in the study of ordinary explanation and explanatory reasoning, or for whom such things are at the nerve centre of what they think is important about social life. We start out in the cognitive heartland of experimental social psychology and push away from its shores into the less static seas of talk, navigating thereafter by the light of explanation (in its various senses) as it is done in ordinary speech (and, occasionally, in written texts).

In Chapter 2 we shall be looking at cognitive social psychology's representation of ordinary explanation as the mental choice among causal candidates: it casts it as a scientific enterprise and represents it as (crudely speaking) the private answer to the question 'why did this event happen?' I shall dig into the roots of its major exponent, *attribution theory*, to see how it took up some, but not all, of its progenitor Fritz Heider's 'common-sense' psychology. I shall also try to show how (as many critics have complained) the kind of things it could tell us about explanation is limited by its perhaps too incautious investment in a certain model of explanation, and in too dead a sense of language and language exchange.

Attribution theory has been revived by the injection of linguistic theory via the 'conversation model', which we shall look at closely in the first part of Chapter 3. The conversation model keeps faith with explanation as an answer to a 'why did such-and-such an event happen?' question, but plays fairer to the wider context by pulling back to reveal that the question does issue from somebody who might have some guessable knowledge about the event. That establishes closer contact between questioner and explainer than did classic attribution theory. The model of explanation is refined from 'why did such-and-such an event happen?' to 'why did this event *and not that event* happen?'

The conversation model's greater respect for linguistic context is an enormous step forward but, once we start taking language seriously, we have to open the debate up to aspects of linguistic exchanges beyond the operation of the principle that talk is cooperative (important as that may be). By the end of Chapter 3 we will have turned to Edwards and Potter's (1992) 'discursive action model' to pull onto the stage a cast of characters to surround the immediate pair of questioner and answerer. To make sense of the ensemble we have to take stock of their relative positions, their navigation about each other and the stagecraft which regulates their exchanges. To break the metaphor: we begin to realize that there are things about explanations which are not fully understandable as private transactions between honest scientists (as even the conversation model of attribution nevertheless insists), but which make more sense as tactical constructions serving not only local, but perhaps social or cultural ends. That knocks down the barriers between explanations to 'why' and all others, and gives us licence for the broad programme in the rest of the book.

In Chapter 4 we take the road to explanation as something that 'does' something; obviously enough, to start off with, the 'doing' of excusing and justifying. The literature on justificatory accounts has a tradition of trying to corral explanations into a taxonomy of various types of exoneration, and we pause to review how well it shepherds the flock, and at what cost. Recalling the advice that we ought to avoid too much abstraction and idealization, we take to task the speech-act theory of language that guides much of the traffic in the accounts area. Instead, we see what can be learnt from attending to the structural organization of the talk.

This moves us on, in Chapter 5, to a fuller account of *conversation analysis* and what it has to say about explanations. On the one hand, it promotes explanations up from their rather inferior status of self-interested tactics to the status of logically necessary clauses in the communicative contract we have with each other. That covers accounts as they feature in a large variety of negotiations about which other theoretical approaches would have little to say. On the other hand, conversation analysis also has something to say about more considered, larger-scale explanations: it shows that, like stories and jokes, they march to certain drumbeats of sequencing and conventional regulation. We will have reason to refer back to the spirit, if not always the technical purity, of the conversation-analytic programme in much of the rest of the book.

In Chapter 6 the accounting is done with a wider palette of cultural reference, and we see how some analysts turn to the formalizations of metaphor and narrative to ground their interpretations of the *social construction* work that accounts do. At this time I reprise the lessons of conversation analysis to offer an account of such storied explanations that tries to free itself from too heavy an investment in cultural interpretation, and commits itself instead to the less taxing, and more public, job of identifying explanatory force through conversational organization.

We had said something, back in Chapter 3, about the power of explanations to construct versions of events, and we take this up in Chapter 7 with a description of *discourse analysis*. Its central notion is that an account does more than merely satisfy a simple request to make something plain: an account, by selecting its vocabulary from available cultural themes and concepts, and by its choice of their arrangement, makes positive claim to a certain vision of the world. The job of the discourse analyst is to discover, by inspection of the vocabulary and its arrangement, what claims speakers are making about the world, and how they are grounding them; and, as at least some discourse analysts might say, who benefits from, and who suffers the consequences of, the world that is thereby constructed.

In Chapters 8 and 9 I shall be rather more explicit than I have been here concerning what it is about argument that manoeuvres such an apparently philosophical discourse into the empirical sights of this book. We turn to explanation in its sense of backing a claim, or warranting one's assertions and judgements, and see that formal models in (certain kinds of) logic and argumentation theory, and in rhetoric, put such explanation squarely into the context of quarrels and arguments.

By the end of the book I hope that I will have demonstrated the range of interests that a study of ordinary explanation can serve. Some of those interests, especially perhaps the social constructionist interest in the way language constitutes reality, would be as well served by studying talk other than explanations as such (though these would seem to have an edge over more neutral exchanges); but others – especially the study of exonerative accounts, on whatever scale – can hardly proceed by analysing anything else. Equally, I hope that I will also have shown that whether one's interest in explanations is as causal reports, exonerations, discursive accounts or claim-backings, understanding the work they do can be helped by inspecting their actual exchange. I shall, throughout the book and in the internal development of most of its chapters, summon up real conversational exchanges as evidence for that claim. The span will reach from the politeness of paper and pencil exercises to the ruder world of raw talk, and we shall see that some of the early problems suggested by abstract analysis fall away to be replaced by more significant and worldly issues when the talk turns real.

2

Attributing Cause

Interviewer: What from your point of view are the causes of unemployment?
Interviewee: I'm sure the world recession has had a lot to do with it, and I
think on top of that the very tight monetarist policies of the
government have exaggerated this to some extent. Whether one
can believe half the effect being caused by the world recession
I'm not sure. I would like to know much more about economics,
but when I think that the professional economists themselves
can't find a uniform approach I wonder if I ever will
(extract from an interview reported in Antaki, 1988: 64)

The interviewer in the talk above has broached a social question of some
complexity, and the man being interviewed is fulfilling his part of the bargain
by responding with a judicious and considered account. What might we want
to know from a social psychological study of the way people solicit and offer
explanations like this? How do they compare with all the other elliptical,
laconic and casual ones that pepper people's everyday dealings with each
other? We should want to know what explanatory vocabulary people use,
when they use it, and to what purpose; what systems of reasoning they
invoke in arriving at explanations from information given or imagined; what
personal, interpersonal and societal constraints affect their giving and
receiving explanations; and how they use explanations to construct and
delimit their social world.

We can't address all these issues at once, though they will gradually
emerge from the shadows over the course of the book. Since we need to take
one thing at a time (at least to start with), then we should begin where
empirical social psychological research is thickest, and go on from there.
That is why the example above turns on explanation as the identification of
'cause'. It illustrates what the cognitive mainstream of social psychology has
taken to be the prototype of explanation, and signals the mechanism by
which it thinks the prototype operates.

This way of representing ordinary explanation – under the umbrella term
'attribution theory' – promised at its inception some thirty years ago to be
fertile and useful for a certain class of explanation and, since then, has
indeed generated prodigious amounts of empirical work. We shall, in this
chapter, concentrate hard on the theory and its history. By the end we shall
have learnt something about the cognitive approach to causal explanations;
but we will also have learnt something of its shortcomings, and they will
serve as pointers towards safer ground.

Attribution theory

The literature on attribution theory is too massive for it to be surveyed in anything like a comprehensive way here, so in this chapter I shall describe the main strata (and what may be the faults) in the steady build-up of attribution theory's account of cognitive process, and I shall say something about its application to social phenomena. Consideration of some of its newer shoots will need to be left over to the next chapter, where I shall have a close look at the 'conversation model' of attribution theory, and see how it can be extended to cover causal attributions in talk. For the moment, though, let us concentrate on the foundations of attribution theory, the vocabulary of ordinary explanation that it bequeathed to social psychologists, and how the functions of explanation have been conceived.

The origins in the work of Fritz Heider

One of the main tributaries which streamed into attribution theory was the notion that people made inferences about the world around them and the people in it. That is to say, that the way that people interacted with the world was scientific, deductive and empirical. This attractive notion was responsible for a great deal of empirical work in person perception and impression formation in social psychology, close cousins in the 'new look' in perception and developmental psychology. It was in this atmosphere that Fritz Heider published his classic contributions to what was to become attribution theory (Heider, 1944, 1958). Heider saw his contribution as being the personalizing of social psychology, a reaction to the social psychology of groups, crowds and other conglomerates, the usual subjects of social psychology in the war years and immediately thereafter. His work on the individual's perception of causality and his analysis of everyday interpersonal language brought into close focus the psychological subject's cognitive apparatus, and turned the psychologist's attention onto the way the ordinary person made sense of the world.

Heider and the basic units of lay psychology

Heider's starting premiss in *The Psychology of Interpersonal Relations* (1958) was that the professional psychologist interested in interpersonal relations should look first at the way in which such relations are embodied in ordinary talk. Ordinary people have rich ways of expressing themselves about what they and their neighbours do, and that expression should be the psychologists' first port of call – but they should not take what they hear at face value. Greatly influenced by positivist philosophy, Heider thought that psychology could never be as scientific as mathematics until it too, like mathematics, had at its disposal a pure stock of unit terms. Ordinary terms needed to be stripped down to basic units, and his book was meant to 'offer suggestions for the construction of a language that will allow us to represent

. . . interpersonal relations. . . . This task will require identifying and defining some of the underlying concepts and their patterns of combination' (1958: 9). He was committed to searching for 'the' meaning of the terms of lay psychology, and to assembling complex combinations from securely identified atoms.

At the very outset Heider gives a linguistic analogy. Suppose we wanted to understand the basics of a set of terms which clustered around the term 'give'. According to Heider, we would go about the task by looking for the root meanings that the set shared and stripping them down to the basics. Thus 'lending', 'borrowing', losing', 'relinquishing' and 'finding' reduce to variations on the simple directional relation between a person (p) and an other (o). Hence to lend is $p \rightarrow o$; to borrow is $p \leftarrow o$. If one could do this for words, reasoned Heider, one might also be able to do it for the narratives of human relationships. As a pre-theoretical example, he takes us through the fable of the fox and the cheese. This could be rewritten as a series of prototypical acts or basic units: the fox 'perceives' the cheese, which 'belongs' to the crow, he 'wants' it, he 'fails' to climb the tree to get it, and so on. Heider's book is then devoted to the explication of what he considers to be a reasonable first pass at the prototypical units – like 'perceive', 'belong' and 'want' – of lay psychology.

In all, Heider identified ten such prototypes out of which the lay psychologist built his or her account of the social world:

> People have an awareness of their surroundings and the events within it (the *life space*), they attain this awareness through *perception* and other processes, they are *affected* by their personal and impersonal environment, they *cause* changes in the environment, they are able to (*can*) and *try* to cause these changes, they have wishes (*want*) and *sentiments*, they stand in unit relations to other entities (*belonging*) and they are accountable according to certain standards (*ought*). (1958: 17)

Combinations of these italicized prototypes made up the social world in the same way that combinations of colour and angle made up the perceptual world. Heider devoted a chapter to most, and two each to 'perceiving' and 'being affected by'; but it was 'causing' that attracted three chapters, and which went on to influence a generation of psychologists.

Heider's view of language and explanation

Heider assumed that the core sense of a word was so powerful that it would overwhelm any variations due to context. Such a belief would be unfashionable now with greater recognition of the cultural variation in allegedly basic units of meaning, and a general move away from lexically based semantics. Yet it was the analogy with which Heider approached talk about human interactions. He thought they could equally be stripped down to core meanings and built up again by a combination of unit terms. It meant that the 'meanings' he identified would always be liable to being overridden by contextual factors out of purely lexical control (and we shall see how this returned to haunt attribution theory later).

Moreover, his picture of what ordinary people counted as a human action did not extend to anything conducted on a purely verbal plane. Paradoxically, although the stimulus for his project was a linguistic analogy, he had no place for his subjects' perception of such linguistic behaviour as promising, threatening, begging and so on. He saw his subjects as being concerned with comprehending their neighbours' behaviour understood as discrete physical actions (rowing, struggling with a weight) and their everyday social transactions understood as given packages (buying a railroad ticket, giving a present and so on). That is to say, though his analysis extended to the linguistic description of acts, it did not recognize acts which were themselves linguistic, setting another fence of restriction around the range of phenomena his successors could expect to explain.

These are general criticisms which give, with the luxury of hindsight, a sense of the understandable blind-spots in what was, after all, a social psychological enterprise meant to stimulate an interest in common-sense psychology. As such, and had subsequent psychologists followed Heider in the broad sweep of his programme, new elements would have been recruited to bring the linguistic apparatus up to date, and the project might have gone on to resemble other mappings of 'common-sense psychology'. These have left social psychology at some distance, and locate themselves on the boundaries of cognitive psychology, linguistics and anthropology. We shall see more of some of these later, especially the work on metaphor (Lakoff and Johnson, 1980). The closest in spirit to Heider is the work of Sabini and Silver (for example, 1982); we shall later come across their criticisms of the line that attribution theory was to take.

But Heider's linguistic analyses were not taken up and the fate of his writings was rather different. One passage will serve as an introduction to two very important latent messages, specifically to do with explanation, which smuggled their way into subsequent psychologists' readings of Heider and became the keynotes of what became known as attribution theory.

> It is an important principle of common-sense psychology, as it is of scientific theory in general, that man grasps reality, and can predict and control it, by referring transient and variable behaviour and events to relatively unchanging underlying conditions, the so-called dispositional properties of his world. (1958: 79)

This passage captures the spirit of what was to become the entire attributional programme. There are three things to say about it. The first is that it makes explanation, or the grasping of reality, a private business. It is a matter of our constitution as ordinary people that we explain, as it were in spite of ourselves, with no particular reference to local context. Where the 'scientist' speaks formally as a scientist, the lay person has no particular role or context, and is simply manifesting her or his 'natural' psychology with the general aim of controlling and predicting his or her world. The ordinary person is as committed to a realist philosophy of the world 'out there' as is the realist scientist. All this idealizes the ordinary explainer. It drives our interests as psychologists inwards, towards the silent mechanisms by which the individual privately grasps at reality, and discourages us from thinking that the individual may be actively and publicly constructing it. As Harris and Harvey (1981) and Abraham (1988) point out, there is a lot more to Heider than this, but that is how posterity dealt with him.

It might be objected that Heider, by ascribing to the ordinary person the scientist's concern to 'predict and control', does indeed acknowledge purpose and local context. One should be able to see individuals using their explanations to predict something happening, and to control the outcome of events. In fact, examples of control and prediction are rare in Heider's account; what are much more common are cases of post-diction and interpretation. Heider speaks much of individuals asking themselves why certain things come to pass – say, why they like Kansas. If they enjoy Kansas more in winter than in summer then they will attribute the reaction to seasonal variation. Such examples are legion in the book. But they do not really approximate the official objective of 'prediction and control' which Heider ascribes to ordinary person and scientist alike. They are, in spite of their advertisement as matters of prediction and control, private reflections.

The account of explanation according to Heider allows two human roles: the scientist and the ordinary person. The scientist is given a role to play and some vocabulary to use. The ordinary person is left undifferentiated, identified only negatively as not being a scientist. This means a starting assumption that the ordinary person is a unitary being, operating with transcendental faculties on a unitary world. It is a conception perfectly in tune with the cognitive psychology that was starting to be so influential in Heider's time. But it was rather perverse to acknowledge that there was such a persona as the scientist and yet deny (implicitly at least) that there were other personae as well: the historian, the debater, the confidence trickster and so on. The ordinary person was not allowed to inhabit such roles or to have at their command such powers of expression; she or he was detailed the role of 'ordinary person' whose failure as a scientist was their complete description. Now the attributionist might argue that these alternative descriptions – the historian and the confidence trickster and so on – are no more than the ordinary person under different hats; that the attributionist's job is to describe 'ordinary-person' cognitive processing, and perhaps later go on to look at how the results of that processing pass through the various extra filters that social roles allow or demand. But to insist that the world is primarily and neutrally seeable through 'ordinary' eyes is to make the huge claim that 'ordinary preception' is the staple fare of knowledge, and that all else is a matter of its various flavourings; this, as we shall be seeing in some detail in later chapters, is far from being obvious, or even plausible.

The third thing to say about the point of view manifested in the passage quoted is that it seems to be saying something empirical about ordinary psychology, namely that it is a search for underlying dispositions, with the intention of controlling and predicting the world. Heider advances no empirical evidence that this is in fact what 'the ordinary person' typically does. It is tempting to believe that, in spite of the quoted passage's implicit inductive discovery that the ordinary person is like the scientist, Heider, in common with his rationalist cognitivist contemporaries, was disposed to deduce the ordinary from the prestigious rationality of the scientific. In other words, it is likely that the claim that people sought out unchanging dispositions was no more than a claim of good faith in ordinary people's ability to reach the heights of rational investigation.

Heider's legacy of reasoning and vocabulary

We might find fault, then, with three things at the very basis of Heider's account of explanations: that they are matters of private, individual business; that they are performed in only one of two possible roles; and that of those two, the role of scientist is the ideal. How dangerous were these three faults in the geological strata that Heider meant to lay down as a foundation for the social psychology of human relationships? As we go through the work of Heider's inheritors, we shall see that they pass unrecognized, but are latent within each generation of theory.

Commentators (for example, Ross and Fletcher, 1985; Hewstone, 1989) pick out four things to mark as Heider's legacy to attribution theory:

1 The emphasis on dispositional causal properties of people.
2 The distinction between such personal causes and things in the environment which might frustrate them (the seeds of the internal/external dichotomy, about which we shall have more to say later).
3 The ordinary tendency to believe that personal dispositions are more causative than are other causal factors.
4 The sketch of J. S. Mill's method of difference as a candidate for the mechanism by which causal factors are weighed.

What is interesting about this list is that it concentrates, reasonably enough, on the positive and fertile proposals that attribution theorists picked out from Heider's work; but it skates over some equally important omissions.

The list is witness to the fact that Heider established the proposition that the lay perception of personal causation is an important element in people's understanding of the social world. In that sense he can be said to have succeeded in his aims. But he is likely to have been chagrined to find that this single proposition gained popularity at the expense of the broader framework into which it was meant to fit, and which gave it sense. The programme of reducing lay psychology to a set of pure prototypes was forgotten in the rush to elaborate this single prototype; the others were ignored and their existence buried under the avalanche of empirical work elaborating in great detail the operation of this one prototype. It is extremely hard to find, in the volumes of attribution theory work after Heider, any reference to causation as a prototypical perceptual unit.

Why was causation more popular than the other nine prototypes? One clue is in Heider's own textual emphasis on causation as being 'of great importance', but there were at least two other terms nearly as favoured, and a case could be made for the investigation of any of the ten. Why then causation? One seductive answer lies in the resonance that this particular aspect of lay psychology had with psychologists' own ways of thinking. Ordinary professional psychologists are trained to be expert in 'what causes human behaviour' and it is understandable that they should want to exploit this expertise in studying how it appears – possibly in corrupt or under-developed form – in the psychology of the untutored lay person. In other words, psychologists, in picking out for special study the ordinary under-standing of personal causation, are playing to their professional strengths.

The most vivid example of this playing to strengths is visible in the way the most schematic of the four proposals – that causal candidates are computed according to Mill's method of difference – grew to be the signal mark of the most widely cited of theories following in Heider's wake.

Perhaps on reading Heider, Kelley recognized his own professional activity in Heider's description of the lay person's attributional reasoning:

> The cause of a difference resides within the variant condition rather than within the conditions common to the diverse instances. . . . In the Asch experiment . . . the variant factor is quickly located in the deviant subject – everybody else sees that the two lines are equal while the subject sees one as longer than the other. Therefore the subject becomes suddenly aware that what he sees has to do with himself in an idiosyncratic way. (Heider, 1958: 69)

In this brief passage Heider ascribes to the individual participant what is essentially the reasoning behind the statistical tests of analysis of variance (or, more properly, co-variance) which forms part of every experimental social psychologist's armoury. If this was indeed the essence of how people reasoned, then, in the absence of a statistician, who better to lay out the formalities of the system than the statistically sophisticated social psychologist?

To take this aspect of lay psychology and make it the keystone of an empirical programme (Kelley, 1967, 1973) was to confirm the view of language and science that had been latent in Heider's face-value conception of the 'ordinary person' and the search for unvarying causes. But attributionists went further than that. Where Heider had at least given the (undifferentiated) ordinary speaker a voice more or less on a par with the scientist, Kelley, by taking the method of difference as the ideal form of reasoning, reduced the speaker to being no more than the scientist's imitator, interested only in reporting the effective cause for a given phenomenon, but not likely to be able to do it very well. At a stroke this rolled up the three faulty threads in Heider's theory into one mass, making the separate strands difficult to disentangle. Now that the previously undifferentiated ordinary person had been equated with a poor scientist, and the search for underlying causes had been reduced to the competent or incompetent application of the analysis of variance, it seemed to the social psychological community that research on ordinary explanations could reach top speed. Now, released from the linguistic analysis for which the psychologist might be untrained, it was a question of setting naive respondents a series of tasks – the explanation of other's actions via the analysis of variance – which the social psychologists themselves were rather good at.

The attributional reasoning paradigm

Once the focus was narrowed to the judgement of causes, and the analysis of variance had been established as its model, research proceeded apace. During the 1970s and early 1980s such research packed the pages of experimental social psychology journals. Attribution theorists themselves recognized that much of the work was atheoretical, and merely used causal attribution as a handy variable in an extension of traditional person-perception and impression-formation experiments, or in new approaches to people's reactions to success and failure. We shall skirt the broad mass of empirical work and concentrate on the research that was meant to throw light on the process through which the respondent made her or his causal judgement. This was the proper test-bed of the post-Heiderian attributional conception of explanation, and it is this that we need to focus on. The methodology used in such experiments is extremely instructive as a manifestation of the three faults that lay in Heider's strata, which were increasingly hidden from critical view as the years' sediment of empirical work accumulated.

The paradigm attributional event was (the written account of) a person reacting to some stimulus. We should note at the start that 'reacting to some stimulus' was, in the beginning, a commitment to genuine reactions, but quickly yielded to any action or experience. Thus a paradigm event would be of the style *Pat enjoys eating Indian food*. The strict tests of the theory – or developments of its detail – would involve manipulation of three kinds of information about the to-be-explained event. How often the person did that action (or experienced that effect); how often she or he did it (or experienced it) in the given circumstances; and how many others did it or experienced it too. The typical experiment would present to a respondent, usually typed on a piece of paper, or in some other non-negotiable form, a short account of some hypothetical person's behaviour. The experimenter would make sure that these accounts systematically varied one or more of the above three factors; for example, how often the protagonist had behaved in that way before, or how many other people behaved in the same way. The respondent was instructed to indicate her or his explanation of the behaviour in, again, some non-negotiable way, usually by making a mark on a given rating scale, perhaps marked with anchors like 'completely to do with the individual' at one end and 'completely to do with the situation' at the other. Variations in the responses would then be correlated with variation in the factors manipulated. A typical conclusion would be that respondents were prone to see the individual as being the cause of the behaviour if she or he had a history of performing it, or that pre-existing causal expectations reduced the impact of new information about the degree to which the behaviour was common to other people.

Context, the language game and descriptive explanations

I should say that such research on explanatory reasoning is not co-terminous with 'attribution research'; in fact, it forms only a small proportion of it, and is surrounded by a large and atheoretical penumbra. However, I shall not describe the accumulated results even of this more primary research programme. Excellent accounts of the centre and the periphery are available elsewhere (Hewstone, 1989, is a comprehensive survey). We can, rather than worry over the shortcomings of one study or another, go directly to what critics say are the questionable assumptions that underlie the empirical work as a whole.

The 'dispositional' context

It has long been a complaint of critics that the attributional paradigm is artificial and reductive, but that by itself is no sin. Plenty of social psychological phenomena work as well in the laboratory as anywhere else, or, if they can't be perfectly mimicked, their laboratory mock-ups do at least give suggestive evidence as to what might be happening in the outside world. That happens when the theorist has approached the design of the experiment with a set of hypothetical constructs which genuinely do represent something that might be going on in the real-world phenomenon, and do so without suffocating restriction. This, as the first wave of critics pointed out, is not the case with attribution theory.

Harré (1981) took issue with the insistence on the very limited version of the 'scientist' that the paradigm expected ordinary people to approximate. Harré identified, in the documentary, non-negotiable statistically based problem-solving task, a clear imitation not of the full range of scientific endeavour, but of only a small and possibly comparatively insignificant part. Harré proposed that the experimentalists produced this paradigm principally because it mirrored their own positivist procedures. Compare, he suggested, the real work of the genuine scientist; she or he is as interested in defining and cataloguing the world as in manipulating it to produce demonstrations of its causal relationships. Moreover, the epitome of explanation in at least some highly prestigious sciences is not the identification of regularity (by Mill's method or whatever other means), but rather the identification of elements which, through their systematic interaction, produce a structure which is the phenomenon at issue.

If you wanted to explain the formation of a water molecule, for example, you would probably not be satisfied merely by finding, through trial and error, that it was caused by the conjunction of hydrogen and oxygen (and not any other combination of elements); you would want to explain it by describing what it was about the make-up of those elements that allowed them to combine in just that way. Even within attribution theory people have started to wonder whether the kind of 'dispositions' identified by the causal mapping ('something to do with John') are really anything like the causes that scientists or ordinary people actually use or find helpful (see, for example, Hilton and Knibbs, 1988).

Attribution experiments were tests of problem solving, where the problem and the solution were of the experimenter's own devising, and where the respondent could only go along with what she or he was presented with and hope for the best. If the behaviour presented for explanation was analogous to water, the explanation into which the respondent was forced was analogous to the 'explanation' that the water was 'caused' by hydrogen and oxygen.

The limited language game

As well as being cornered into a certain kind of science, the respondents were cornered into a certain kind of language game with the experimenter. In the same way as they could not negotiate the meaning of the vignette presented to them, they could not argue with the need for explanation at all: they were committed, by experimenter–subject protocol, to make up some answer to the explicitly stated or covertly implied question 'why did this happen?' whether an answer was necessary or not. This peculiar fold in the experimental landscape was a direct result of the geological faults of treating explanation as private apperception, and of conceiving of the explainer as a non-specific, contextless ideal. If explanation was unspecific private apperception, then it took place in all contexts and the experimenter could feel justified in generalizing the context of the laboratory to all other contexts. Peculiarities of the paradigm – the denial of debate, the insistence on an answer – were immaterial.

The earliest complaint that attribution theory set the explainer down in a featureless landscape was made by Sabini and Silver (1982). Their point was that attributionists talked of people wanting to explain their 'reactions' in the sense of (say) having heartburn after a meal. Now although such 'reactions' are indeed part of social life and may well trigger the search for an explanation, they are very different from 'reactions' like thinking someone is dishonest, or judging a play to be exciting, and so on. These 'reactions' are, in a word, *arguable*; the heartburn may be caused, but it is not arguable. Attribution theory is about heartburn-type reactions, and all its process is a process that would only be relevant to finding a cause for that kind of reaction. It has nothing to say about the 'reaction' of judging a play to be exciting or dull, an issue in explanation we shall come back to when we look at assessments and their backings in Chapters 8 and 9.

It is probably true to say that Sabini and Silver (1982) were too literal in their reading of the early attributionists as really meaning 'a person's reaction' as their gloss on action; certainly subsequent attributionists were in no way committed to anything other than the broadest possible meaning of 'action' (and, thus, ironically, incurring the criticism that they confused actions and occurrences). But although Sabini and Silver's objection was hung on the wrong peg, there is still a powerful force to their message that 'Actors are sometimes concerned with whether [evaluations] are correct. They discuss them, argue about them, find support for them or try to refute them' (1982: 87). By uncapping argument, Sabini and Silver let flow a whole river of human explanation which will not easily run down attribution theory's course of causal judgement.

What is being explained?

Kruglanski (1975, 1988) and later theorists acknowledged that the description of the to-be-explained event exercised a powerful influence on its explanation. Voluntary action, for example, required a different explanatory vocabulary from involuntary action. But, 'voluntary' or not, the event was still considered to be non-negotiable. The theorists stopped short of allowing the respondent to drop the mask of reporting scientist in favour of the mask of the debater, the agenda-setter or the troublemaker. Yet it is a commonplace in any linguistically informed view of social exchanges that the medium of language makes events negotiable; and that the description claimed for the event has certain powers. Any event can be presented in language that suggests that it is (for example) voluntary or involuntary. The detail of the language can specify its potential explanation in broad class or close detail; or it can pre-empt the very possibility of explanation.

Without acknowledging this aspect of explanations, we shall not be able to make sense of people's disputes about what Billig (1987) calls the 'essentiality' of an event: not its cause, but what is really important about it. For example, I could claim that the cause of a mutual friend's current moroseness is his precarious financial situation. You, on the other hand, are quick to agree that his finances are in a bad way, but claim that he is not (exactly) 'morose', more 'flat'. We agree about the cause, but disagree about the effect it has actually brought about.

The attributional paradigm, then, construed the experimental subject as a causal mapper, even though this notion would be rejected as too limiting even by philosophers of science. The non-negotiability of the experimental paradigm, in which it would be unthinkable for the respondent to argue with the wording of the behaviour described on the documentary vignette, cornered the respondent into reporting on a given state of affairs rather than being able, as a genuine scientist, to explore different interpretations of the behaviour and try to identify how its constituent parts fitted together. The respondent was forced to become a passive calculator rather than an active investigator. Any patterns that emerged might well be reproducible

(though, intriguingly, attribution theory research has a history of unrepro-
ducible effects, even when these are apparently merely formalizations of
common sense, such as the actor–observer difference or the fundamental
attribution error). But they would demonstrate not what people did in
constructing a world to be explained, or in negotiating the meaning of the
explanation, but rather their competence in mimicking the analysis of
variance reasoning around which the attributional paradigm was consciously
constructed.

Vocabularies of ordinary explanation: internal and external causes

The attribution theory project was selective in taking from Heider a certain
theoretical goal – the uncovering of the mechanism of causal attribution –
but, by casting ordinary explainers as passive, scientifically backward
problem solvers, it reproduced the three geological faults in Heider's
foundations. The discoveries that the project could in principle produce
were necessarily limited to its own stiff language game, and promised little
application to the mercurial world of talk. In describing the attributional
paradigm, we have so far spent more time on its conception of the
explainers' role and task than on the language in which their explanations
were to be cast. That casting, too, has some lessons for the study of ordinary
explanation, as we shall now see.

The dispute within attribution theory over the description of ordinary
explanation as being by appeal to cause is framed by the following question,
whose terms date back to Heider: 'can every explanation of social
phenomena be understood as identifying a cause either *internal* to the
person or *external* to them?'

It was central to Heider's scheme that ordinary people's explanations
could be located in two broad classes of causes: things within the person and
things coming from outside. This was not an empirical finding on Heider's
part: like his belief in people's basic rationality, it was evidence rather of his
willingness to ascribe to ordinary people the positive aims of the scientist.
Hence: 'In common-sense psychology (as in scientific psychology) the result
of an action is felt to depend on two sets of conditions, namely factors within
the person and factors within the environment' (1958: 82). Later on, Heider
betrays the origin (or, at least, the more recent origin) of this division of the
causal field by recalling Kurt Lewin's famous description of behaviour as
being a function of the person and the environment.

This attractive division was enthusiastically taken up by theoreticians and
(especially) by experimentalists, who were quick to do two things: first, to
refer to both the 'person' and 'environment' terms in the equation as
'causes'; and, secondly, to enshrine the terms as the classic dependent
measures of the attribution paradigm. Explanations in purposive terms
were, nominally at least, excluded, and this would strike us now as being
rather odd, but is consistent with the attributionists' ascription of scientific

determinism (which Heider, recognizing reasons and intentions, had avoided) to ordinary people. Perhaps it is not surprising, as Harré (1981) pointed out, that they attributed to ordinary people the kind of causal language that they themselves favoured. Michael (1989: 233) puts it in rather a less charitable way: 'could it be', he asks, 'that the sovereignty of the individual implied in these models is a projection of the assumed sovereignty of intellectuals (e.g. attribution theorists)?'

In any case the dependent measures caught on and empirical work blossomed. Experimental subjects would be asked to indicate their explanation of the event on scales which would (in the crudest version) be anchored with 'something to do with the person' at one end and 'something to do with the situation' at the other. Dependent measures proliferated without any clear standard, and odd results started to be thrown up. Partly in reaction to these and partly in recognition that the old Lewinian formula had outlived its heuristic elegance, critics were soon to chip away at the internal–external distinction. The critics were of two kinds: those who wanted better dependent measures for the same attributional project; and those who wanted to do away with the distinction and with its attributional *raison d'être*. The problems they identified all stemmed, ultimately, from the central problem of what counts as ordinary explanation. As Semin put it at the time 'the ambiguity of the two-fold cause classification . . . is precisely the loophole which enables the attribution theorist to achieve an "intuitive leap", namely fitting what people say into what attribution theory suggests people to mean' (Semin, 1980: 293).

What do the terms mean?

Miller et al. (1981) set out a number of misgivings about the internal–external distinction. The list, still live (see, for example Hewstone, 1989; White, 1991), settles down to three main concerns: (a) that the two classes of cause are not mutually exclusive; (b) that categorizing any given cause as one or the other is hard; and (c) that the terms 'internal' and 'external' cover too much ground. It is worth adding to the list the problem of whether 'internal–external' is a pair of detached categories or two ends of a long, but joined up, spectrum.

It was soon found empirically that Heider's version of the Lewinian equation was mistaken as a description of ordinary explanation. Heider had assumed that the relation between internal and external causation was 'hydraulic' in the sense that the more you attributed an event 'internally', the less you would attribute it 'externally'. But when respondents expressed their attributions on separate rating scales, one for internal and one for external attributions, it became clear that the two were far from being perfectly inversely correlated: respondents would happily do things like rate the event as being caused by internal and external factors equally highly. That made people realize that 'internal' and 'external' were not straightforwardly exclusive categories, at polar ends of a single spectrum.

Methodologists complained that they could never be sure just what was meant by each other's dependent measures. Some researchers anchored their scales with the pairs internal–external; some with personal–situational; some with dispositional–environmental; and many with *ad hoc* phrases that were peculiar to the particular event being explained, and were only intuitively related to the internal–external distinction. Moreover, if they didn't use rating scales, it was hard to see how they categorized explanations written in respondents' own words: if you asked two different people why they go to Spain for their holidays and one replies *because it's hot* and the other says *because I like the heat*, did those answers really represent two different categories?

Careful methodological work revealed the rather alarming finding that there was no satisfactory consistency between different ways of measuring the categories. If one asked respondents to write attributions in their own words, for example, and to respond to varieties of rating scales, putting together the various results did not form a coherent picture. A respondent might explain her or his holiday by writing *because I like the heat*, but on a rating scale would indicate 'something to do with Spain'. (A look at the context of the respondents' talk would make the two consistent, of course, but respondents' talk was not recorded; we shall come back to that.)

What then, did the terms 'internal' and 'external' actually cover? Heider had meant to call things like (say) 'duty' and 'ambition' internal causes only as a first step, in preparation for the later discovery of how the mix of basic prototypical ingredients was subtly different in each case. With the immediate take-up of the internal–external split, that careful work never came, leaving all manner of subtleties – not least the difference between two presumably 'internal' causes like 'duty' and 'ambition', as well as more substantial explanations like reasons and motives – unexplored.

Dimensional solutions

How did attributionists go about trying to solve these problems with the internal–external division? The first lesson – that internal and external causes were not inversely correlated – was learnt reasonably early on, and it would be unusual nowadays to find a study which used one rating scale with internal at one end and external at the other. But the other two problems have not been acknowledged to the same extent. Rating scales are indeed still used, and the internal–external division is still the dependent measure of choice.

The second lesson – that it was not clear what fell into the internal and external categories – received a rather intriguing, if ultimately evasive, answer. On the face of it, you might expect that if a theory claims that people explain events by attributing them to causes which can be classified as (say) internal or external, then such causes should actually appear in ordinary talk. But attributionists have traditionally taken the position that these are *underlying dimensions* of cause, not expected to be superficially obvious.

That being the case, it is perhaps not surprising that some people have tried to improve the subtlety of the internal–external distinction not by explicating it conceptually but by throwing more dimensions across it. The principal two-part distinctions proposed to supplement it (but not replace it) are the dimensions stable–unstable and controllable–uncontrollable; whether the cause is stable or not, and whether it is controllable or not (Weiner, 1986). The idea is that the respondent conceives of causation as being somewhere in the cognitive space crossed by these dimensions, so one can forget entirely about individual words like 'ability' or 'effort' and so on, and get the respondents to go straight to making a dimensional judgement. Russell (1982), for example, has developed a scale on which respondents indicate how internal, stable and controllable the cause they are thinking of is.

The trouble with this solution is that it asserts what it is meant to show: that the internal–external dimension is indeed a coherent one, understood in the same way by ordinary people and psychologists. By not asking for explanations in words, it avoids any embarrassing revelation that people might not agree with the experimenters. Yet if a comparison is done it does reveal puzzling differences: in Krantz and Rude's (1984) study, for example, half the respondents thought that 'luck' was an internal cause, and half thought it was an external cause. Even such an (apparently) obviously 'unstable' cause as the effort someone puts into a job can be seen by some people as a wholly stable personality trait (the person may be the kind of person who generally works hard). What can a 'causal dimension' mean if luck or effort can lie at either end of it?

Rather than clarifying internal and external causation, fastening on more dimensions just adds more layers of assumption. The internal–external distinction is still cast in the same terms as before, so we are no further forward in understanding what it means. If anything, the problem has been made worse, because we now also have to worry about equally slippery concepts like stability and controllability. More thoroughgoing attempts at sorting out the internal–external division had to face up squarely to the fundamental question of just what it means to say that a cause is 'internal'.

Causes and reasons: category-based solutions

Miller et al. (1981) pushed the issue an important step forward by reminding us that *what* is being explained is an important consideration. According to them, an action attributed to an 'internal' cause was one which was freely chosen by the actor, and an action attributed to an 'external' cause was one constrained or induced by the outside world. This is reasonable enough so far as it goes, but there was still further that one could go. As White remarks: 'the solution . . . was supposed to save the basicity of the internal/external distinction (if not its unidimensionality) *by selecting a particular interpretation of it*, as a chosen–not chosen distinction' (1991: 260, emphasis added). White points out, in other words, that Miller et al.'s solution stands by the claim that there is indeed one dimension at work separating internal from external. Other critics (including White himself) want more than one dimension, and all their proposals turn on Kruglanski's (1975) early acknowledgement that explaining 'actions' is not the same as explaining events or 'occurrences', and on the recognition, following Locke and Pennington (1982), that the word 'cause' is a generic term, and can comfortably include reasons.

White summarizes the various candidate proposals like this: 'the internal/ external . . . distinction is not one distinction but two, because both halves of it confound the distinction between conscious, voluntary action explained in terms of reasons and unconsciously deterministically caused behaviours explained in terms of causes other than reasons' (1991: 261). White's own version is the most accessible: he proposes two pairs of explanation types, one pair for voluntary actions and the other pair for involuntary ones. Voluntary actions can be explained by internal reasons (for example, *you went into a shop because you wanted to buy a book*) or external reasons (*you sent your parents a card because it's their wedding anniversary*). Involuntary actions or things that happen to you can be explained by internal causes (*you ran away from a dog because you were terrified*, or *you blushed because you were embarrassed*) or by external causes (*you let go of the kettle because it was scalding hot*) (White, 1991).

White's analysis looks immediately plausible (a feeling shared by his respondents, who agreed that the four examples above were indeed different in the way he describes). As evidence of its plausibility, the scheme also solves the traditional riddle over apparently synonymous explanations like going to Spain *because I like the heat* and *because it's hot*. The first is, in White's account, an internal reason and the second is an external reason and, indeed, there would be no redundancy in saying *it's hot and I like the heat*. It also solves, as White observes, the long-running dispute over whether it is the case that people attribute the cause of their own behaviour 'externally' and the cause of others' behaviour 'internally'. Rather than get into unresolvable fixes about the attribution of cause, we can ask the sensible question of whether people see their behaviour as being of the same sort (voluntary and conscious) as that of others.

There the situation with regard to attribution theory's internal disputes over categories of cause rests at the moment. It remains to be seen if White's recent categorical solution will appeal to experimentalists where previous solutions have not. Experimentalists have tended to stick with the straight internal–external distinction partly, one presumes, out of habit and precedent, and partly because of its intuitive appeal (traced, by some critics, to the Western heritage of a split between self and world). The system may be good for how people understand causes in static vignette descriptions, but it leaves some hanging worries which we shall come to at the end of the chapter, and which come into sharp focus when we look at what happens when one tries to put attributions into some kind of non-reporting context and identify their use, or function.

Functions of attributions

As I mentioned before, Heider and his immediate successors conceived of the explainer's task as 'predicting and controlling the world'. This personal ambition was as vague as it was grand. The first wave of necessary specification sharpened the individualistic focus by proposing that people sought causal attributions for egotistical reasons: to preserve their self-esteem and to present themselves well to their neighbours.

One would have thought that such intuitively plausible propositions should have been easily and widely confirmed. Hewstone's careful survey (1989: 121–8) shows, however, that the evidence was decidedly patchy. It is true that certain patterns do look as if they have been empirically reliable: 'Broadly speaking, egotism is especially likely in competitive interpersonal contexts, self-presentation is typical of evaluative public settings; and egocentrism is most likely to occur when respondents are asked to recall behaviours first and then estimate their own and their partner's contribution' (Hewstone, 1989: 128). But close inspection of this broad trend reveals peculiar inconsistencies. The prediction that people would claim successes for themselves (that is, attribute positive outcomes internally), for example, is not always borne out. It might be that the reason for the apparent inconsistency is that we don't have a sufficiently long list of variables which, together, explain the occasions on which the bias will or won't appear.

But there is a more economical possibility, and that is that the theories simply aren't able to specify the meaning of the attribution: just when an internal attribution for a positive event will be 'self-serving', and, similarly, when a contrary external attribution will be the opposite of self-serving. One respondent might 'self-serve' not by a (vainglorious) internal attribution to ability, but rather by a (modest) external attribution to luck. The same person might switch tactic faced with a different audience, or faced with slightly different dependent measures. Another person may believe in their own abilities but attribute their success to hard work specifically to avoid the accusation of making a 'self-serving' attribution; yet they may be accused of boasting by a friend who believes that a capacity for hard work is nevertheless a personal achievement. The range of meaning of an 'internal attribution' is wide, and experimentalists were perhaps fatally optimistic in believing that their experimental subjects would take the dependent measure rating scales at face value.

The search for 'personal' selfish functions of attribution, then, is troubled by difficulties in specifying what is, and is not, good selfish strategy in changing circumstances. Might there be other functions, less open to dispute and the operation of uncontrolled variables? Attribution theory took a turn towards 'group' functions in European social psychology (Deschamps, 1983) when it was acknowledged that the attributer could be moved by desires that served her or his group. This loosened up the insistence on the attribution distinction between external circumstances and the individual actor, replacing them with the polar opposites of 'my group' versus 'their group'. The positive benefit was to introduce the rather contextless attribution machinery to the weighty social psychological issues of group conflict articulated by theory elsewhere (in, for example, social identity theory; see the application of attribution principles to group perception in Hewstone and Jaspars, 1982; Hewstone et al., 1982).

One positive result was to generate a brief acknowledgment of the pre-attributional process of categorization and representation (Deschamps, 1983). In spite of this, the move to group functions brought with it no great shift in research practice, and the empirical work tends to cluster around a fairly flat reworking of attributional vignette experiments. Respondents' group membership is acknowledged and the vignettes are manipulated to present them with opportunity to manifest various kinds of ingroup favouritism and outgroup prejudice. Thus, for example, one might make the straightforward claim that people will attribute a bad act performed by an outgroup member to that person's dispositions, and a good act as being due to the circumstances; and vice versa for ingroup members (Pettigrew, 1979). Supportive evidence for such a claim comes from studies on, for example, Chinese and Malays' attributions for each other's positive and negative behaviour (Hewstone and Ward, 1985).

This kind of 'social function' stays within the broad camp of cognitive understandings of explanation, though clearly it does extend motivation from purely individualist concerns (self-esteem and so on) to wider issues of group identity. But all the criticisms we saw above apply: we have no landmarks to help us navigate to the places where group function would be served by group derogation or where it would be served by celebration.

Moreover, the language game in which the explanation is offered is still resolutely limited to the idealized players of attribution theory's scientist and reporter. Michael (1989) observes that the ostensibly group functions at issue (the maintenance of self-esteem, the presentation of a positive image) are as resolutely individualistic as Heider's original proposition that the explainer is out to predict and control the world. As Michael puts it,

> explanations have wider ramifications. Not only will they affect the explainer, they will also affect other, more or less proximal agents . . . the likelihood of this happening is proportional to the power attached to that explanation, or rather the complex array of institutions and discourses that are the conditions for the emergence of that explanation. (1989: 235)

The explainer still fills the screen in close up, and we do not see her or his interlocutors, or the stage on which they play out their roles, as part of the image.

The contribution of classic attribution theory to the study of ordinary explanation

I have tried to show in this chapter that what is now known as 'classic' attribution theory has come some way from Heider's original enterprise.

Heider wanted to mine the seams of ordinary language as the raw material of social psychological understanding. In one sense one could say that subsequent developments brought advances. Heider's exploratory analytical machinery has been replaced by a technology of testing equipment built for a very specific job. That job is to take very seriously the ordinary explainer as a certain kind of scientist, pursuing a certain kind of causal reply to a certain kind of question. In another sense one could say that these technological advances were bought at the expense of the understanding of the raw material itself; that although the tools became more sophisticated, the language practices they were applied to became narrower and less real. Let us recap the misgivings one might have about Heider's legacy, and look forward to the developments in the next chapter.

The last section, in which we briefly looked at the 'functions' that an attribution might have, identified a problem for any theory of explanation which was committed to the fixed meaning of given words or phrases. We saw that it was difficult for an attribution theorist to specify, out of context, how any individual speaker might deploy 'internal' and 'external' attributions to present themselves in the best light. Were one interested in that aspect of ordinary explanation, it might be more profitable not to chart patterns of such attributions (even were they to be exhaustive) but rather to explore what it means socially to exchange an explanation at all, and how such malleable social excuses, extenuations and mitigations can be accomplished in ordinary talk.

That diagnosis and recommendation is a specific variation on the three general themes which have been running through this chapter: that we might learn from Heider's legacy that an account of explanation that was fixed on causation is impervious to context; that it has a restricted and restricting conception of language, and language exchange; and that the rather rigid methods that are built on its theoretical base are not likely to pick up much variation in the ebb and flow of explanation in talk.

What, then, might we expect to see in a fuller account? The last section of this chapter gave a strong hint that we should look to see if we can do something to place the explanation more securely in its particular context. With that in mind we can turn to developments which address the specifics of conversational interchange. In the next chapter we shall turn to the 'conversation model', and let developments there take theory on to what we shall see is a more contextualized story.

3

Causal Talk

Interviewer: I'm asking you *why* you dis*tort*ed those facts (0.2)
Interviewee: Well we didn't distort them
(Heritage and Greatbatch, 1991: 105; transcription simplified)

In this exchange between interviewer and interviewee, the response challenges the very presumption of the question, and diverts (or tries to divert) the exchange onto less dangerous territory. Suppose that an exchange like the one above had taken place not (as it did) in a television studio, but in the well-ordered world of the psychological laboratory. I think it would be safe to say that the response in the real example – challenging the facts as set out by the interviewer – would be very unlikely. The laboratory is well ordered to the point of rigidity, and experimenters are in a position to lay out their questions in unchallengeable ways: on paper, on a computer screen, or read out without interruption to a class of subjects attending a group session. Subjects tend to reply to the question as given; those few who risk social disfavour by declining to do so – who score through the printed instructions or write their objections in the margins – are quietly dropped from the analysis.

That rigid interaction between didactic experimenter and constrained respondent is, however, one that fits well with the rigid conception of explanation we saw in the last chapter. We traced the account of the causal logic of explanation from its roots in linguistic analysis to its modern concentration on a certain kind of abstract causal reasoning. We had cause to ask what foundation in language, and linguistic exchange, would support the abstractions of theory, and ended the last chapter looking forward to seeing what we could make of some hanging issues of language once we had set explanations more firmly into their real-life context.

Now we need to bring ourselves up to date with developments in attribution theory which come round again to linguistic analysis, although this time of a sort different from that used by Heider (see Chapter 2). We shall look closely at the development of an explicitly 'conversational' model of attribution and ask whether it satisfies the queries that hang over the abstractions of the classic model. In answering that question we shall rely more and more on extracts from real-life exchanges of explanations, and begin to open up the range of analyses that such talk demands.

The bulk of the chapter will be devoted to describing the conversation model of attribution (Hilton and Slugoski, 1986; Turnbull and Slugoski,

1988; Hilton, 1990, 1991) and seeing how it stands up to the stresses and strains of explanation exchanges in real life. At the end of the chapter we shall introduce Edwards and Potter's (1992) radical re-think of what the conversation model is trying to account for, and take that as a stimulus to a still closer reliance on everyday talk in its raw form.

The conversation model of attribution

We left two issues hanging from our inspection of classic attribution theory and the taxonomies of the account literature: the language game the explainer was playing, and the conversational context in which it was being played. There has been a recent movement within attribution theory, started by Lalljce (1981), to pull the camera back and allow us to see conversational context. This apparently simple step back from close-up to medium shot gives us a dramatic a view of the linguistic character of explanation. By locating the explainer in a conversational context, Lalljee immediately recognized three embarrassing lacunae in attribution theory's conception of explanations: the undertheorized relation between the explanation and pragmatic demands; the knowledge assumed in the person to whom it was addressed; and the vocabulary in which it was expressed. More to the point, the location in conversation promised a way forward which would make sense of existing attributional phenomena, and also move the theory out of the laboratory and the written page and into the real world of talk.

In what follows I shall briefly trace the development of Lalljee's original conception and describe its current formalization in the conversation model of attribution (Hilton, 1990, 1991). I shall argue that the new conversation model departs rather sharply from the direction set by Lalljee, and that its new route might not avoid going over some of the terrain distorted by the geological faults in Heider's strata. We shall be seeing, towards the end of the chapter, whether or not it looks likely to be applicable to explanations in actual exchange and, if not, what a less cognitive alternative might look like.

Two key features of the conversation model

There are two, rather separate, strands to the conversation model of causal explanation (as expressed in Hilton, 1990, 1991): a restatement of the explainer's task as being the identification of 'contrast cases' and 'counter-factuals', and a setting of counterfactuals in conversation, ruled over by Gricean maxims of cooperation. We shall go into what these terms mean immediately below. Just before doing so, though, it is important to note that, as parts of an attributional theory, these two strands have equal weight, and that they follow a certain sequential order. When I come to make comments in the model, I shall argue that another order is possible, but let us take it in the official sequence first.

Contrast cases and counterfactual explanation

Work by Hilton and Slugoski (1986) and Turnbull and Slugoski (1988) sharpened the linguistic focus to a point where Lalljee's (1981) proposals gelled into a strong model of attributions as responses to questions. Hilton takes up the thread of argument to make the point that an explanation is made in response to some question – and that the question contrasts two states of affairs explicitly (as in *why did you do this rather than that?*) or implicitly (as in *why did you switch off the TV?*, rather than, implicitly, leaving it on). This neatly leads on to the elegantly simple principle that the explanation merely picks out something that did happen in one of the two cases and didn't happen in the other: the 'counterfactual condition'.

Counterfactual explanation, as White (1990) points out, is a modern version of old 'regularity' theories, which, like Mill's method of difference, infers causation from regular association. The rule of thumb when giving a counterfactual explanation is to take the event to be explained – say, why the *Titanic* sank immediately on collision with the iceberg – and compare it with an alternative – say, that it stayed afloat for a few hours. Then you identify one thing (which has, of course, to be at least potentially causative) which was true about one alternative state of affairs but not about the other. So you might reveal that the hull was holed at a point just below the waterline, knowing that had it been holed above that point it would have taken some time for water to enter the ship with the rise and fall of the swell, and that rapid shipping of water does cause catastrophic listing. The point at which the ship was holed is the ingredient which discriminates the two cases (the counterfactual condition) so it stands as the explanation. This distinguishing ingredient is obviously a candidate for explanation in a way that something which is common to both cases could not be. You could not advance as an explanation the fact that, say, no look-out had been posted that night, if that had been true both in the case of the ship being holed above the waterline and in the case when it had been holed below it.

The advance over traditional attributional conceptions that Hilton points out is that it states the overarching principle of which the method of difference is one example. This means that we can look around for further examples which might make sense of some problematic findings difficult for the standard attributional account to explain. One such example is the overlooked method of agreement, which is a better description of the attribution of dispositions – a central concern of attribution theory – than is the method of difference. We need not go into the details here, but Hilton makes the point that to attribute an event to (someone's) disposition (the standard case since Heider) is a special case of attributing it to one among many possible candidate causes. If the explainer's task is to get to a dispositional judgement (rather than to reach a less restricted conclusion) then Mill's method of agreement is a better description of the reckoning process through which the explainer has to go.

From the model's point of view then, the counterfactual principle is an advance within traditional attributional theory even were the argument to be taken no further than this. But it does go further. Hilton is obliged to notice that the counterfactual principle is silent about which of the many possible cases is chosen by the explainer. One needs to make a principled choice.

Implied contrast cases

Hilton follows Lalljee's identification of 'surprisingness' as the principle through which the explainer chooses which contrast case to orient to. Since, as Lalljee (1981) points out, an explanation will be called for when something unusual prompts it, the explainer has a natural alternative (namely, the normal state of affairs) to consider when looking for a counterfactual. The counterfactual condition is simply picked out by whatever was strange or untoward about the to-be-explained event (the 'abnormal condition'); everything else, since it was 'normal', is ignored as being causally uninformative. So if you ask me to explain why I am late for work, I will tell you what was unusual and what distinguished today's journey from yesterday's (say, that I took my neighbour to the doctor's); it would be pointless telling you about something that was the same today as it has always been.

Implicit causality

It is worth noting here that various event-descriptions have been established empirically to predispose certain causes. Social psychologists have concentrated on the predisposing effect of verbs, and Semin and Fiedler (1988) give a thorough review of the phenomenon within their comprehensive linguistic-category model. An example of the effect is that empty phrases like *John bores Sandra* suggest to readers (if one asks them) that the cause is John, whereas *Andy admires Rebecca* implies the cause is Rebecca. This is helpful, up to a point, to the conversation model, which would recast it as the verb restricting certain contrast cases and their implicit counterfactuals. To say *John bores Sandra* is conventionally to express the contrast case of John-as-opposed-to-others boring Sandra. Thus, if any explanation is called for, it will pick out something to do with John. But the conversation model goes further than that, using the speaker and audience's mutual knowledge to specify just what it is about John that is boring: his obsession with football, his monotonous voice, or his habit of speaking as if he were addressing a public meeting. The verb by itself does not say.

The insight that verbs carry implications about causality is useful, and it is important to know that the conversation model encompasses such implication. But we should be wary of reading too much into that at the moment, since verbs are not the only features of speech that have this kind of predisposing effect, and such predispositions can be overridden by syntactic markers and by pragmatic and by discursive context, as we shall see later.

Conversational maxims as 'quality control'

Having established the operation of the abnormal conditions/counterfactual principle on data from the standard attributional paradigm, Hilton then moves to consider how it might fare in more naturalistic settings. So far we have seen some welcome tightening up of the previously undertheorized relationship between the event to be explained and the proper candidates for explanation, as hinted by Lalljee. We have been looking forward to an equivalent expansion of what we saw as the real power of Lalljee's insights, the location of the explanation in genuine conversation, as the title of Hilton's model promises. It is at this point that the argument undergoes a curious sea-change. We are expecting an analysis of talk, but that is not how the model proceeds.

The model identifies Grice's conversational cooperative principle not on the empirical basis of what explainers say and when they say it, but rather as the principled last step in an idealized cognitive package. It is the quality control filter through which an explanation must pass before it is deemed satisfactory. The principle has four maxims: be clear, be informative, be relevant and be honest. The model claims that the explainer first generates a host of likely causes and then selects the appropriate one by testing it against each maxim. Hilton (1991) uses the example of the puzzle of the *Challenger* space-shuttle crash to make the point. Suppose someone who had never come across the story asked *why did it crash?* and was told *because of cold weather on the eve of the launch*. The account fails, according to the conversation model, because the speaker is not properly adhering to one of the maxims – that the account be informative. The speaker has failed to tailor the explanation to the listener's knowledge, so although the account is true, relevant and clear, it is not anchored in anything the listener knows about the case so it remains uninformative. The function of the Gricean maxims, then, is, as Hilton puts it, to 'constrain and tune' the explanations that the speaker has generated for the event in hand. The maxims are a final stage in a cognitive process, brought in to satisfy the final demand of conversational competence.

The model, then, looks like this: an explanation is triggered by a comparison between a certain state of affairs (probably an unusual one) and another state of affairs (probably the normal one). A range of things that occur in one state but not in another (probably including 'abnormal conditions') is generated, and standards of relevance, truth, informativeness and clarity are invoked to choose among them. The choice is made and the item is chosen as the explanation.

The conversation model is not conversational enough

The counterfactual principle and the contrast-case selection device make the conversation model a powerful improvement to the contextual awareness of attribution theory. By acknowledging that explanations are given in conversational exchange, it reveals them as responses to some contrast case set up by the request; and by allowing a cause to be any counterfactual condition it corrects the standard attribution insistence on causes as being limited to things 'to do with' this or that part of the environment.

It might be, however, that the attributional legacy is still a hindrance to the full realization of the conversation model's promise, and there might be room for still more 'rules of conversation' to be integrated into the model. In the next sections I shall look down a number of possible avenues along which the model might be extended; in summary, they are these. It can be difficult to see in ordinary talk the workings of a counterfactual principle; it might need tailoring to cope with explanations given in a monologue, and about event-descriptions which are not, by themselves, wholly deterministic. What may be cast as a causal question (and implicit contrast case) may be answered with a non-causal explanation, renegotiated, or rejected entirely; the model relies on the cognitive operation of the Gricean maxims whereas, as conventions, they set up the conditions for any response to be cooperative, so are in that sense untestable; and, finally, what may seem to be a causal answer to a causal question may orientate not to the propositional surface of the question but to some aspect of its pragmatic force. I will go through each of these in the sections below, using some illustrative examples from real conversations.

Causal attributions in talk are not always obviously counterfactual

Here is an example of a good candidate for the model:

> (In the context of talking about having friends in different places)
> A: (. . .) I haven't had an awful lot of friends to sort of go around with much because it's been terrible lugging Karl about, you know
> B: Well [*2 to 3 syllables unintelligible*]
> A: And it wasn't worth it for the last, in the last few years
> (LL S1.10, p. 258, 501)[1]

This is a good example of a counterfactual: one could reasonably easily cast *having Karl to lug about* as being the abnormal condition which distinguished having few and having many friends, assuming that all participants knew that what is terrible about lugging someone about is the time and effort it takes and (if she or he is an invalid or a child, or perhaps even a pet) the responsibility for looking after her or him.

Here, on the other hand, is a difficult case for the model:

> (In the context of an anecdote about Sir Garnett Wolsey, a figure in British military history)

A: Everything was all untidy and Crimean before him, and after him it was
        all very snappy and . . and and everything you see and so soldiers used to
        say
B: It . . it means all proper
A: It was all Sir Garnett when everything was all tidy and proper
(LL S1.10, p. 249, 62)

There are two potential causal explanations here. One is an explanation of why things were tidied up and made 'snappy'. That is attributed to Wolsey. That attribution is then used as an explanation of why the soldiers refer to neatness as *all Sir Garnett*. In the first case, Wolsey is put forward as the cause of the clean-up, but is he a counterfactual? The explainer seems to be using a rather different philosophy of causation: Wolsey was the intervening variable between the state of affairs at time 1 and time 2, so is taken to be the cause. This is much more like 'efficient' causation than causation inferred from regularity, including counterfactual causation. In the second case, the 'cause' of the soldiers calling something *all Sir Garnett* is their perception of its similarity to his achievement. This is an odd kind of cause, if it is a cause at all; in any case, it looks most unlike a counterfactual.

Syntactic influences on event-description: the 'new' and the 'given'

The conversation model is committed to explanations being restricted by the immediate informational content of what precedes them, whether by explicit comparisons (*why did you buy Gorgonzola and not Parmesan?*); by implicit comparisons with normality (*why was the train late?*); or by the predisposing effect of verbs (*why does John bore Andrea?*). The question is whether these local descriptions (the implicit or explicit contrast case; the choice of verb) are special cases of a more general class of linguistic pointers.

There are powerful linguistic devices that signal that something is 'new' in the utterance: 'new' in the sense of worthy of psychological or discursive attention, or at least signalled for further take-up by the text or the speaker. Such markers, in English, include the use of the indefinite rather than the definite article, being grammatical subject rather than object, the early rather than late appearance in the sentence, and certain patterns of intonation. These may all work in concert or in competition to make something salient or worthy of attention. They are powerful in the sense that they cannot (in the normal way) be overridden.

Let me illustrate with an example using the articles *the* and *a*. In whatever (non-absurd) context, *the* marks the given and *a* marks what is being introduced as new. Imagine an event described, perhaps in the first line of a novel, as *A van drew up in front of the house*. The use of *a* and *the* suggests that the story's development will take up the reference to the newly introduced van and give more information about it (*it was sputtering and stalling*, and so on) and that if an explanation of the event is solicited, it will be cast in terms of the van and not the house (*it was delivering a parcel*). Swapping over the articles so that it reads *the van drew up in front of a house* reverses the effect. Now it suggests that what follows will be something about the house (*it was large and imposing*) and, if an explanation of the event is required, it will be cast in terms of the house (*it was the address they were looking for*). In the case of an ambiguous pairing like *A van drew up in front of the house. It was yellow and white*, readers and listeners would normally infer – perhaps without realizing that there was a choice – that what was yellow and white was the van, not the house.

The point to make is that the conversation model's contrast-case devices (explicit and implicit comparisons, causally predisposing verbs) look like being special cases of markers like the definite or indefinite article – and *can be overridden by them*. Take the verbs. In a story about the likes and dislikes of a class of children, the verb *to bore* in a sentence like *she bored the class* does, as Brown and Fish (1983) claim, do a lot of work to imply that the boring person is the explanatory locus: that it is the teacher who is boring. But in a different story, this time centred on a history teacher's experience in school, the sentence *she bored a class*, while probably not wholly absolving the teacher of responsibility, does at least partly signal the children as causally important; she might have bored one class, but not others. A fuller model would need to accommodate event-descriptions being overridden, or determined, by a much wider (and more powerful) range of syntactic determinants.

Monologue explanations

The model is committed to the case of the explainer's cognitive processes being triggered off by the contrast case set by another person's request for an explanation. It is an open question whether the kind of process sparked off there has anything to say about what happens when the speaker presents an event and explains it her- or himself (which case, we shall see later, is probably by far the more common in conversations). In self-generated attributions the explainer is, as it were, judge and jury; if there is any question of cognitive process, it is in the individual's decision to bring up the causal event at all, since we assume that the causal solution offered is part of the package, not an actively novel deduction. This is not a fatal problem for the conversation model, since the form of the attribution may be counterfactual; but it does raise the question of *when* the cause was actively processed.

> (In the context of what words mean and what associations they conjure up)
> *B*: No it's terribly . . terribly cultural — in fact you can't separate yourself from — natural free associations about each word [*5 to 6 syllables unintelligible*]
> *A*: Well I can because I've lived in two [s] two very different countries
> (LL S1.10, p. 253, 263)

Speaker A sets up a case for explanation: she can do something that speaker B claims can't (normally) be done. It looks as if what she is pointing to is meant to be an abnormal condition (whose abnormality is signalled by the intensifier 'very'). But what evidence have we that she has actively processed the explanation in response to the demands of a given contrast case? It is equally plausible that the setting up of the contrast case (*I can even though others can't*) and the causal attribution (to living in different countries) is delivered as one conversational package under her own control.

Apparently causal questions may be answered by non-causal explanations, renegotiated or rejected entirely

In the following exchange (taken from a newspaper forum in which readers' queries are answered in succeeding weeks by other readers), the 'answer' simply subverts the 'problem' in the original question, and effectively stops the debate or forces the questioner to reformulate what they mean:

> Q: Why are tax discs round?
> A: I think the answer can be found in Collins' *Concise English Dictionary*, page 215: 'Disc. Any flat, circular thing'
> (Rimmershaw, 192: 248)

The following exchange, on the other hand, is an example of a less radical renegotiation. A direct causal question is asked, but the respondent takes advantage of his turn to renegotiate the terms in which the event is cast. There is then a battle over the answer.

> (Interview between patient (Pt), head psychiatrist (HP) and two other doctors who do not appear in this extract)
> 1   *Pt*:   [*Long complaint about his treatment*]
> 2   *HP*:   What got you down here?
> 3   *Pt*:   They sent me down here for observation
> 4   *HP*:   Why?
> 5   *Pt*:   They, they thought I, I, went to see a social worker, and I saw a psychiatrist, they said that well why don't you go down there. Because I had an old problem
> 6   *HP*:   You felt the coffee was poison and you felt that people were mixing you up in your thinking, you were shaking
> 7   *Pt*:   Not so! The only part that's true is the coffee (. . .)
> (Mehan, 1990: 174–5; introductory remarks and transcription simplified; turn 1 paraphrased)

In line 2 the psychiatrist asks a direct causal question. But note that the expression *what got you down here* pragmatically orientates the answer towards something inevitable (the patient's illness, for example). The patient refuses this implication by casting the answer in terms of 'they'. The psychiatrist asks why, implying that the patient's answer is insufficient. Out of the patient's reply to this question the psychiatrist chooses the last phrase to expand on, bringing out the patient's condition as being the cause he was searching for all along.

And, in the example which we saw at the head of the chapter, the causal question is simply rejected:

> (A broadcast of a news interview: the nominal interviewee, JG, asks the question of the ostensible interviewer, IR)
> *JG*:   I'm asking you *why* you dis*tort*ed those facts (0.2)
> *IR*:   Well we didn't distort them
> (Heritage and Greatbatch, 1991: 105; transcription simplified)

A rejection like this is not fatal to the conversation model, which would hardly force speakers to give explanations at gunpoint. But it does remind us that more can be done with a causal question other than simply respond to its propositional content, a point which we shall go into in more detail immediately below.

Grice's maxims as normative background

The Gricean cooperative principle is that speakers and listeners will orientate to certain normative rules. For any utterance, the listener assumes that the speaker is abiding by the maxims and is saying something relevant, clear, informative and honest. Equally, the speaker knows that what she or he says will be treated by the listener as being relevant and so on.

The model treats this as a hurdle the speaker must foresee and jump; it commits the speaker to thinking hard in order to make her or his explanation relevant and so on. But there is a quite different reading, consistent with Grice's own belief that the principle is a normative, prescriptive one. The speaker can simply exploit the listener's expectation that what is coming is a relevant explanation. No special tailoring is necessary.

Attributionists would complain that we would never then be able to distinguish between 'good' and 'bad' explanations. According to that point of view, *because the spaceship was launched in cold weather* is a bad explanation (for the *Challenger* disaster) because 'without further information of various types, the truth, informativeness, relevance and clarity of this explanation remains to be established' (Hilton, 1991: 68). This is the wrong way round. The explanation is 'guaranteed' to be relevant by the operation of Gricean expectations. A listener who knew nothing about the *Challenger* affair would assume good faith on the explainer's part and suppose that the cold weather must have had something to do with the disaster (did it crack something? was a pipe frozen?). The explanation is 'bad' only in the sense that the listener's elaborations may be wrong or diffuse. It is good in the sense that the Gricean maxims, simply by being in place, ensure that it is counted as an explanation. Even if the answer was something like *well, you know what they say about Dallas technology*, that would be a successful explanation. We don't know the first thing about 'Dallas technology', but since we assume the reply is relevant, we take it that it is notoriously faulty, and that that caused the crash in some way. The model is committed to 'good-looking' rational use of the maxims, but since *any* filling of the post-question gap counts as an explanation, the rational calculus of the model will be no guide.

Causal answers can orientate to aspects other than the surface proposition of the question

There is another oddity in how the cooperative principle is used in the model. The explainer must tailor the candidate explanation to a guess about the other person's knowledge of the causal background of the event. This is true to the fundamental attributional belief in explanation as a matter of non-negotiable reporting. But in a real conversation, the prescription to 'make it relevant' (and so on) would involve the speaker in reacting to very much more than the propositional content of what has gone before.

Suppose A asks B why she or he came in at 2 o'clock last night. It is taken for granted by any pragmatic reading of language that the 'question' will mean a variety of things according to a range of factors, and there will be a consequential variety of cooperative responses. In one scenario the questioner is a worried parent and explainer B is a fifteen-year-old adolescent. In another A is the night shift superintendent and B is an employee. And so on. And for any one set of characters there will be a variety of facts which may or may not be salient: some of these are facts that might constrain a causal story (for example, whether it was raining outside, or whether the buses weren't running). These are the ones on which the conversational attribution model is based. But there are others, which will constrain not the causal story, but rather such things as the authority to ask the question (for example, the fact that the parent has herself just got in, or that she had said nothing about a deadline previously, and so on) or the speaker's obligation to answer it (for example, that the adolescent is, or may claim to be, *too tired to discuss it* and so on).

Responding to the request for an explanation will certainly mean adhering to the maxim of relevance, but the reply may be relevant not to the proposition and its attendant contrast case (which might be *why did you come in at 2 o'clock and not earlier?*) but rather to the question's deep store of pragmatic presuppositions. This notion of relevance might even come out openly: the parent might reject the child's answer as being 'impertinent', literally not relevant, but not relevant to what the parent wants it to be relevant to. For the child it *is* relevant, but to the parent's authority rather than to the request for causal information.

If we acknowledge that explanations can advert to non-propositional aspects of the question or utterance that sets them up, we make sense of causal explanations when they are 'impertinent'. In the following extract the critical question is, or seems to be, *why shouldn't you respect your mother today?*, and the response looks 'impertinent'.

(Henry and Zelda are a married couple in their mid-sixties; Irene is their neighbour in her mid-thirties. All are Jewish. Prior to the extract, Henry and Irene have been arguing about intermarriage between Jews and Gentiles. Henry has just told a story about how his brother was prevented from dating a Gentile woman by his mother years previously. 'He' in the first line is the brother.)

   1 *Henry*: But he– the fact is that he listens. T'my mother. And, he did her wishes. We respected our mother to the hilt

   2 *Irene*: But that was *years* ago

→ 3 *Henry*: But *why* shouldn't you respect your mother today?

   4 *Zelda*: Wait a– wait a minute. That's *his* opinion!

   5 *Henry*: Why should it be different?

6 *Irene*:   All right. Right. That was *years* ago. I don't feel that the kids– I
                  don't think
7 *Henry*:   D'you agree with me?
8 *Irene*:   The kids
9 *Zelda*:   heh?
10 *Henry*: D'you agree with me?
11 *Zelda*: No, don't agree with him. He has his own beliefs
(Schiffrin, 1987: 246; introductory remarks and transcription simplified)

In line 3, Henry makes what is ostensibly a request for an explanation, which could in principle be satisfied by a cause or a reason. Even if we leave aside the way it is immediately treated by Zelda and look at what happens when Henry repeats it in line 5, we see that the response it gets from Irene can't be accommodated by the conversational attribution model. She does not orientate to the propositional surface of the utterance – its appearance of being a request for an answer to a 'why' question – but rather to something else about it. Her *all right* concedes something, and it is tempting to see it as a concession that mothers should still ('today') be respected. This reading is corroborated by Henry asking Zelda (we suppose) not whether she can give an explanation, but whether she agrees with him. This confirms his earlier 'question' as really being a statement about mothers deserving respect. The 'explanation' Irene gives in line 6 is not an explanation of what could cause it to be the case that mothers ought not to be respected today, but rather a reaction to the legitimacy of raising the question at all.

Causal attributions in ordinary talk

We started at the origins of attribution theory with Heider's view of language and explanation. The positive stimulus of interest in lay accounts of social relations was tempered by a restricted view of language. The notion of explainer-as-scientist conceived of explanation as private apperception, of the explainer as one of an undifferentiated mass of ordinary persons, and of causation as a matter of dispositions inherent in a human agent. The middle period of empirical work on attributions used a paradigm which cemented these assumptions firmly into place. The conversation model did reach out to correct one of the assumptions – the causal problem the explainer had to solve – but left the other two unaddressed. It still assumes, on grounds distorted by old geological faults in the foundations of attribution theory, that the explainer's task is to causally explain the non-negotiable, literal event being presented by an interlocutor.

Of course, there are particular settings where such strictly informational, businesslike and 'cognitive' exchanges might take place: in a courtroom, say, or a scientific conference, or an inquiry into an accident. That is, indeed, just the kind of case the cognitive conversation model seems to be applicable to. It could be assumed, at least in principle, that in such a case there is nothing else going on but the disinterested search for the abnormal condition that discriminated between what did and didn't happen. But ordinary conversation is not so restricted, and indeed, as we shall see in later chapters, even in courtrooms and scientific laboratories the story might not be as straightforward as it might seem.

Edwards and Potter's discursive account of attribution

Edwards and Potter (1992) thicken the critical mixture above – which binds together various linguistic and pragmatic complaints that the conversation model is not conversational enough – by adding in two very potent ingredients of explanation which are missing. One is the observation that an explanation might renegotiate the puzzle it's meant to be solving: Edwards and Potter whip this up into the claim that the explanation (or the discourse of which it forms a part) is not so much a thought that has merely found expression in words, but is rather an 'action' in its own right, or in concert with other actions; as such it goes actually to 'constitute' the reality other analysts might take it just to be describing. The other ingredient they throw in is 'partiality': when explanations matter, Edwards and Potter point out, they matter *to* somebody or other, and are a means to some end; an explanation will be on somebody's side. These two ingredients are part of Edwards and Potter's 'discourse action model', and, as we shall be making reference to it at various points in the book, it is worth just taking a moment to describe what it says.

Edwards and Potter's discourse action model (Edwards and Potter, 1990, 1992) crystallizes the anti-cognitivist feeling that talk has been rather underplayed in attribution theory, 'social cognition' and in cognitive psychology more generally. The model redresses the balance by emphasizing action over cognition, interest over neutrality and the concerns of an interaction's participants over those of the spectating researcher. That is to say, it advises us to drop our worries about what individuals are thinking and attend rather to what they are visibly doing – excusing, blaming, reporting and so on – and recognize that, in ordinary life, the 'truth' and 'falsity' of what they do is a matter of management and arbitration rather than a matter of accuracy against an experimenter-set norm. Participants in interactions are accountable to each other, and they know it; they tailor their words and deeds to the expectation that each is keeping various sorts of tabs on the other: legal, moral and general or contingent, localized and specific to this or that subculture, speech event or transient interest. Edwards and Potter put all this in the form of a 'model' not to promote a recipe but as a salutary reminder that the term – and the precision and rigour it implies – has not wholly been lost to the other side; they would be just as happy with some description like 'a set of policies and recommendations for discursive enquiry' (1992: 155) were it not rhetorically to yield ground to the cognitivists and their claims to a proper programme for accumulating facts.

What keeps all this in reasonable order – from our point of view – can be simply put: explanations *do* things. That gives us a theme for the rest of this book. Throughout, we shall want to see how explanations do things in Edwards and Potter's three senses: how they are part of action, how they display 'interestedness' and how givers and receivers of explanations play to each other's expectations that each is accountable.

To start us off, we can usefully turn to Edwards and Potter themselves for an illustration of the kind of analysis that such a programme suggests. We shall not always be bound by it when we come to further chapters, but it will give us a helpful pole to push us off from the cognitive shores of attribution theory.

Discursive management of evidence: consensus

For the attribution theorist, consensus information is a given which affects social judgement of the cause of the disputed action. The more there is 'consensus' about the reaction to an 'entity', the more the entity caused the reaction. Hence if 'everyone' laughs at the comedian then one person's laughter is caused by the comedian, and not by peculiarities of the individual. Edwards and Potter's point is that consensus, in the real world, is not given but managed, and managed for rhetorical purposes. It is an achievement which is part of the performance of discourses of 'fact'. In other words, they take 'consensus' out of the realm of the vignette and into the interactional world of talk by interested parties.

The particular episode they use as a demonstration of their point is a minor verbal scuffle which happened in 1988 between Nigel Lawson, the then Chancellor of the Exchequer (the British minister of finance) and a group of journalists whom he had privately briefed. The journalists filed stories suggesting that the British government was contemplating a certain course of action which was controversial. Lawson denied it, and the reporters insisted not only that it was true but that it was based directly on their contemporaneous notes of what he had said to them. Contradictory versions of reality circulated: the reporters and their newspapers claimed one thing and Lawson and his office claimed another.

The crux of Potter and Edwards' argument is that if you look at the actual texts and talk produced by both sides – alive to the three notions of interestedness, actual exchanges and the constructive power of talk – you will see the very same consensus was used by both sides to campaign for two contradictory versions of reality. The newspaper reporters used the consensus among themselves as proof that the fault was not of their making (how could so many of them have misheard the Chancellor?) and that the 'cause' of the divergence between them and the Chancellor was not 'them'. So far this invokes the same notion of consensus that attribution theory invokes: the more people who see *X*, the less *X* is peculiar to any viewer. But their antagonist the Chancellor invokes consensus in a radically different way: the fact the reporters all agreed is proof that they actively colluded to make it up.

Mr Lawson: Oh yes, they will have their shorthand notes and they will know
                it, and they will know they went behind afterwards and they
                thought there was not a good enough story and so they
                produced that
(Edwards and Potter, 1992: 116)

Consensus, in the politician's usage, is not the passive reception of what the world provides; it is the active, and mischievous, invention of it. In attributional terms, it is as if the 'everyone' in the vignette 'everyone laughed at the comedian' was suddenly revealed to be a pre-arranged claque. Crudely speaking, the journalists inhabited (or claimed rhetorically to inhabit) the attribution theory world of impartial reporting, whereas the politician tactically committed himself (on this occasion at least) to a world in which facts are made up. The attributions of both sides are not fully describable in terms of attribution theory, either in its classic or its conversation model.

Looking forward: real language and social construction

What sense of ordinary explanation does a discursive analysis suggest, what problems does it see, and how are its methods meant to help? The following is in the nature of a trailer for things we shall be seeing in greater detail later on. A discursive account like Edwards and Potter's discourse action model (1992) offers us a view of human life which insists on 'action', or rather, 'action through the medium of talk'. In this they are, of course, in the tradition of other social scientists who have large claims to make about language and social life; we shall see more of the story in later chapters. Moreover, they propose that parties to such talk are alive to the interests it might promote, and that they appreciate that it makes them accountable; this is, on both counts, a recapitulation of theory elsewhere in the social sciences and a signal of work to come. According to Edwards and Potter, certain things, once the province of cognitive psychology (like memory, or causal attribution) now stand revealed as essentially reports which do discursive duties. Their particular pass on these duties is to understand them as representing the speaker as an accountable member of society – as we saw just now, through the promotion of her or his credentials as a factually unimpeachable observer, arriving at truthful explanation only after navigating responsibly through the tricky waters of self-interest.

Another lesson to learn is what to do about method. In the middle part of this chapter, our criticisms of the conversation model of attribution relied very heavily on examples from real-life exchanges between two people. Sketchy as it was, it was at a different grain of analysis from the more fully discursive approach which, as we saw briefly in Edwards and Potter's example above, is informed by a wider cultural, political and ideological reading of the context in which the text occurs. Both proceed from the same general principle: that everything uttered is uttered as a matter of choice, and the choice is more significant than a matter merely of personal idiosyncrasy.

We shall be seeing, in subsequent chapters, how one might proceed separately down both of these tracks to tell, on the one hand, a very minute, utterance-based story about explanation which invokes the notion of systematic rules in talk (the mechanics of which we shall see a great deal). On the other, there is a kind of a story to be told which is much more willing to go above exact wording and is friendlier to interpretation and exegesis. To start us off, we shall, in the next chapter, follow Edwards and Potter's discursive approach and turn our attention to how explainers manage the 'interestedness' of explanations, and what role these explanations can play in propping up, or rescuing, a speaker's social accountability.

Note

1. Examples labelled LL come from the author's analysis of the London–Lund corpus of unobtrusively recorded private conversations among mostly middle-class native English speakers, held as a computer database, but referred to here in its printed form (Svartvik and Quirk, 1980) for convenience. The first number identifies the conversation, the second the page and the third the point at which the extract starts.

4

Explanations in Exoneration

I wasn't feeling well at the start. The lights were in my eyes, and I thought he was going to foul me. I'm confident that I was the better man. It wasn't his blow that knocked me out, it was the impact of my head on the floor of the ring. I'm ready for Louis or Schmeling now. I wasn't fairly beaten. I won the first round on points. I think I slipped just before he hit me in the second round. I was going to hit him with all my might when it happened. I wasn't well, and my gloves weren't on properly. I had him beat, then I slipped up. I don't think he hit me at all. My shoes were slippery, and the floor was dangerously slippery, too. I think I won on points.
(fictional; from Frayn, 1963: 239)

In this chapter I shall take up the sense of explanation, satirized in the above extract, as being given when one is 'accounting for oneself'. In the last chapter we saw that there is a good deal of conversational room for manoeuvre in the exchange of an explanation, both linguistically and strategically. We saw that there were pragmatic conventions that a questioner and an explainer can exploit, and Edwards and Potter's (1992) discursive action model reminded us that, in the ordinary exchange of talk, speakers can always be seen as having interests to promote: that their talk can go some way actually to constructing various strategic versions of reality. All of these extra handles on explanation promise a firmer grasp of the phenomenon than might be possible with a traditionally cognitive account.

I shall be tracing the origins and development of social psychological work on the use of explanations as 'accounts' which are meant to excuse, justify or otherwise exonerate the speaker from socially sanctionable behaviour. In the literature on accounts we should find a recognition that explanations have a complex relation with the linguistic situation they appear in, and that they betray motivations other than the scientific model of honest reporting. We shall see, as the chapter progresses, that we are guided towards considering the exact manner and context in which explanations are exchanged.

Explanations given in times of trouble

Explanations given in exoneration are those that we give when we are in some trouble, or faced with some kind of accusation. The offences that we commit and the accusations that are thrown at us can range, in principle, from murder to a trivial gaffe, and an account offered in mitigation can be anything from a complicated insanity plea to a graciously simple apology.

Explanations and accounts of such apparently low denomination can be very valuable to the researcher interested in how people conceive of, and perhaps actively construct, their social worlds.

Existing work on exonerative accounts tends to concentrate on those offered for mundane failures, embarrassments and mistakes, and on the kind of account that is given in, or can be captured by, a single word or phrase. Certain kinds of exonerative accounts will fall to be discussed more naturally in other chapters: accounts given in the moral run of work and other social interaction in Chapter 6, and accounts people give of themselves and the lives they lead in Chapter 7. What I shall do in this chapter is stay fairly closely to accounts given for specific blameworthy action, and refer to them as 'exonerations' to keep them separate from these other meanings that the word 'account' can have.

Foundations

The 'accounts' literature has traditionally been concerned to develop classifications, or taxonomies, of types of exoneration. These taxonomies are sometimes put to the test in questionnaires, controlled experiments and, occasionally, in observational studies, but the spirit in most of the central work is exploratory and classificatory. There is a very different literature in ethnomethodology and sociolinguistics which insists on non-classificatory empirical examination of real talk in situations of real social breach, in the spirit of understanding not so much the order of the exonerations themselves as their place in their users' lives. The two traditions have common roots but have diverged. In the early part of the chapter we shall see how the modern, rather idealized, 'accounts' literature developed. In the latter part of the chapter we shall turn to concrete realizations of accounts as conversational performances.

'Vocabularies of motive'

'Men discern situations with particular vocabularies, and it is in terms of some delimited vocabulary that they anticipate consequences of conduct' (Mills, 1940: 906). The way people explained their actions, according to Mills, was the way they constituted themselves as people. His promotion of explanatory talk as a proper subject of social scientific interest prepared the ground for the social constructionism that was to come a generation later (and which we shall see more of in Chapter 7). For the moment we need only note that it successfully laid the ground for motive-talk – what people said about the reasons for what they did – to be considered as a profound source of evidence about social action. By, we could note in parentheses, sociologists; it is instructive to see how Heider's similar call was less well heeded by psychologists (see Chapter 2).

Mills' strong claim was taken up by those who wanted to use their respondents' accounts to explore why they acted as they did and how their reasons offended conventional mores. In that sense 'accounts' would become a methodological tool to help get the measure of a given social problem. Sykes and Matza (1957), for example, assimilated the notion of 'motives' into a theory of delinquency. This, the precursor of what was to become the 'accounts' literature, uses accounts in this stronger sense. If respondents' accounts were to be used as primary evidence of the boundaries to their social world – if people's explanations of their lives revealed the blueprints of the way they ran them – then, Sykes and Matza claimed, one could use the explanations given by delinquents to guess at the springs of their antisocial behaviour: 'These justifications . . . precede behaviour and make deviant behaviour possible' (1957: 666). To be a delinquent was precisely to behave in ways that were justifiable according to criteria different from those in the dominant culture. Delinquents would neutralize offences by appeal to the 'wrong' criteria: appeal to loyalty to other, equally delinquent, gang members; redescription of the offence as 'mischief'; and so on.

For theorists like Sykes and Matza, the account and the social phenomenon it meant to exonerate were equally important. The interest of the 'techniques of neutralization' their delinquents used was the insight it gave into the springs of their social action. The concern with explanations for large-scale social breaches – social breaches as a way of life – was soon jostled aside by an eagerness to study accounting as a phenomenon in itself – what its outlines were and how it worked as a general repairer of (anyone's) social breach. We shall see in Chapters 6 and 7 how accounts resurfaced as measures of the social construction of identity. But in the search for general mechanisms of everyday exoneration, specific contexts like delinquent talk were subordinated to cultural universals which could apply to offences across the social board.

Accounts for offences: Goffman and 'self-presentation' in talk

Erving Goffman's early observations on repairing embarrassment (1956), and on 'self-presentation' more generally (Goffman, 1959, 1971), were not so committed to the strong version of Mills' position: he was less sure that there was something internal and longstanding about people's lives that could be captured by their transient accounts. He certainly agreed that accounts constituted some part of reality, but it was the fleeting reality of day-to-day encounters: an account would do local work – crucial, but quickly over.

Goffman began a research project on repair which is still far from finished. We should take stock first of how he wanted the project to go, because succeeding generations have not always tackled it the same way. One very important likely confusion we should clear up at the start is that what Goffman meant by 'self-presentation' was rather different – more sociological – than what is meant by the modern social psychological literature which uses the same term. Goffman saw presentation as part of the continual joint construction of meaningful activity. To self-present was perpetually to monitor the fit between one's social identity and that demanded by the situation. Some social psychologists, on the other hand, take it more unilaterally and literally to be a question of the 'self', motivated by ego-promotion or ego-defence. They normally frame self-presentational behaviour as being by definition insincere, and set it down to personal, and rather ignoble, needs: the need to be liked, to have influence and to show off.

The consequence of this is that it encourages them to think of self-presentation as a personality variable, and to that degree independent of the social stream: the research they do tends to measure or manipulate people's various 'drives' and see how they affect their behaviour in given circumstances; thus, for example, it is found that people anxious about their performance perform badly when made to face threatening audiences (Schlenker and Leary, 1982). This means that the actual instrument of self-presentation – the exoneration, apology and so on – is for them merely a behavioural expression of the inner motivation and not of much interest in its own right. The consequence for us is that we can't turn to the self-presentation literature in social psychology for much help with *forms* of exonerations, though, if we were interested, we could turn to it for speculations about people's personal motivations for using them. Even then, we should have to accept models which have rather untheorized images of personal motivation, a problem we met when we sorted through the related literature on self-serving attribution.

To return to Goffman, then, and to set exonerations firmly in the social stream: disturbances, according to his way of thinking, are smoothed over by self-presentational practices designed to preserve the faces of *all* concerned. Some of these practices are retrospective (apologies, say, or excuses) and some are prospective (warnings, requests). Some, like these two, are done by, or on behalf of, the offender. Others are done by the audience (acknowledging the offender's defence, say, or deliberately not noticing that there was an offence at all). Exonerations make sense not as individual solos but as orchestrated ensemble performances, as part of the 'corrective cycle' which fills in the breach and moves the interactional sequence back onto firmer ground.

The exoneration was, according to Goffman, one part of the event, one device among many. But it was exonerations that received most attention in the subsequent take-up by sociologists.

Exonerations

The first classic paper in what came to be known as the 'accounts' literature was the schematic, but very suggestive, listing of accounts by Scott and Lyman (1968). They abstracted Sykes and Matza's (1957) 'techniques of neutralization' from the specific case of the delinquent and added it to their own list of what were, now, to be 'accounts' for any piece of social deviance, from a gaffe to a crime. An account, according to Scott and Lyman, was 'a statement made by a social actor to explain unanticipated or untoward behaviour – whether that behaviour is his own or that of others, and whether the proximate cause for the statement arises from the actor himself or someone else' (1968: 112). They were out to identify the most general parameters of accounts so as then to locate specific versions in specific contexts of actors and audiences.

Hindsight allows us to note two things. One is that they used the term 'accounts' to cover only exonerations for specific behavioural offences. This cut off their theory from other offences and other sites of accounting. The other is that they restricted themselves to exonerations achieved by explanation, putting out of bounds other forms of prevention and repair which Goffman had gone to some trouble to identify as part of the corrective cycle. This puzzling restriction – and the trifling citation of Goffman, hardly used – was only corrected late in the day when, as we shall see, social psychologists put accounting talk back into its situational context. Until then, Scott and Lyman's taxonomic template – more general than Sykes and Matza's theory of delinquency, and with much more heuristic detail than Mills had offered – dominated the 'accounts' field, and their preference for a-contextual rules dominated its ambitions.

Excuses and justifications

Scott and Lyman (1968) began their taxonomic split by separating 'excuses', exonerations which denied that the actor had responsibility for the act, from 'justifications', exonerations which accepted responsibility for the act but gave permissible reasons for it. The split is taken from J. L. Austin's linguistic philosophy in 'A plea for excuses' (1961), a source of a great deal of the ideas implicit in this and subsequent 'accounts' work, though here relegated, like Goffman, to a cursory footnote. Neither Scott and Lyman nor their successors were eager to seek philosophical authority for their project, which, in the drive for rough and ready classification, never reached the subtlety of Austin's witty probing. Austin was aware of the lurking dangers and had kept to the task of clearing the undergrowth; Scott and Lyman and their successors were unashamed about building on whatever ground they could find. If that meant hasty definitional decisions and the likely consequent semantic muddles, then so be it; a policy which, as we saw in Chapter 2, ultimately proved ruinous for their contemporary colleagues in the neighbouring field of causal attribution.

What was, then, Scott and Lyman's taxonomy of exonerations? Among 'excuses', they distinguish (in, as I remarked, a rough and ready way) between straightforward claims that the offence is an accident or that it is 'biologically driven', and the excuses of 'defeasibility' (*I didn't know it would lead to this*) and 'scapegoating' (*it was all so-and-so's fault*). Among 'justifications', they have the denial of injury; the appeal to (higher) loyalties

(*I did what I had to do for the sake of the gang*); the denial of the victim (or rather, a claim that the victim somehow deserved the injury); and the condemnation of condemners (*the police are worse*). Again, these require no special comment. Scott and Lyman add 'sad tales' and 'self-fulfilment', and these do perhaps need a little unpacking; a 'sad tale' is one that reveals hidden reasons for sympathy, while 'self-fulfilment' is to offer evidence that the act was personally fulfilling.

Since Scott and Lyman's treatment of each of these is not meant to be waterproof, it would be wrong to dwell on definitional difficulties. (In what sense is it a 'justification' to condemn the condemners? Is a sad tale of personal incapacity an excuse or a justification? and so on.) Theirs is a heuristic list, not meant to be exhaustive but to promote 'accounts' as a researchable area.

The invitation was duly taken up by Hewitt and Stokes (1975) who, in the same urgency to build rather than to check the foundations, added their own wing ('disclaimers') to the accounts edifice. Disclaimers were devices which could be used (unlike retrospective exonerations) to repair a breach before it happened. Hewitt and Stokes offer a list of disclaimer types in much the same spirit as Scott and Lyman. There is the 'hedge' (*I'm no expert . . .*); 'credentialling' (*Now I generally like your work, but . . .*); 'sin licences' (*I know this is against the rules, but . . .*); 'cognitive disclaimers' (*I know this sounds daft, but . . .*); 'appeals for the suspension of judgement' (*Now don't get upset, but . . .*). Again, like Scott and Lyman, Hewitt and Stokes follow these up with various suggestive notes about how these disclaimers might be given and countered, and what their implications are for actions chosen and forgone. Equally, the virtue in what they say is not the specific detail but the fact that they come up with a plausible story to tell about another facet of explanation-giving as a form of social regulation, so further extending its researchability.

How the taxonomy grew

The generous design of the original Scott and Lyman taxonomy guaranteed that its boundaries would never be stable. Many people offered suggestions and variants on one part or other of the scheme. One profitable byway, for example, was to develop Sykes and Matza's (1957) notion of 'redescription' as a means of exoneration. This has been a thread weaving in and out of the accounts literature (Backman, 1976; Harré, 1981), with forays into attribution theory territory (Howard and Leventhal, 1985).

More thoroughgoing refurbishment was done independently by Schönbach (1980) in his empirical work on escalation in 'account phrases' and by Tedeschi and Reiss (1981) in their theoretical review of how 'predicaments' are managed. Both Schönbach and Tedeschi and Reiss marshalled the variety by bundling together subtypes of excuse and justification under a new, middle-level order of families. Tedeschi and

Reiss, for example, grouped the accumulated thirty-eight discrete exonerations into a more manageable ten families (so 'scapegoating' and 'condemning the condemners', for example, became subtypes of 'social comparisons').

In spite of this marshalling work, the list was growing, and with it the danger that empirical verification of the exonerations taxonomy would always be trumped by further elaboration. It would be easy to forget that the motive force for looking at exonerations was the insight they would offer into social action, and that the taxonomic listing should only have been a preliminary phase. Fortunately some order, and a sense of perspective, was brought onto the site by Semin and Manstead's comprehensive survey in 1983.

Semin and Manstead's review of the exoneration taxonomy

Semin and Manstead (1983) tidied up the accumulated excuses, justifications and so on into a comprehensive scheme (which appears in Table 4.1). They kept Austin's basic geographical split between excuses and justifications, and put the bulk of Schönbach's (1980) and Tedeschi and Reiss's (1981) lists on either side. They systematized the middle-level clusters of subtypes and filled in minor niches, occasionally cropping a duplication and finding a better label for a sub-account. Semin and Manstead also cleared up some of the conceptual difficulties left hanging from the earliest days: thus, for example, a 'sad tale' is recast more convincingly as an excuse rather than a justification (as Scott and Lyman, 1968, originally had it). By improving on Schönbach's and Tedeschi and Reiss's middle-order classifications (e.g. 'denial of injury' and 'minimization of injury' are both subsumed under the more general justification that 'the effect has been misrepresented') the list has been made more coherent and exhaustive.

Semin and Manstead's more important achievement, though, was not the tidying up of the exonerations list but, paradoxically, the relegation of exonerations back to the role of supporting players in Goffman's 'corrective cycle'. They followed Schönbach in reminding us that exonerations occur in sequences of action, but widened the perspective to include the range of 'motive-talk' devices that Goffman had originally envisaged. Thus they bring into play apologies, requests, acknowledgements and the ensemble of practices that go to make up the management of social breaches. The offence is back into centre stage and the rest of the ensemble deployed around it. Intriguingly, a review by Nichols (1990) came independently to the same kind of restatement of the accounts event in temporal terms. Nichols distils accounts into eight types and organizes them into four that precede the offence (disclaimers, pretexts, explanations and neutralizations) and four that come after it (admissions, excuses, justifications and denials). In any case, the important thing is that the account is put firmly back into its place as one element in the cycle of offence, restitution and acceptance.

Table 4.1　*Semin and Manstead's (1983) typology of accounts*

A　Excuses

>　A1　Denial of intent
>　　　　Accident or unforeseen consequences
>　　　　Identity of target person mistaken
>　A2　Denial of volition
>　　　　Physical or psychological causes
>　　　　Lack of authority
>　A3　Denial of agency
>　　　　Mistaken identity or amnesia
>　　　　Joint production
>　A4　Appeal to mitigating circumstances
>　　　　Scapegoating
>　　　　Sad tales

B　Justifications

>　B1　Claim that effect has been misrepresented
>　　　　Denial or minimization of injury
>　B2　Appeal to principle of retribution
>　　　　Reciprocity of harm
>　　　　Derogation of victim
>　B3　Social comparison
>　B4　Appeal to higher authority
>　　　　Powerful person(s) commanded
>　　　　Institutional rules stipulated
>　B5　Self-fulfilment
>　　　　Self-maintenance or self-development
>　　　　Conscience
>　B6　Appeal to principle of utilitarianism
>　　　　Law and order or self-defence
>　　　　Benefits outweigh harm
>　B7　Appeal to values
>　　　　Political, moral or religious
>　B8　Appeal to need for facework
>　　　　Face maintenance
>　　　　Reputation building

Source: Semin and Manstead, 1983: 91–2; somewhat simplified

Do people use these accounts?

The accounts literature, in its narrow or wide form, would have nothing to recommend it were it not properly to represent what actually happens when people give and receive exonerations. What is the evidence that people use the excuses and justifications so painstakingly classified? Ashworth (1979: 153), reviewing Mills' legacy, complained that 'hardly a start had been made' on this chapter of Mills' programme of accounts research. By the time of Semin and Manstead's review (1983) some evidence had started to accumulate, but, even now, a decade later, the pile is not high, and is of variable quality. We shall look over some typical research then move on to ask why progress has been so patchy.

Paper and pencil studies

At no point in the field's development, it seems, has anyone checked empirically to see if the list of exonerations current at the time was exclusive or exhaustive. What little empirical work was done accepted the contemporary list (or some workable version of it) at face value and concentrated on testing how effective the various exonerations were. In a small literature the majority of studies are paper and pencil tests. Experiments like those of Mehrabian (1967), Blumstein et al. (1974) and Schlenker and Darby (1981) presented subjects with information about an offence which would be manipulated one way or another. Respondents would be asked to rate how acceptable they found various exonerations given by various offenders and it would be found that, say, acceptability varied with 'the moral worth of the offender, his penitence, his superior status relative to the demander, and the offensiveness of the violation' (Blumstein et al. 1974: 551).

Reviewing this kind of empirical work, Semin and Manstead felt able to offer only this cautious summary: that 'one consistent feature of the findings . . . is that accounts are limited in their power to stem negative evaluations of the offender' (1983: 114). Otherwise, little could be said, and even then the conclusion had to be qualified with a reminder that the data came from paper and pencil quizzes. Semin and Manstead looked forward to research that asked 'how frequently the elements distinguished in typologies of motive talk are employed in naturally occurring offerings' (1983: 115).

Seven years later, two reviews (Cody and McLaughlin, 1990; Nichols, 1990) added some more examples of empirical work on perceived acceptability. The hypothetical offences in these new studies ranged from late essays (Hale, 1987) and other 'social predicaments' (Holtgraves, 1989) to politicians' corruption (Riordan et al., 1983). There has also been some work on children's understanding of exonerations in vignettes (e.g. Bennett, 1989). All these are subject to the same reservations about verbatim usage, and are still some way from answering Semin and Manstead's question.

Experiments

The few experiments that have been done to test the efficacy of exonerations have been equally second-hand, relying on the experimenters' operationalizations of what they thought were good examples of various kinds of exonerations. The typical method is for a confederate to commit some offence and present an exoneration. Respondents' behaviour is secretly monitored to see if the exoneration has worked. Thus, for example, Langer et al.'s confederate (1978) prefaced a potentially impolite request to jump a photocopier queue with various justifications, one of which was (allegedly) 'meaningless'. Ungar (1981) got his confederate to knock over a suitcase on a railway platform then offer an excuse (*you shouldn't have left it there, someone might have tripped over it*). Weiner et al. (1987, studies 3 and 4) had their confederate proffer excuses for turning up late for an experiment. It is a shame that there are not more of these controlled excursions from the laboratory; it would have been intriguing to try to knit together the results they came up with. But since the available studies each use their own definitions of justifications, excuses and so on, it would be premature to work too hard at joining them up. They would have benefited from being laid more carefully into the exoneration inventory available in the taxonomies of Scott and Lyman and their successors; perhaps we shall see such programmes in the future, though, as we shall see, there are some difficult questions of operationalization to be resolved.

Studies of reported exonerations

All of the research mentioned above filters talk through the researchers' operationalizations. There have also been a few studies that solicited actual exonerations or, more accurately, reports of exonerations, in respondents' own language. Those that ask about very real offences tend to classify the exonerations in a way appropriate to the specific aims of the study, but in consequence lose generalizability. Hence, Felson and Ribner (1981), for example, coded the formal pleas given by men jailed for murder and assault simply into 'legal' and 'other' excuses and justifications. The more typical laboratory studies impose more elaborate category schemes, but the offences may be fictional or comparatively trivial and the exonerations they elicit necessarily less authentic. Schönbach's project of mapping exonerations in their proper place in the corrective cycle, for example, depended on respondents making written judgements about retrospective or hypothetical situations (e.g. Schönbach and Kleibaumhüter, 1989). In McLaughlin et al. (1983), probably the most thorough and sensitive of these experiments, student respondents provided retrospective narratives which were then filleted into sequences of reproaches and exonerations, each being carefully subdivided into constituent types.

In all of these examples, the data were solicited and generated in a documentary, written-down spirit. A closer approximation to exonerations in the raw is Cody and McLaughlin's study of exonerations given by motorists in situations of genuine accountability – when stopped at the roadside, for example (Cody and McLaughlin, 1985) or when accused in court (1988). In the latter, student observers wrote down summaries of the defendants' courtroom statements, which were later coded into various types of exoneration. Results included, for example, the finding that excuses were the most frequent exoneration, but were less effective than logical proofs of the defendant's innocence. This study raises very interesting questions about the language of accounts, and we shall come to it again below.

The model of language implicit in the accounts literature

McLaughlin et al.'s studies come nearer than the paper and pencil studies to the spirit of Goffman's project of charting the efficacy of real accounts in real situations, but there is still something amiss. Semin and Manstead (1983) had hinted at the problem when they complained that the linguistic grain of most studies was rather coarse, and Nichols (1990) makes those doubts stronger by complaining about the confusion in the literature between accounts as single statements and as lengthy presentations. Perhaps most seriously, critics of Langer's study (Langer et al., 1978) which claimed to show the effectiveness of allegedly 'mindless' justification (for example, Shotter, 1981: 166) pointed out that, in an accounting context, the function of the utterance is not always readable from its surface form.

These two complaints – that the linguistic grain was too coarse, and that context was devalued – are familiar to us from our consideration in Chapter 2 of attribution theory's conception of language. They send up a cloud of doubts about the accounting literature's implicit model of language and language use.

Fortunately, the problem has been spotted by Buttny (1993) who crystallizes it like this: 'Relying on the researcher's intuitions or re-spondents' reconstructions and hypothetical evaluations results in broad glosses of the phenomena, and . . . [results] in a conception of a person offering "*the*" account, as though accounts are invariably achieved in a *single speech act*' (1993: 30). In other words, Buttny neatly identifies the trouble as being due to the implicit reliance on a certain view of language: that the explainer can achieve her or his ends by the judicious use of certain words and phrases, and that the researcher can stand to one side and make an inventory of such words and phrases as they pass by.

It must be said that nowhere in the accounts literature is the case for treating exonerations as speech acts made quite so explicitly, but Buttny is surely right in his observation: it is the only theorization that makes sense of the enterprise of listing and classifying exonerations. Let us take a brief look at the theory of speech acts before turning to see how they might be applicable.

Speech acts

The same Austin who had unwittingly given the accounts literature its principal organizing device – the split between excuse and justification – was also the source of its principal (if implicit) model of language: that utterances 'do things' (Austin, 1962).

Austin observed that there are many things that we say which are not reports of states of affairs, and so not a matter of being true or false: to order a drink, to warn someone, or to christen a baby are actions in their own right, and they have effects on the world around the speaker: in Austin's terminology, they were 'illocutionary acts', which had 'perlocutionary effects'. Of course, properly to utter an illocution, you had to be suitably authorized: you couldn't name a baby without being a priest and doing it at the due moment at a formal christening, nor could you promise someone something you knew that you didn't have in your power to give, and so on. This, in fact, is the way they are assessed – not by virtue of their truth or falsity, but by virtue of their 'felicity'. Your right to perform the act, your sincerity, the obligation and ability of your hearer to respond in the appropriate way; these are general 'felicity conditions', and every specific speech act adds some more on top.

Are promising, warning and so on – what Austin calls 'performatives' – just a subclass of language, identified by certain special verbs, always in the present tense (*I warn you!* or *you are hereby invited to the Queen's garden party*)? And, if so, might we then be able to spot excuses and justifications? Not at all: even *she warned you last week that the chair was broken* could serve perfectly well as a warning right now (just as, say, you were about to sit down on it, momentarily forgetting). There is no hard and fast test of vocabulary or grammar that will separate performatives off from 'ordinary' statements. Just about any form of words will serve as a performative in the right (felicitous) conditions: *it'll tip over!*; *we're taking that chair to the refuse-tip tomorrow*; *don't!*; *Camilla fell off that this morning*; *whoah!* and so on. That means that we have to consider the felicity conditions of any and every utterance we come across – merely asking whether it's true or false won't reach the limit of its possible meanings.

This establishes, then, that performatives don't form a separate identifiable class; but what about those statements which, even when we look at them carefully, don't seem to have any performative function: *she warned you last week that the chair was broken* said in some neutral context (say, in an enquiry about just when the chair was discovered to be broken)? Surely these are outside the remit of the theory, and are simply true or false? Austin replies that even this utterance must observe felicity conditions: there are certain things which must obtain before the speaker can sensibly make it – in this example, that there is indeed a 'she', a chair (in fact 'the' chair) to warn someone about, a 'you' to be warned, and so on. If one of these conditions did not obtain, then what I am saying is not true or false; it is as senseless (or infelicitous) as my saying that *the President of Scotland warned you that the Pope's wife was coming*. We have to treat even the apparently bland 'act' of making a statement in the same way as the richer 'acts' of warning and so on, and subject them all to tests of felicity.

To sum up, then: all utterances do things. The most 'basic' is merely 'doing' reporting, but even this needs to be felicitously done. On top of this, and more interestingly, there is a certain kind of 'doing' which, if it follows certain conventions, will count as a social act in its own right: a speech act. This speech act will have consequences in the world: perlocutionary effects.

Does it help to think of exonerations as speech acts?

In what follows I shall try to pick at some of the problems that come along with the notion of exonerations as speech acts, but, since the issue is not one dealt with explicitly in the accounts literature – we don't know which particular version of speech-act theory, for example, would be acceptable to the accounts theorists – my remarks will have to be general, rather than specifically addressed to one or other candidate theory.

The exoneration Buttny's (1993) observation that accounts theorists are, ultimately, committed to a speech-act theory of exoneration identifies the danger of reification – of treating as independent something that only made sense as part of a larger ensemble – that had been present ever since Scott and Lyman pulled out accounts from Goffman's corrective cycle. Buttny asks: if an exoneration is a speech act, that is to say an utterance that performs a certain social action, how can one recognize it? How do we know that such-and-such an utterance stands alone, and functions as an appeal to insanity, a blaming of the other, or any other entry in the exoneration grid?

The first standard problem is that not all speech functions need exclusively to be performed in speech. Exoneration could be accomplished non-verbally: the verbal taxonomic approach strays from Goffman's original observation that the corrective cycle was a performance the objective of which could be achieved not just by the spoken scripts but by nods, winks, 'body language' and the whole range of stage business at the command of the sophisticated social performer. This bedevils verificatory research because many exonerations will have some kind of elliptical analogue, which might, in the right circumstances, be wholly non-verbal. It is certainly possible to imagine 'apology' and 'denial', for example, being acted out in mime.

The deeper problem is the set of objections which can be levelled at speech-act theory as an analysis of *any* verbal device. We had reason in Chapter 2 to query whether an attributional account of 'self-serving bias' could satisfactorily guide us on how people would use internal and external attributions in varying circumstances, and we see that that was a specific instance of this general problem of identifying speech acts. If exoneration is a speech act, the theorists would have to propose something along the lines of the rules that constitute them; but if they did so (and the nearest they get is the exemplifications they give to the subheadings of their taxonomies) then they would be proposing iron definitions too rigid for ordinary usage, just as attributionists insist that self-interest could not be served by making an internal attribution for success. Even Nichols' (1990) proposal that re-searchers should look out for combinations of account, as well as their basic forms, is committed to the view that the accounts are definable as individual atoms out of context.

Levinson puts the general case against breaking conversational talk down into moves or speech acts like this:

> Single sentences can be used to perform two or more speech acts in different clauses, and each clause . . . may perform more than one speech act. Further, there are many sub-sentential units that occur as utterances and it is possible for non-linguistic vocalisations (e.g. laughter) . . . to perform appropriate responses to utterances . . . [It] is impossible to specify in advance what kinds of behavioural units will carry major interactional acts: rather the units in question seem to be functionally defined by the actions they can be seen to perform in context. (1983: 291)

Applying the general case of recognizable form to such exonerations as apologies, Coulter (1979: 184–5) points out that 'If the rules were truly constitutive, then all of our communicative actions should be accessible in terms of correctness or incorrectness; but how could one be said to apologize "incorrectly" or to insult "correctly"? They do not have these adverbial tolerances at all.' The upshot is that we cannot be sure that any of the 'accounts' in the existing inventories are actually used by anyone, since the way they are described rests too much on the notion of easily identifiable acts.

The offence   Once Buttny has spotted the speech-act issue as a problem for categorizing the account, we see that it can also be a problem for identifying the offence. What does it mean to speak about 'the offence' for which an exoneration is being solicited? Theoretically, the taxonomic tradition takes the offence generally to be an offence against some kind of social norm: the offence is referred to, variously, as 'untoward behaviour' by Scott and Lyman (1968); the 'failure event' by Schönbach (1980) and Cody and McLaughlin (1985); the 'undesirable event' by Schlenker (1980). That the offence offends is incontestable, but the question remains as to how people go about signalling to each other that some norm has indeed been breached. Semin and Manstead (1983) afford the offence centre stage, but do not ask how it comes to be constructed *as* an offence.

In practice, the verificatory research finesses the issue by simply presenting respondents with offences ready framed. This is obvious in such experiments as Blumstein's or Ungar's, in which the offence and accusation are written or acted out. It is also true in observational or documentary studies: in Cody and McLaughlin's (1985) study the offence is set up by the judicial surroundings and the formulas of the law. In McLaughlin et al. (1983), students' written recollections were searched for 'reproaches' which were coded apparently unproblematically into six categories (for example, 'projected excuse': 'My husband said, "Where the hell have you been? Did you forget to wind your watch again?"' McLaughlin, 1990: 235). Schönbach and Kleibaumhüter (1989) presented respondents with vignettes which varied the accusations operationally (for example, 'derogation of self-esteem': 'How could that have happened to you? Apparently, you were occupied too much with yourself!'). Such coding and operationalization is very plausible but we might, as analysts, want to know more about the interpretative work that has gone into it. Moreover, if we look back at Scott and Lyman (1968) we see a disturbingly wide range of 'offences' – 'being a homosexual', for example – whose social sanction is obviously variable in place, time and culture. The question of what an 'offence' is should not be dismissed *a priori*. We need to have a theoretical perspective which will acknowledge that there will be as much going on in accusing as there is in exonerating the offender.

Identifying accusations and exonerations in talk

To be proof against these complaints, the literature on accounting would have to have principled ways of identifying the speech acts of accusation and exoneration in talk. But it has not really faced up to the question of how one goes about recognizing accounts, of whatever sort, in ordinary language. Those few recent studies in the accounting literature that do collect ordinary language do not address accusations at all, and demote the difficulties in interpreting exonerations to a matter of coding. Assuming that they can look for 'the' exoneration utterance, the coders break up the text into chunks and then assign each chunk to a discrete category. The preliminary chunking, as Nichols (1990) complained, presents serious problems in its own right (does one categorize a whole sentence? one word? a paragraph?). The further, and the more fundamental, challenge is to assign the candidate unambiguously to one category, and to have that category filled with a finite and exclusive set of items. That challenge is not, as the accounts theorists uniformly assume, merely a methodological one. It is theoretically weighty, since the very notion of categorizing an utterance makes sense only on the assumption that exonerations are performed as speech acts. But what if one cannot read off the function of the utterance from its surface content, and what if one saw that a given exoneration type could be realized by very different utterances?

We could turn to anthropologists to give us examples from other cultures to show that the surface form of what someone says can't be tied literally to the function we naïve hearers might take it to have. But let us stay within anglophone culture recognizable to most readers of this book. If we go back to Cody and McLaughlin's study of courtroom exonerations, we recall that what the defendants said was summarized by an observer before being turned over to the coders. Let us assume, for the purposes of interpretation, that the report is completely faithful. The summary is given in the form of a dialogue, as in this part-extract:

> *Counsel*:   Reckless driving. What is your plea?
> *Defendant*:   Guilty as charged
> (Cody and McLaughlin, 1988: 120)

The account the defendant gives is coded by the authors as a 'concession': 'those cases in which an actor admitted guilt or stated that she or he would not contest the ticket' (1988: 120). That is surely reasonable, but only because we know that the phrase is being uttered in the tightly constrained circumstances of a courtroom where certain formulas have well-established meanings. Even here, though, Pollner (1979) reports that in some courts there is more latitude than others in how one is allowed to concede guilt. In one court only 'guilty' or 'not guilty' were permitted. In another the judge would accept 'guilty in part sir . . . with extenuating circumstances' as a plea, and in a third court the judge would accept no explicit plea at all, or treat no plea as a kind of 'not guilty'. So there is more than one way to communicate a concession. The converse is also true: that an apparent concession of guilt may mean other things. Suppose the phrase had been uttered in this context:

> (Hypothetical talk among friends)
> *A*:   So – I see you've been elected to the country club
> *B*:   [*embarrassed laugh*] Guilty as charged

In this (admittedly invented) example, we read the phrase *guilty as charged* as a kind of apology. It works by explicitly agreeing with A's potential valuation that being elected to the country club is a dubious honour; not only does B's 'guilty as charged' formulation avoid an immodestly boastful confirmation (which could have been done by a neutral *yes, just last week*, say), but it debases the election into a 'crime'.

If context is the hidden frame that supports the meaning of even such an apparently straightforward phrase as *guilty as charged*, how much more important, then, is context when the utterance is less formulaic? Let us see the whole of Cody and McLaughlin's extract, adding turn numbers for convenience:

> 1   *Counsel*:   Reckless driving. What is your plea?
> 2   *Defendant*:   Guilty as charged
> 3   *Counsel*:   Were you under the influence of alcohol at the time of the arrest?
> 4   *Defendant*:   I had two beers at dinner
> 5   *Counsel*:   Oh, the old 'just two beers' story
> 6   *Defendant*:   Yes, your honour
> 7   *Counsel*:   Well, the charge will stand, but I want you to attend 12 AA meetings, and [take] a \$406 fine [and] 36 months' summary probation
> 8   *Defendant*:   Isn't that a little bit harsh?
> 9   *Counsel*:   Not for someone who is a threat to other drivers on the road

(Cody and McLaughlin, 1988: 120; bracketed insertions in original)

For Cody and McLaughlin, the defendant's second turn (line 4) is 'typical of the category' of concessions, which 'could include apologies, offers of restitution and promises that the behaviour would not recur' (1988: 120). But deciding whether the defendant is offering one of these is very different from deciding whether he or she is 'conceding'. *Guilty as charged* is one of a very small number of possible answers, each of which has fairly fixed (but not wholly so) courtroom meanings. The content of turn 4, on the other hand, is not fixed in the same way. The defendant's choice of what to say, and how to say it, is significant in a way that the guilty or not guilty plea could not be.

If we shake off our preconceptions and simply look at what is actually going on between the two speakers, we soon see that *I had two beers at dinner* is not quite the exonerative speech act that Cody and McLaughlin have in mind. It seems to work rather as an acknowledgement, and a repair, of the further offence implied by counsel in turn 3, committing the (already conceded) offence under the influence of alcohol. Although the reply avoids overt disagreement (the defendant could have, but did not, merely say *no*), it repairs the disagreement, as Pomerantz has shown (1984b), by offering an account (claiming the smallness of the quantity of alcohol, and the legitimizing context in which it was consumed). Taken together it adds up to a turn which we could gloss as *I am conceding that I had drunk alcohol, but in legitimate circumstances, and in insufficient quantities to impair my driving.* In other words, this turn constructs counsel's preceding turn as an accusation and, at the same time, offers a redescription of its premiss.

The cultural context

Just as a fixed vocabulary of explanation drove attribution theory down a narrow, perhaps rather artificial, path, the accounts literature risks losing its original application to real exchanges by its development in abstract speech-act categories. We saw in the last section how explanations offered in exoneration were hard to pin down to specific words and phrases. To say something about exoneration, we had to make some attempt to describe the language game, or speech situation, in which the speaker and hearer found themselves. The need is more obvious when we step outside our own culture and familiar landmarks are lost: the tourist's outrage at (what to him or her seems to be) insultingly inadequate exoneration or restitution is the strongest possible signal that there is a problem of interpretation.

> I am drawing my car up to a parking space to park parallel with the curb when a man in a small car that fits the space easily slipped in behind my car. Angry, I got out and spoke to him about it. It was as though I were not there at all. The man's face was completely blank and he seemed to be 'staring through' me. I returned to my car, and it was only when I was about to drive away that I heard a voice behind me, but in a low tone that gave me to understand that he did not intend to say anything in reply. (Morris, 1981: 96)

Even if the ethnographer solicits the respondents' own views of the meaning of exonerations, the cultural difference still has to be bridged. Herzfeld (1985) gives an illustration of how Cretan shepherds reveal that an account has formulaic meanings perhaps not obvious from the bare utterance itself. In this extract a villager is evaluating a sheep-stealer's excuse that he had not realized to whom the animals belonged: the excuse, Herzfeld's informant says,

> is a [statement of] cause, a phrase, so to speak, a justification which justifies everything. And it does make you wonder . . . He gives you the impression that . . . perhaps he really didn't know. In other words, this is a rule, a justification. He can't very well tell you 'I didn't do it, and *that* fellow stole them from you!' There should be 'reasons'. He comes and tells you 'Yes, I did take them'. If there are 'reasons'. When there are none, however, what can he say to you? [Would you want him to say] 'I want to begin a family quarrel with you, because I just *want* to?' That's out of the question! (Herzfeld, 1985: 184)

The studied ambiguity of the claimed excuse is sanctioned in this Cretan community, for which the 'offence' of sheep stealing is not a simple legal matter with simple motives of greed. On the contrary, it can be socially cohesive:

> He may do it deliberately. There is a strong possibility, however, that he may wish [for an alliance], when you are strong . . . He may want to be friends with you, so he comes and steals your animals intentionally, so to speak, so as to establish ties with you. (Herzfeld, 1985: 184)

In such a situation, then, the act of 'exoneration' takes on a ritualistic meaning that it would not have for offences which carried less of a social charge than does sheep stealing for these villagers. Without that proper cultural translation of the speaker's community's normal practices, we should be at a loss to make something of the account.

Although these are second-hand reports of exonerations, they do point up the difficulties of arriving at hard and fast semantic rules of spotting what counts as potential exoneration. In the last section of the chapter, we take heart from the sketchy analysis we made of the courtroom example above, and see if there might be something about the exact way in which the participants knit and weave their words (and silences) together that might help us to see what sense they are making.

The organization of exonerative accounts

As Pollner (1979) remarks, the courtroom is a site *par excellence* of disputes about reality and which version of the truth holds; and, since the participants are engaged in accusing, defending or arbitrating, their behaviour will tell us something about exoneration and its management. Arbitration has been looked at (for example, by Philips, 1990) but more work has been done on accusing and exonerating (by, for example, Pollner, 1979; Pomerantz and Atkinson, 1984), and it is on this that we shall concentrate.

The classic study by Atkinson and Drew (1979) gives us an extended treatment of exonerations to contrast with the taxonomic tradition, and what we now recognize as its commitment to the speech-act model. They report that 'the close examination of most court data . . . reveals that there is no single component which carries all the work which a witness or defendant does to defend his action' (1979: 139–40), so we shall necessarily see them identify exonerations by other means. The key to their approach is to see that it is the *placing* of the utterance that turns it into an 'exoneration'; in many of the examples we shall see, what the speaker seems on the face of it to be doing is 'describing', but if we attend to the implications of the descriptions, we shall see that they work to replace the questioner's version of what happened with a reality more favourable to the speaker.

All the examples that follow are taken from Atkinson and Drew's analysis of a tribunal of inquiry into violence and civil disorder in Northern Ireland (for details, see Atkinson and Drew, 1979: 106). In the following example, the soldier in the arrowed line is saying something that looks forward to a future turn. As an account, it only makes sense as a 'pre-sequence' which ensures a certain exoneration being possible were it to be called for.

C: So when you baton charged the Catholic crowd for the second time you knew, because of your previous experience, that the Protestant crowd were liable to follow you?

W: I did

C: How far did you drive the Catholic crowd at the time?

→ W: I stopped in Dover Street and nobody went very far past me and no-one went on Divis Street from the Protestant crowd

(Atkinson and Drew, 1979: 141; C means counsel; W means witness, a soldier)

By establishing here the close limits of the Protestant crowd's advance the soldier can be taken as pre-empting the accusation (perhaps already signalled in counsel's reference to the soldier's knowledge that the crowd would follow him) that his behaviour incited, or at least allowed, the crowd's incursion into Catholic territory. His guess that this is an issue is borne out as the extract proceeds:

C: No-one got very far past you, you say?

W: No-one got more than a few yards past me

C: So some people went past you?

(Atkinson and Drew, 1979: 157)

Just in case we are not convinced that the soldier, at least, construes the question and answer sequence as an accountable one, we see that his next utterance pulls out the accusative implication by offering what can only be an exonerative explanation.

W: I was hit in the leg by a stone and went down and that is why they went past me

(Atkinson and Drew, 1979: 171)

This longish example shows how sequence aids us in understanding certain features of exonerating work: it helps us see how a turn might prepare the ground for a later exonerating turn, how one turn pulls the accusative implication out of the preceding one, and so on. Let us see if we can use this contextualization in other illustrations of how the idealized exonerations in all the taxonomies from Scott and Lyman onwards might be affected by their sequential positioning. It would be too long a task to go through all the byways of Semin and Manstead's taxonomy (which we detailed on p. 49), so I shall concentrate on one example of an utterance that seems to have the effect of an excuse and one example that seems to have the effect of a justification.

1 C: You saw this newspaper shop being petrol-bombed on the front of Divis Street?

2 W: Yes

3 C: How many petrol bombs were thrown into it?

4 W: Only a couple. I felt that the window was already broken and that there was part of it burning and this was a re-kindling of the flames

(Atkinson and Drew, 1979: 155; renumbered)

In the above extract we can follow Atkinson and Drew in reading the description in turn 4 as a pre-sequence, in which the witness is pre-empting a potential accusation that his actions might have underestimated the seriousness of the situation. His utterance makes sense only as a rebuttal of this implied accusation. If we had to guess what kind of grounds he is invoking in exoneration, it might be what appears in Semin and Manstead's classification as a justificatory 'claim that the effect has been misrepresented' but, of course, he is doing so without this representation having yet been made.

> C: What did you do at that point?
> W: I was not in a very good position to do anything. We were under gunfire at the time
>
> (Atkinson and Drew, 1979: 161)

In this extract, we might be tempted to read the witness's description as either an example of the excusing 'denial of volition', subtype 'physical or psychological' (e.g. fatigue, drugs, illness, arousal) or 'denial of intent' subtype 'accident or unforeseen consequences'. But, again, we are glossing the fact that the speaker is doing a cocktail of things at once: setting up a potential accusation (that he culpably did nothing) and, at the same time, taking a preparatory step to disarming it. In this example, as in all the others, the bare facts of the transcript show that the witness is describing a state of affairs: *it is only through knowing its place in the sequence that we can read it as having its exonerating effect.*

Managing exonerations

Atkinson and Drew showed how in courtroom talk there was a running index of blame: the offence would shift as new aspects of the reported event came up in the talk (thus, as the description of the riot progressed, different aspects of the soldier's action or inaction became blameworthy). This conceives of offences as being at a fairly atomic level (allowing the crowd to go too far; not calling for a shop fire to be put out; and so on). This grain of analysis will need to be superseded when we want to understand how a series of exonerations is managed and how the vocabulary of exoneration might be manipulated. In this last section of the chapter we shall look in detail at two examples of that kind of content-enriched analysis, which will try to put back into the mechanics of conversational organization some of the substance of exoneration – what counts as excuse and justification – that stimulated the accounts literature in the first place.

Conley and O'Barr (1990) report an analysis of different styles of accounting in a US small claims court. In these courts, people can carry out their own defences and are less constrained than in more formal judicial proceedings. There is usually ample room for speakers to present whatever exoneration will, as they see it, defend their case. This will give us a useful complement to the restricted exonerating work studied in the tighter constraints of the public tribunal that was the source of Atkinson and Drew's analysis.

Conley and O'Barr show that not all the genres or styles used by plaintiffs and defendants are equally appropriate to the legal milieu in which they find themselves: they distinguish between those they call rule-orientated accounts, which stick to the legally relevant facts, and relational accounts, which (from the court's point of view) deviate into social, personal or moral relations irrelevant to the strictly legal question at hand. In the case below, the plaintiff Broom is suing Grumman for unpaid rent. Part of Grumman's defence is that the heating equipment that he had replaced should count in lieu of rent. We take up the case as Broom, the landlord, is taking advantage of the judge's prompt to explain why he does not accept that Grumman's replacement was an improvement:

> *Q:*   (. . .) Then let's back up to, where's the furnace at this date?
> *Broom:*   It's, it's discarded, was put in the dumpster, sir. I had to remove the furnace because, uh, this is a, uh, I went over to the city of Parkwood and uh, did some further, uh, leg work on this. I have found this is a garage, it has a garage door. This is a garage repair type of facility, and when Mr Grumman moved in we had just installed prior, three months, ninety days prior to his taking uh, commune of that area, a new overhead hanging furnace which is about oh, six feet above the floor and this was a 90,000 BTU furnace which is adequate to heat this thousand square feet. Now he removed that furnace and threw it in the back and I subsequently installed it in another area of the same building. It's working fine today. He had a used house type furnace that he put into this area and he, uh, cut some ducts and ran some ducts through the ceiling of this, of the leased area and put this furnace in the back area. Could I, could I show you some pictures perhaps?
>
> (Conley and O'Barr 1990: 186)

As Conley and O'Barr observe, Broom's talk is full of measurements, legal or legal sounding terminology ('a garage type facility') and other markers of orientation to courtroom evidence. These are like the 'logical proofs' that Cody and McLaughlin found were the most effective form of defence in traffic courts. Had Conley and O'Barr wanted to be more specific, they could have used Pomerantz's (1984a) analysis of descriptors to identify just what it was that made Broom's talk more formal. Broom uses what Pomerantz calls 'official' descriptions: the kind of description that would work out of context and would use full names, numbers and so on (for example, 90,000 BTU, ninety days). Compare that with this extract from the defendant Grumman's testimony:

> *Grumman:*   Well to start with, I didn't rent the building, lease the building on the date that he stated. American Builders, uh, American Wood Products had the building leased and I didn't know where he was at, at the time I was looking for a building. I leased the building from the other man at a cheaper rate and a cheaper deposit. Because the roof was leaking it had a dirt floor in the back and it had inadequate heat. It had a broken window and

	another one cracked and the stool was leaking out the back of it and it had two big piles of trash in the back of the building. After I got it all cleaned up and everything, he comes back, raises the rent, raises the deposit, and 'you can take it or leave it'
Q:	Who did you have a lease with at the time?
Grumman:	His pre–, uh previous tenant, which was supposed to have a lease on it
Q:	Did that previous tenant assign it to you or how did
Grumman:	Yes he did
Q:	Do you have a copy of that with you?
Grumman:	I don't, I can't find a copy, but I had one
Q:	How long did that lease run?
Grumman:	For about
Q:	American Wood Products lease?
Grumman:	I don't know when his lease run out

(Conley and O'Barr 1990: 188)

Grumman uses non-official descriptions, what Pomerantz calls 'relational' descriptions, which refer to things obliquely and in relation to something else (the other man, a cheaper rate, a cheaper deposit, in the back, another one, raises the rent, raises the deposit), and 'characterizations' which describe the thing within limits (on the date he stated, at the time I was looking for a building, big). (Pomerantz's term 'relational' is more specifically linguistic than Conley and O'Barr's.) When asked to specify an official description (*who did you have a lease with at the time?*) he gives a relational answer (*his previous tenant*), and when asked for an official length of time (*how long did that lease run?*) he gives, or starts to give, a characterization (*for about . . .*).

The difference in lexical style shows Grumman's general orientation to the moral, as opposed to the legal, aspects of his situation. This orientation causes him to pick out the 'wrong' aspects of the case against which to mount a defence, as this extract (which immediately follows the last one) shows:

Q:	Do you remember the date you took over [*the lease*]?
Grumman:	But uh, according to Mr Elrod [*a previous tenant*], the man, that was there with Products, he was supposed to have authority from Mr Broom to lease the building at what, at the same rate as what he had it for such and he rented it for 200, uh $200 a month, more than what he had been paying
Q:	The first of May rolled round, of '83, and we have before us what appears to be a business lease form, which purports to have your signature on it. Did you at that time lease from the, uh, plaintiff in this case, Mr Broom?
Grumman:	Yes I did. Uh, I really had, I'd already moved into it and didn't really have too much choice. I'd spent two weeks plus fixing the roof

(Conley and O'Barr 1990: 188)

What Grumman is doing in this extract is taking the judge's first turn to imply an accusation: that he was ill advised to sign the lease. This is not what is at issue and so Grumman's exoneration in the second turn is not an acceptable answer; the judge repeats the question more explicitly in the third turn so as to establish the signature. Even then Grumman can't forbear to add an exoneration. His perception of what he is being accused of is radically different from the issue facing the court, so his exoneration centres around his moral standing (what a previous tenant did or did not say, his record as a conscientious improver of the property). These are facts only very tangentially relevant to the legal question of whether he was at fault in his repayments to the landlord. In other legal systems such evidence may be acceptable (Philips, 1990, quotes Gluckman's observation that the Barotse legal system encouraged such information). In the US system, however, Grumman's insistence on his moral, as opposed to his legal, status, does not help his defence, and the landlord duly wins the case.

Conley and O'Barr's kind of analysis fuses the sequential organization of talk that we saw in Atkinson and Drew's work with something like the search for 'types' of exoneration. But note that we have not gone back to the categorization of discrete exonerations, as was the style in the taxonomic systems above. Rather, this kind of analysis is concerned to map the constellation of devices which cohere into genres of exoneration, not individual speech acts. At this distance from particular speech-act exonerations for particular offences we are coming closer to conceiving of exoneration as the presentation of a *case*. The focus has shifted from the social repair of a blameworthy social breach to the presentation of forensic argument in favour of one position or another, in which simply 'blame' is only one element of a complex negotiation.

Let us take this case-making further and see what we can make of the negotiation of exonerations. Fisher and Groce's (1990) study of doctor and patients' talk gives us a good illustration. Their interest is in the power relations implicit in the doctor–patient interaction, and they collect transcripts of the explanations that are exchanged in the typical consultation. Some of these are marked as exonerations, and Fisher and Groce suggest that these are used systematically differently by the two sides in the interaction. Here the patient construes what the doctor says as implicit blame for some action she did or failed to do, and her reply is understandable as an exoneration:

D: Do you drink milk now?
P: No, but if you tell me that I should, I will. Like I said I love milk. I only gave it up because I thought it just that much more of a dairy product that I wasn't supposed to have 'cos of my spastic colon and I also thought milk was constipating, so I gave it up two years ago and started drinking water all the time

(Fisher and Groce, 1990: 231)

D: How much [were you smoking]?
P: Half a pack
D: uhhuhh
P: I'd start smoking about a pack and a half a day when I get nervous. The more nervous I get the more I smoke

(Fisher and Groce, 1990: 239; simplified)

The doctor, by contrast, hardly ever volunteers that type of exoneration, and patients hardly ever ask for it. When they did, the doctor would respond in a way that reiterated his or her professional dominance. That is the key to the reading that Fisher and Groce make: the mismatch in power between patient and doctor is mirrored in the differences in the amount, and kind, of exonerations that they ask for and provide. This is a nice echo of Conley and O'Barr's study of rule- and relation-orientated exonerations in the courts. Just as in the small claims court, some exonerations key into the approved vocabulary, and others do not; using one or the other signals the speaker's social standing within the interaction, and all are achieved in sequences.

A simpler conceptual structure of accounts?

The moral that Buttny (1993) draws from the demonstration of the sequential organization of accounts is that 'accounts may be seen as produced as a function of . . . the conditional relevancies arising from the antecedent blame' (1993: 45). In other words, we should attend to the context which makes the utterance understandable as a response to implicit or explicit blaming. Moreover, such 'constructions [of events] are possible because of the cultural's group's assumptions, vocabularies, and ideologies of right or practical action which are applied . . . through the use of folk logic' (1993: 51). This is a reprise of Scott and Lyman's (1968) notion that accounts work by meshing with the 'background expectancies' held by the audience. But it does mean that, apparently in spite of the blow-by-blow negotiation sense of exoneration we have just seen, we do have to return to some sort of inventory of account devices, and if we look back at Atkinson and Drew's analyses we see that this is inevitable.

Atkinson and Drew's analysis showed how identifying the account as such depended on knowing its place in the sequence of affairs. This cannot be the only, or last, step in the identification of the account, however, since we have to recognize that the account does appeal to *something* as authority for exoneration. Atkinson and Drew have shown that speakers are concerned, as Wooffitt (1992: 2) puts it, to 'influence the range of inferences which the overhearing jury will arrive at'; they want to reduce the inferences to those which have the effect of mitigating the offence. A witness is clearly setting up inferences which invoke some kind of excuse, and it would be odd to proceed without recognizing that. This means that we shall have to return to the taxonomic tradition for at least some kind of idealized accounts inventory. The difference is that now we shall be alive to the fact that whatever level of categories we choose, we shall have to admit that they can be realized in a huge variety of ways, and that any candidate utterance may well serve the functions of any of the categories on the list.

The safest way forward is to keep the category system as simple as possible, and to keep in mind always that what we analysts think matters less than what the participants in the interaction make of it. This means going in the opposite direction from the accounts literature and cutting away all the superstructure it has built over Austin's basic distinction. Our argument has been that it is pointless to have such an elaborate inventory when it is impossible to identify utterances that represent each category, and that *a priori* category construction prejudices a view of what actually happens in talk. Better then to work with the simpler and more tractable notions of excuse and justification, and see how those basic forms of exoneration become realized in the detail of conversational interaction.

We have to keep clear in our minds what the ambition of a structural analysis is. A structural analysis can't do away with the notion that there *is* some determinable set or family (however subtle, complicated or ramified) of exonerations. Societies proceed on reasonably clear understandings of what counts as excuse and justification. They might well be different in different discourses (legal, moral, casual and so on) and between different societies and epochs; nevertheless, there is such a thing as (say) the appeal to madness, or to coercion, and so on. One is acquitted because one was temporarily insane, or was at knife point. Being insane or at knife point works as an exoneration. Structural analysts have no quarrel with this. What they do say, though, is that idealizations – like the defences of 'insanity' or 'coercion' – are not identifiable simply from the speaker's choice of words even within one culture, and that even a brief excursion into another culture is enough to show that the problem is a profound one.

What happens in ordinary exchanges is that a large mass of ordinary reasoning is manoeuvred to make a bridge between the utterance and the abstraction it is realizing. If the utterance's context is hidden from the analyst – as it is in any taxonomic system – the analyst's own reasoning has nothing to work with, and the bare listing of the taxonomy can't cope. So, while there is no bar to the mapping in principle, the failure of the idealizations to provide us with templates of width sufficient to take in context means that the project will face enormous difficulties.

We leave the taxonomic enterprise half satisfied with what we have. A catalogue of exonerations helps as a very rough approximation of the kinds of things one will encounter, but offers no guarantee that one can use it infallibly to arbitrate on every case; like a guide intended for travellers to a strange country, it may lead to confusion unless supplemented by local knowledge. Clearly an understanding (preferably an ethnographic one) of the concepts available to be used as exonerations is necessary, but there is a big gap between just listing them on paper and identifying them in actual practice. Perhaps one should leave the cultural work of conceptualizing ideal exoneration types to anthropologists and ethnographers, and move instead to what is tractable. We can make progress on the interactive dynamics of exonerative talk, and that is what we shall be doing in some detail in the next chapter.

5

Explanation Slots

Sherri: You didn' get an *ice*cream sandwich
Carol: I know, hh I decided that my body didn't need it
Sherri: Yes, but ours did
(Schegloff, 1988: 128)

That little exchange between Sherri and Carol is a fragment of an episode we shall be looking at in some detail shortly, because it illustrates people's subtlety in managing the delicacy of blaming each other and justifying themselves. That management is the business of this chapter, and I shall be showing how explanations – like Carol's above – can sometimes be set up and filled as questions of interactional regulation. A speaker can call for an explanation, or can signal that she or he is about to give one; both cases are matters, as we shall see, of marking out shifting positions.

The question of position came up in the last chapter, when we noted the long shadow that Erving Goffman cast on the more sociologically minded of later account researchers. Goffman pioneered the close, almost microscopic, inspection of the passing signals of everyday encounters, and his writings are full of descriptions of people offering accounts and otherwise shoring up their moral position. We saw in the last chapter how his notion of the 'offence cycle' influenced a generation of researchers eager to track down and classify the various ways in which people repaired the breaches of everyday life. But although he inspired much work on accounting, Goffman has been taken to task for failing adequately to ground his insights in the actual linguistic practice of his respondents – actually to quote them, or describe in detail what it is they say and how they say it. The worry is that this might miss something fundamental about just what it is they are doing. A newer breed of analyst insists on having the backing of the detailed talk, because they doubt their own (and others') ability to reconstruct what happens without reductive simplifications. The conversation analysis that they champion aims to discover what talk-in-action is like in the raw.

Conversation analysis will come up again in Chapter 7 when we see what it might tell us about how people transact the business of giving each other accounts more generally; that is to say, how they manage stories which aren't specifically exonerative, but nevertheless are called up to do some sense-making work in the interaction. Here, though, I shall introduce the main ideas of conversation analysis (some of which we've already seen, in passing, in previous chapters) and stick to exonerations. This chapter is about what conversation analysis has to say about the exchange of exoneration as people weave the fabric of ordinary talk, and I shall be describing how people set themselves, and each other, explanation 'slots' which need to be filled, sooner or later, by suitable accounts.

Conversation analysis

The flag that conversation analysis flies is that the organization of conversations – what comes after what – is the most direct evidence possible about people's social reasoning. To respond to what has just been said, people have to have understood its significance, and must be aware – at some level – that the different responses available to them will take them in different directions. They will exploit the rules of the local management of conversation – turn-taking, timing, and so on – to signal where they are and get to where they want to be.

The floor-plan of the local management system is the way people offer and take up opportunities to speak. Certain kinds of utterance (like questions, invitations and orders) are regularly followed by certain kinds of responses (which in these cases would be answers, acceptances and compliances, respectively). And if these don't follow immediately, they follow eventually, after some other sequence has been inserted into its brackets. These pairs of utterances are the staples which pin conversation together.

So far this is straightforward, but conversation analysts exploit the notion, known to us also as Grice's cooperative principle (see p. 31), that the background regularity of such pairs of statements ('adjacency pairs') sets up expectations so powerful that they can actually determine meaning. If I ask you a question, I should receive an answer; so anything you say will be taken to be either an answer, or a comment on the lack of an answer: there can be no escape from the expectation that you *will* orientate to what I say. If I say *have you done the washing up?*, your reply will be taken as some comment on the question, whether you like it or not. It might be *yes*, *no* or *not yet*; even if it is *what a rainy day it's been* it still stakes out a position on the matter.

Equally, the expectation works in reverse: the answer will be trying to recast the utterance it responds to. To respond to the first part of a request–acceptance pair with the second part of a greeting–greeting pair is to try, for whatever reason, to turn the original question into a greeting. So to say *what a rainy day it's been* is to try to recast the original question about the washing up as something else (a greeting, perhaps, or a comment about the weather; something other than a prompt about the washing up, in any case). *OK, I'll do it* would turn it into a request; *it's not my turn* would turn it into an accusation, and so on. It is important for conversation analysis that we see that the conversationalists are constantly giving each other context, and that that context can be so powerful that it changes the meaning of what it surrounds.

This gives us a very important analytical tool for taking apart meaning. Looking at conversations we often find that a question can be 'answered' by something that is clearly not an 'answer' in the required sense: it might be a refusal to answer, a redirection to somebody else, a challenge to the questioner's right or competence to ask that question, and so on. If the participants in a conversation are alive to the signals that their utterances give, then we should see them take active steps to mark out what they are saying as meeting or not meeting what is expected of them. If one collects and compares a dossier of unexpected and expected answers – that is to say, answers which do, or don't, interrupt the smooth flow of the conversation – they turn out to be reliably different. If the second part of the adjacency pair is not a 'normal' response, then it will be done a bit less readily, and generally 'marked' in some way – by a hedge, or a request for clarification, or both. I may ask *why don't you come to our housewarming party on Saturday?* and you may say – without pause, and without elaboration – *sure*, and the conversation passes fluidly on. If, on the other hand, the proceedings have snagged, it will be because you have given what is a 'dispreferred' response, marked (it is empirically found) by a certain amount of umming and ahhing and an account of why you didn't give the expected response: [*small pause*] *well, I'd like to . . . but I've got some friends staying over.* It is these dispreferred responses, and the accounts that are important features of their marking, which we shall be looking at in some detail in this chapter.

It is important to note that conversation analysis presents itself as discovering patterns 'empirically'. It doesn't start with a theory about what speakers are up to; in fact, conversation analysis objects to other linguists' theorizing before the facts. These facts are regularities, from which conversation analysis will draw inferences about the rules to which the participants are playing. Once those rules are understood by the analysts, they can look at a particular play and make a guess at what function it served. A reasonable metaphor would be learning the rules of a game by watching it over a period. You pick up certain regularities (for example, that play is stopped if the ball is passed to a striker who is behind the opposition's players) and you suppose that the players knowingly orientate to the rule that underpins the regularity. Once you know that, you see why, for example, a team tries to make sure it has all its players in front of the opposition's leading player so that the ball can't be passed to them without 'off-side' being called. Conversation analysts, like any other group of worrying academics, do, though, constantly ask themselves whether they haven't imported too much interpretation into their observation; whether it is not too impetuous to use terms like 'team', 'player' and 'ball', for example. But they reassure themselves that they have to start somewhere, and if they keep to the least presumptuous descriptions possible then they shall risk least danger.

The application of all this to explanations is plausible enough. In a general way, it cautions us to be wary of interpreting what explanations are doing before we have a full view of the regularities of their organization. Conversation analysis is a sensing instrument by which the exchange of any explanation, like any piece of communication, might be monitored. It points to participants' own agenda and their disposal of what comes up on it: it is methodologically open and theoretically democratic. Given our concerns in this book, conversation analysis is specially useful in so far as it shows that the organization of talk throws up interactional grounds for exoneration: if a turn at talk invites one kind of response, then, when some other response appears instead, it ought to be accompanied by an account as a signal of its unexpectedness. This kind of motivation for exoneration is all but invisible from the traditional 'accounts' perspective we saw in the last chapter, but plays a powerful role in talk, as we shall see.

Example of a conversation-analytic reading of exoneration

The best way to start, now that we have a rough idea about the basic notions of adjacency pairs, and the principle that unexpected responses are marked in some way, is to see conversation analysis in operation.

This is an analysis from Schegloff (1988). In the following extract, Carol returns to her student friends Sherri, Ruthie, Karen and Mark after going out to fetch a certain kind of ice-cream (an 'ice-cream sandwich'), and is greeted by a complex interplay of accusation, justification, retraction and acceptance. Schegloff is out to show that the participants are indeed living out their moral lives, but that were we analysts to gloss the participants' actual words and pauses, we would immediately import our own prejudices. To see how participants build the exchange of exonerations which are so crucial in establishing their social relations, we need to respect their vernacular architecture. Not to use their actual talk would mean that we would crush the participants' own delicately meshed constructions under the weight of our own interpretations.

```
                 [door squeaks]
152    S:    Hi Carol =
153    C:    = H⌈i::
154    R:      ⌊CA:ROL, HI
155    S:    You didn' get an icecream sandwich
156    C:    I know, hh I decided that my body didn't need it
157    S:    Yes but ours did
158/9/60    [2 or 3 voices laugh]
161    C:    hh Awright gimme some money en you c'n treat me to one an
162          I'll buy you all some⌈too
163    S:                         ⌊I'm kidding, I don't need one
164          (0.3)
165    ?:    hhh
166    C:    I WAN' ONE [in 'whine' voice]
167          [1 or 2 voices laugh]
168    C:    [laughs]
169    C:    No, they didn' even have any Tab
170          [1 voice laughs]
171    C:    This is all I c'd find
172          (0.2)
```

```
173  R:   Well then there's ez many calories that prob'ly in en ice cream
174       sanwich (so) yih jist, you know
175       (.)
176  C:   I know an icecream sanwich is better, (b't) I d'n feel like going
177       down tuh 'P' an' seeing all those weird people an' have them
178       st⌈are at me
179  R:      ⌊In yer slippers
180       (0.3)
181  C:   Yeah
182       (0.8)
183  C:   I don't want them tih see me when I look this good
184       (0.4)
185  R?:  hhuhh hhhh
186/7 C:  No-one deserves it
188  ?:   tch hh
189  C:   I'll see you all later
190  R:   Awright
191       (1.4) [door opening]
192  M:   Where were we
```
(Schegloff, 1988: 128; transcription simplified; for the notation conventions of this extract and others we shall be encountering subsequently, see p. ix)

It would be perfectly possible to tell all this in a story along these lines: Carol has failed to bring back the ice-cream sandwich that she was sent to get. Her competence and good faith in question, she comes out with three different excuses. None is accepted by the others so, crestfallen, she leaves. But this story, to an analyst, smacks too much of the all-knowing author's voice: too much unverifiable interpretation has gone into its telling. So, instead, we might say: Sherri complains (at line 155), provoking Carol to give a justification (156) which Sherri doesn't accept (157), and then an offer to go out again (161); Sherri retracts (163), but Carol insists (166), then gives another reason why she came back without the ice-cream but with something else (169). Ruthie casts an aspersion (173), prompting Carol to give yet a third reason why she didn't get ice-cream (176–8). This is left hanging and Carol announces her departure (189).

Schegloff's point is that even this isn't right, because we haven't got down, yet, to the description of just what it is that makes what Sherri says a 'complaint', what Carol offers a 'justification', and so on. As socially competent readers, we have a rough idea of how the talk goes; but the job of the analyst is to get in under the bonnet and see exactly what makes it work. We won't go into all the mechanics of it (which, though Schegloff calls it 'abbreviated', takes up nearly a dozen pages), but it turns on the speakers' subtle and flexible use of the simple adjacency pair we mentioned earlier. The very first pair of utterances sets up an expectation which sets the tone of the whole interaction, and makes it what a traditional social psychologist would gloss as this or that social interaction – a 'negotiation among friends', say, or 'a mini-dispute'. What conversation analysis does is give us a pass directly to what is going on, without misleading or pre-emptive abstraction.

First, then, Sherri's utterance at (155). In idealized models of accounting (as we saw in Chapter 4), we would have skated over this as an accusation without troubling ourselves too much about how we identified it as such. But Schlegloff observes that this is precisely the question – why do we (and, of course, the actual participants) see it as a significant 'noticing'? We are, in fact, mobilizing two things. First, from the Gricean principle that what people say to each other is always relevant, we infer that what Sherri has chosen to notice (the lack of the ice-cream) is relevant, and we further infer that there was an expectation that Carol would have brought that ice-cream. Secondly, we as analysts (and the participants as ordinary reasoners) know that it is significant that Sherri 'notices' the lack of the ice-cream, rather than make a comment about what Carol has actually got in her hand (which is alluded to in line 171); and she 'notices' it as a failure. We know as analysts (empirically) that these are two features that are generally found in 'complaints' – that is, utterances the normal response to which is some kind of apology or acknowledgement.

By attending to the organization of the talk, then, we see how Sherri's utterance is potentially a noticing and a complaint. We would predict that the response should ratify those readings, and we know from elsewhere that noticings are taken up with acknowledgements, and complaints with remedies and excuses. In other words, we come to Carol's turn with more than just the notion that (somehow) she is being criticized; we know that it is a complaint, we know how Sherri did it, and we know what, in general terms, Carol has to do. This is a powerful example of conversation analysis exegesis.

Carol does, indeed, orientate both to the noticing and to the complaint: *I know, hh I decided that my body didn't need it* (156). The utterance ratifies the noticing and the complaint, but to Carol's ('moral') advantage. It marks her not-bringing as not forgetfulness but as a decision – known about, and made on a given basis: in other words, rational. Moreover, by turning attention to 'my body' rather than 'I', she brings into the picture a negative self-image – an astute move, since we know (independently, from the collected dossiers) that there are strong norms for hearers to disagree with self-deprecation. Carol is angling for her friends to rush in with a disagreement that her body is a problem, which would distract attention from not having brought the ice-cream.

Sherri has to reply to what Carol has said. We know, again from the dossiers, that disagreements are often delayed or sweetened with an agreement token, and this is what Sherri does. The 'yes', Schegloff interprets, works as a delaying 'be that as it may' before Sherri gets to the disagreement not with the content of what Carol said but with its status as a reply to the implicit criticism of not-bringing. In fact, *yes, but ours did* is a particularly devastating argument that Carol's reason was inadequate, since it uses Carol's own criterion (bodies needing or not needing ice-cream) and asserts that, in fact, some bodies (theirs) did need it, so on Carol's own exoneration she should have got it. Moreover, the laughter doesn't build up during the turn, as it does in turns people want publicly to mark as 'funny' (chuckling in anticipation of a punchline to be savoured by everyone): so

Sherri's turn holds for its entire length a quite serious accusation, its mood only changing right at the end. In any case, Sherri's rejection of Carol's excuse keeps the complaint live: that is to say, Sherri has illegitimatized Carol's attempted second-pair part, so we expect by conversational rules that she will have another go at it. And that, in fact, is the key to how the whole interaction unfolds: it is a series of attempts by Carol to perform an accepted second-pair part.

It would take up too much space to follow Schegloff through the analysis of all the turns (as you can see, all of the above has been on just the first two), but a similar story could be told for each of them. The exercise has really been an account of how a first-pair part (the first utterance of a pair whose second utterance is strongly expected) constrains its response, and how its response can reconstruct the meaning of the original statement itself; and, thereafter, how the participants manoeuvre themselves about the resulting expectations. The social psychologist couldn't ask for better evidence than this: this is where the action is.

Explanation slots

Schegloff's bravura decomposition of the students' talk is based on a lot of groundwork building up dossiers of the regularities of blaming and excusing, and we need to open those dossiers up to get a fuller account of the devices that have gone into his reading. The guiding theme is that blaming and excusing is a routine part of life: that the communication contract we have with each other forces us to have a mechanism for explaining ourselves. Heritage (1988) invokes this contract when he says that speakers give accounts as part of the way they mark what is being said or done as 'unexpected in the circumstances'. Implicit in what I have been saying is that this is not just an empirical observation: unless it was routine for people to account for a non-expected turn at talk, there would be nothing to distinguish between what is expected and what is not expected; in other words, there would be no principle of organization of communicative interchange. Only a system in which nothing ever went wrong would need no markers of problems. In human terms, only a world in which every invitation was accepted, every proposal was agreed to and every request was complied with would need no marker of deviation.

Now, the analyst might feel the need to fuel this austerely structural mechanism with some recognizably human motivation, and the need to preserve 'face' has been put forward as such a candidate; but I shall not talk about the debate (which is elegantly set out in Taylor and Cameron, 1987: ch. 6), because the choice of fuel doesn't affect the actual operation of the machinery.

By its nature, then (and whether fuelled by the need to save face or the automatic pressure to maintain the communicative contract), the traffic of talk will sometimes open up to yield an account-shaped space, or an 'explanation slot'. The explanations that fill them deal with the kind of offence which comes up within the borders of the local interaction: to explain, justify or warrant a puzzle which has arisen then and there, and which needs to be sorted out before proceedings can be resumed.

I have borrowed the notion of a 'slot' from the work of Cody and McLaughlin (1988) and McLaughlin (1990) who, as we saw towards the middle of Chapter 4, brought the accounts literature closer to everyday talk. One of their organizing principles was to put the accounts into what they thought of as being a canonical, or prototypical, sequence: first came the reproach, then the account, and finally the evaluation. I want to keep the notion of the account being set up by its context, but the kind of 'slot' I have in mind is, in the conversation analytic spirit of this chapter, different from Cody and McLaughlin's. The preceding argument has moved us away from the notion, pervasive in the accounts literature, that offences are publicly ratified social failures, which have occurred independently of the running of the interaction. The kind of 'offences' I am concerned with here are of a different order: as dispreferred conversational moves, they come up within the borders of the local interaction, and arise as a consequence of the interactional exchange, and need to be sorted out before proceedings can be resumed. And the disquiet with speech-act theory will also prompt us to move away from Cody and McLaughlin's formulation of account slots as being identifiable through the 'content' of what is said by the offender (*I'm sorry, but the train was held up*; or *I couldn't help it, the knife just slipped*). Rather, as we saw at the end of Chapter 4, the slots are identifiable through the sequence and structure of the speaker's utterances.

In the body of the chapter I shall separate the two main families of explanation slots. I shall talk first about those which are created by one speaker casting something about another speaker as requiring explanation (on the model of Sherri casting Carol as accountable for not fetching the ice-cream). Then, following Heritage (1988), I shall talk about those explanation slots which are created and filled by the speaker her or himself (on the model of Carol setting herself up to mark what she is saying as a dispreferred response). In both cases the spotlight will be on the explanation space that occasionally comes up in a conversation, and the action we shall see will be the conversationalists filling it in.

Setting up explanation slots for another speaker

A speaker can open up a slot for somebody else to fill in. That is to say, there are times when a speaker can dragoon the next person into providing an explanation as a matter of the preferred sequential organization of the talk – either to respond to their direct or indirect request, or to meet some mild or forceful accusation that something is wrong. More precisely, the slot will open up a space for an explanation which, if not forthcoming, will offend against the expectation that it do so, and leave in place the formulation offered by the previous speaker.

All this squarely faces us with our motivating interest in explanations – referred to rather obliquely in Chapter 1 – that they orientate to problematic information, position or status in people's interactions with each other. Since any aspect of human life might be problematic, searching for universal features of problems is chimerical; but we might be reaching for something more solid if we search instead for regular ways in which things can be 'turned into' problems. In the following sections, I shall catalogue some of the main ways in which problems can be signalled and the slots for their resolution opened.

Noticings

We start with one of the fundamental pragmatic principles of conversation analysis: that speakers cooperate with each other; more specifically, that they expect that what is said is appropriate to what is going on. This gives speakers a simple but effective way of making something problematic. If they report a state of affairs when it is redundant to do so, then, given that what they say is meant to be sensible, it must have something to say other than the (patently unnecessary) simple information it ostensibly reports. *I see you've got a new hairdo*, by the very obviousness of the state of affairs it reports, invites an 'account' of it.

This stating of redundant information is called 'fishing' by Pomerantz (1980) or, more neutrally, 'noticing' by Schegloff (1988), and both show how it does significant work in talk. We saw Schegloff's demonstration of how 'noticing' can work as an accusation, where Sherri 'notices' that her friend has returned without the promised ice-cream sandwich, unleashing a series of exonerative accounts. Recall:

> [*Door squeaks*]
> *S*:   Hi Carol =
> *C*:   = H⌈i::
> *R*:   ⌊CA:ROL, HI
> → *S*:   You didn' get an *ice*cream sandwich
> *C*:   I know, hh I decided that my body didn't need it
> (Schegloff, 1988: 128; transcription simplified)

The device of stating the redundant delivers a great deal: Sherri's noticing opens a slot which Carol fills with the account *I know, hh I decided that my body didn't need it*. Here are two variant forms of noticings, 'my side tellings' and 'passes'; both have the same power to open up an account slot.

'My side telling'

Pomerantz (1980) observes that the point of view in 'noticings' which open explanation slots tends to be the point of view of the person requiring the explanation: it states something redundant, but 'tells my side' of it. For example:

```
B:    Hello::
A:    HI:::
B:    Oh:hi:: 'ow are you Agne::s
```
→   `A:    Fine. Yer line's been busy`
```
B:    Yeuh my fu(hh) – 'hhh my father's wife called me [story]
```
(from Pomerantz, 1980, quoted in Bergmann, 1992: 141)

A tells her side of what B must know, prompting B to supply an account resolving the implied puzzle of why her phone was busy (an account beginning *my father's wife called me*).

The speaker could have phrased her 'noticing' in a number of ways, and Bergmann (1992) argues that how one chooses between formulations like *your line seems to have been busy*, or *apparently your line sounded like it, maybe it was busy?* and so on can be significant. He shows how the noticing can be more or less specified; that the noticer can detail the thing they're noticing, or, alternatively, can underspecify it. In Bergmann's corpus of psychiatric interviews, the psychiatrists regularly make their 'my-side-tellings' underspecified by putting them in tentative or uncertain terms, and will further under-report by using euphemisms rather than being frank. Both feature in this example.

   (Dr F is interviewing Ms B for possible psychiatric admission)
→   *Dr F:*   Dr Hollman told me something like you were running across the street
             (not so completely dressed) or something like that
   Ms B: (h)Yes: that's– I am a child of God; I am his child (.)
(Bergmann, 1992: 149; transcription slightly simplified)

The psychiatrist could have said something openly challenging like: *you were running around naked, weren't you?* But his choice of a much more tentative and delicate-looking formulation is not quite innocent: it functions, Bergmann claims, as a Trojan horse into the interviewee's private life. Such a noticing as *Dr Hollman told me . . .* looks sympathetic – after all, it claims uncertainty and it avoids using taboo descriptions like 'naked' or 'mad' and so on – yet, at base, it is still a noticing, and by stating the event at all it knowingly forces the interviewee to account for it. If the interviewee does give an account she is drawn into agreeing that there is a problem; but if she does not, then she will be failing to cooperate as a normal person would. Either way, her behaviour will be evidence of a problem.

Here is how another interviewee, put in the same position by Dr F's underspecified noticing (*you feel angry about being committed . . .*) finds herself drawn into a display of frustration:

   Dr F: 'h thh. You feel angry about being committed by Doctor
             [Kluge [*unintelligible*]
   Ms K: ['hhh No:: I don't feel angry about h– being committed by Doctor
             Kluge 'hh but that you somehow– (1.0)
   Dr F: What? (0.6)
   Ms K: hhh (3.0) Mhh(a)h(a) please
             [*Ms K sweeps the doctor's papers with a wave of the hand off the
             table*]
   Ms K: I:– (.) can't stand you Doctor Fischer
(Bergmann, 1992: 157; transcription slightly simplified)

Bergmann is careful not to impute consciously unfair motives to the psychiatrists as individuals; rather, he prefers to read this double game of linguistic sympathy and control as a microcosm of the same dilemma facing society's relation with mental illness in general. Such speculation is an intriguing move from conversation analysis to the discourse analysis that we shall see more of in Chapter 6, but we don't need to follow it up here; it is enough for our current purposes to see that Bergmann has persuasively demonstrated that one apparently trivial variable in the 'my side telling' domain of noticings can be influential within the interaction and have significant consequences outside it.

Puzzle–pass–solution–comment

Another regularity of noticings is what Schenkein (1978) identifies as their presence in four-turn puzzle–pass–solution–comment sequences, in which the apparently innocuously echoing second turn (the 'pass') works to solicit an account of something in the first turn. In the first example below the solution is accepted sympathetically, and in the second not; but in both cases it is accepted and the puzzle resolved.

	Ellen:	Fine, jus' fine thank you cept for this fucking in*fec*tion
→	*Patty*:	Infection?
	Ellen:	I can't seem to get rid of this fucking, u *uri*nary track infection – it's been dragging on now for a couple of months – and it's driving me up a *wall* hehh hehh heh
	Patty:	They're impossible I know all about it deary believe me
	Caller:	(. . .) My problem, if you would jus' listen for a second has to do with what I need here
→	*Operator*:	What you need?
	Caller:	What I need. I've been trying for more than a month now to get installed one of your multiple input systems?
	Operator:	You're talking to the wrong department sir. Let me connect you wit' Sales

(both from Schenkein, 1978: 70)

In both cases the 'pass' (*infection?* and *what you need?*) open slots for an account (accounting for the special irritation of the infection in one case, or the special reason for calling in the other). It is interesting to note that the apparently empty 'pass' is a common feature of 'non-directive' therapy, in which the therapist 'echoes back' something the client has said. It is possible that the therapist's non-directive pass is working identically to the 'my side tellings' that we saw in Bergmann's collection of psychiatric interviews. That is to say, that, far from being non-directive, it very specifically locates some part of what the client has said as requiring accounting, but knowingly declines the responsibility of naming it.

Problem setting

If all the above were more or less indirect ways of casting something as a problem, we should finish off this section on other-initiated slots with a look at what happens when the 'problem' is made more salient. What would in one context be an invitation to speak on a topic will be, in another context, more appropriately understood as a (mild) accusation and set up an account slot, as happens here:

> *Nancy*: What's doin' (.)
> *Hyla*: a–ah:, noth⌈in:
> *Nancy*: ⌊Y'didn't go meet Grahame?
> → *Hyla*: .pt .hhhhahh *Well*, I *got ho*::me =
> *Nancy*: = u–hu:h?
> *Hyla*: ayu::n:: .hh he hadn' *called* yet 'n there weren't any *mess*ages'r . . .
> (Button and Casey, 1985: 29–30; transcription slightly simplified)

Nancy picks out, in a form of 'noticing', something that Hyla did not mention one way or another (*y'didn't go meet Grahame?*), and by doing so turns it into an accountable event. Hyla responds with an account that makes sense of her inaction (*well, I got ho::me ayu::n:: .hh he hadn' called yet 'n there weren't any messages*). An example, as we have seen repeatedly throughout, of an utterance that takes its explanatory force directly from its sequential context.

Setting up one's own explanation slots

So far we have been talking about setting up slots for another speaker. Now in this section I shall switch over to describing how speakers can, and in fact sometimes must, set up an explanation slot for themselves. The organizing principle here is the need to mark what one is saying as unexpected – not that it is necessarily outlandish or offensive but rather that it offends against the regularities of ordinary exchanges. If one's response is 'offensive' in that sense (and we shall see what this means below) then, given the communicative contract, one opens up a slot for oneself in which an explanatory account must fit. If we recall the ice-cream sandwich episode, it is the kind of account that Carol sets herself up for when she introduces her response to her accuser with the words *I know* . . . and its implicit *but*.

The first part of this section describes the various slots that come about when things go wrong in what Buttny (1993) notes is the more obvious case for accounts in general: when the utterance is somehow wrong in relation to the utterance that immediately precedes it. Later we shall see the same principle apply to explanations that come into play when utterances 'go wrong' at longer range.

Explanation slots in immediate second parts

Given some pairs of utterances which normally go yoked together (a question and answer, say, or a greeting and a reply), then the typical second utterance will be prompt and unmarked, whereas unexpected, or 'dispreferred', responses usually start with a pause, then a hedge, then a palliative

Table 5.1   *First-pair parts and their preferred and dispreferred responses*

First parts	Request, offer, invitation	Assessment, formulation	Question	Blame
Second parts				
Preferred	Acceptance	Agreement	Expected answer	Denial
Dispreferred	Refusal	Disagreement	Unexpected answer	Admission

Source: Levinson, 1983: 336

appropriate to the previous turn (a token agreement, if the previous turn was a claim wanting confirmation; an appreciation of the invitation if there has been one; and so on); next comes the exonerative account and finally an appropriate rejection, disagreement or refusal. Not all 'dispreferreds' will show the whole catalogue of markers but (by definition) no dispreferred will have none of them. A useful way of organizing the illustration of accounts in dispreferreds is to work from Levinson's (1983) list of adjacency pair seconds, shown in Table 5.1. We shall have a look in turn at each of these major divisions of adjacency pairs to see how an account slot is opened when the second pair part is not the normally expected one.

Refusals of requests, offers and invitations

A response which complies with a request is, as we know, delivered promptly and without qualification:

> *A*:   Can I pinch a ciggie?
> *B*:   *Course* you can ((would you like)) a *men*thol or [ei] *plain*
> (LL S2.11, p. 655, 286)[1]

A refusal, on the other hand, will be marked:

> *A*:   (. . .) If you wanted to: 'hh you could meet me at UCB an' I could show yih some a' the other things on the computer, maybe even teach yuh how to program Basic or something
> → *B*:   Well I don't know if I'd wanna get all *that* invo:lved, hh' hhh!
> (Davidson, 1984: 108; transcription slightly simplified)

B's initial *Well* sends up a flare signalling that a space is coming up wanting an account: *I don't know if I'd wanna get all that invo:lved* delivers it. The whole turn gets across the refusal that is conversationally abnormal. Here is another example, this time when the refusal is of one alternative among others:

> 1   *D*:   (. . .) Black or white?
> 2   *B*:   Please– m (.) black please Cedric
> 3   *A*:   Black please Cedric

```
  4   D:   Yes
→ 5   B:   Never touch milk it's against my religion
  6   C:   At all?
  7   B:   Oh I have it in my cornflakes (.) I find they get too soggy if I pour
            coffee on them
```
(LL S2.4, p. 462, 28; simplified)

The rejection of the alternative is marked by a jocular account (*it's against my religion*).

So far it has been the offending speaker who has volunteered (or been made to volunteer) an account. But it can also be the case that an account is offered on behalf of the offender by another speaker, possibly as a way of saving their face:

```
  1   E:   Wanna come down'n have a bite a'lu:nch with me:? I got s'm bee:r
            en stu:ff
            (0.2)
  2   N:   Wul yer ril sweet hon:, uh::m (.) ⌈let– I: have
→ 3   E:                                     ⌊or d'yuh 'av sump'n else
```
(Heritage, 1988: 137; transcription slightly simplified)

E makes an invitation which N starts to give an account for and E finishes off (note that E prefaces the explanation with *or* to attribute N with the implication that had they not had something else on they would indeed have wanted to accept the invitation).

Assessments

We are in the business of cataloguing utterances which have strong expectations of a certain kind of reply, and the second major species is the assessment and agreement pair. Pomerantz (1984b) takes the strong position that ordinary talk is full of assessments and judgements, and that there is a pervasive norm that hearers should agree with these judgements (and to do so unequivocally, by 'upgrading' the assessment), as in the following example:

```
    J:   It's really a clear lake, isn't it?
→   R:   It's wonderful
```
(Pomerantz, 1984b: 60; transcription slightly simplified)

Violation of this agreement norm, like any violation, will need to be orientated to (for example, by hedge and a pause) and warranted by offering something in mitigation or explanation.

```
    L:   Maybe it's just ez well Wilbur
    W:   hm?
    L:   Maybe it's just ez well you don't know
         (2.0)
→   W:   Well/uh– I say it's suspicious it could be something good too
```
(Pomerantz, 1984b: 71; transcription slightly simplified)

W buys time with *hm?* but still needs to mark his disagreement with L's claim that *it's just ez well* with a further silence, a hedge (*well*), and, after he has stated a contradictory position (*it's suspicious*), an explanation, or expansion, of why he thinks so (*it could be something good too*). Pomerantz has a large collection of such examples, in which disagreements are delayed within or across turns (or both, in the case above); and that if they are put off (by gaps, or requests for clarification and so on), they are treated as disagreements by the disagreed-with speaker anyway. They can also be done by weak agreement, which comes to the same thing as outright disagreement.

> *L*:   I know but I, I–I still say thet the sewing machine's quicker
> → *W*:   Oh it c'n be quicker but it doesn't do the job
>   (Pomerantz, 1984b: 73)

There is some debate over just how strong this preference for agreement is, and how liable it is to be overridden by the demands of the time and place (see Buttny, 1993: 38, and a further note when we come to look at quarrelling on p. 163 of this book), but the general principle seems firm. Let us make four subsections of this general heading 'assessments' to consider separately how accounts seem to be called for when there is some disagreement over four things: evaluations; factual claims; choices; and formulations.

Assessment 1: Evaluations   The first subtype of assessment we can think about is evaluation. An account slot will be set up when an evaluation is proposed which makes some marked deviation from a norm. Such deviation is signalled by comparisons against some ideal (*too big, not wide enough*), extreme adjectival (*huge*) or adverbial (*massively*) qualifiers, and intensifiers (*really*); for example:

> *Agnes*:   How's ev'rything at the *rest*'rantee
> *Portia*:   'hh uh Gee we were really *busy* las' night ih was like *sum*mer
>
> *Jenny*:   .hhh Ahnd eh–I like the cabinet ez well b't (.) it's a bit (.) too big I:
>   think fer the wh⌈ere ih ti:s
> *Ann*:   ⌊Uh huh Ye:s
> *Jenny*:   .hhh I would've liked the two:. (0.2) It's a three: cupboard one
>   (Button and Casey, 1985: 12 and 38 respectively; transcription slightly
>   simplified)

Assessment 2: Factual claims   The 'assessment' at issue may be proposed as a factual claim, strongly encouraging an equivalently factual tone to any subsequent disagreement, as happens in this example:

> *B*:   No it's terribly . . terribly cultural — in fact you can't separate yourself
>   from — natural free associations about each word [*5 to 6 syllables
>   unintelligible*]
> *A*:   Well I can because I've lived in two [s] two very different countries
>   (LL S1.10, p. 253, 263)

Speaker A's account (*I can because I've lived in two very different countries*) fills the slot opened up by the starting *well*, and together they accomplish the marking of A's utterance as a disagreement with what B had set up as a factual claim (that no one's word-associations can hope to be free of a particular culture).

Assessment 3: Choices   The making of a choice might require warranting if the assessment of one alternative as better than another might be construable as controversial, or damaging to the face of others. The following is an example of accounting for a choice in order to head off the potential implication that one has chosen something for the (self-deprecating) reason offered by another interactant:

	1	*B*:	What would you like (.) we've got (.) vermouth (.) whisky (.) or wine
	2	*C*:	er (.) Oh dear
→	3	*B*:	Preferably yours
	4	*C*:	⌈Wine
	5	*B*:	⌊It looks a good deal better than ⌈ours [*laughs*]
→	6	*C*:	⌊Yes (.) how about wine cos whisky certainly doesn't go with wine

(LL S2.7, p. 545, 30)

The host B has in line 3 flattered the guest C by assessing C's wine as preferable to theirs. By choosing wine, C risks looking as if she is agreeing with that self-deprecatory assessment, an agreement which is routinely avoided in talk (Pomerantz, 1978); hence her explicit invocation of a quite different, 'face-saving' account in line 6.

Assessment 4: Formulations   A 'formulation' is a form of words that captures, or claims to capture, something about what the previous speaker is trying to say. As Heritage and Watson (1979) show, formulations are signals of what the speaker takes to be the important aspect of the other's talk, as in this example:

	I:	How long did he spend in Rampton
	S:	Well he was in er Rampton and Moss Side hospitals er alternatively until nineteen sixty one
→	*I*:	That's the best part of thirty years
	S:	That's right Now in nineteen sixty one . . .

(Heritage and Watson, 1979: 130)

No account is necessary because I's summary formulation is agreed with by the speaker and the conversation proceeds. Accounts will be necessary when, on the contrary, the speaker disagrees with the formulation, as in this example:

(Young caller (Ca) speaking to counsellor (Co) of 'home troubles' about employment)

	Co:	(. . .) When do you take your O levels?
	Ca:	I take them in June
	Co:	In June
	Ca:	Yeah
→	*Co*:	Yes so you know you will get the job the results and you could get a job
→	*Ca*:	(Well look) you see, it's not just that get's me down, it–it you know, because my mum's she's she's a bit

(Heritage and Watson, 1979: 130)

The caller rejects the counsellor's identification of 'getting exam results' as an acceptable formulation of the state of affairs she finds herself in; in defence of her rejection, she offers an alternative account (*it's my mother, she's a bit. . .*).

Questions

Now that we've had a look at dispreferred responses to various kinds of assessment, we can move onto the next of the major type of utterance pair, the question and answer. Replies to questions will have to include an account when the reply is to be marked as unsatisfactory in some way: in its content, tone or register, or perhaps, as in the example below, because the speaker cannot fulfil the conditions which would have authorized them to give a satisfactory answer.

```
        A:   Yeah (.) does it work ⌈does it get action
  →     B:                         ⌊Well I I I mean I've only just been elected
             ⌈I haven't yet (.) been to a (.) meeting
        A:   ⌊Oh no haven't you (.) er (.) yeah
```
(LL S3.3, p. 805, 46; transcription slightly simplified)

Speaker B's *I've only just been elected* fills the slot advertised by *well I mean*, and the utterance marks the failure to come up with what the questioner expects – after all, speaker B has only just got into post, and can't be expected to give an authoritative answer. In this next example, the speaker again reveals grounds why a second-pair part answer was not possible. This time, however – and just to show how powerful is the expectation that a question will eventually get a reply – a longish insertion sequence intervenes between the two pair parts. See how the interactants work towards a proper resolution of the request in line 1 (*how many tubes would you like sir?*).

```
   1   A:   (. . .) How many tubes would you like sir?
   2   B:   An– uhm (.) what's the price now eh with VAT do you know eh
   3   A:   er I'll just work that out for you =
   4   B:   = Thanks
            (10.0)
   5   A:   Three pounds nineteen a tube sir
   6   B:   Three pounds nineteen is it =
   7   A:   = Yeah
   8   B:   e:hh (1.0) yes u:hm [dental click] [in parenthetical tone] e:h jus–justa
            think, that's what three nineteen That's for the large tube isn't it
   9   A:   Well yeah it's for the thirty-seven c.c.s
→ 10   B:   er, hh, I'll tell you what I'll just eh eh ring you back I have to work
            out how many I'll need. Sorry I did– wasn't sure of the price you
            see
```
(Levinson, 1983: 305; transcription slightly simplified)

The requirement for a request (in line 1) to be followed by an appropriate response is so strong that it lasts a good nine turns, finally to be addressed by the customer in turn 10. In fact, the customer can't come up with a 'proper' answer, setting himself up a slot in which the phrase *I did– wasn't sure of the price you see* works as an account. Note once again how it illustrates the theme of this chapter that the phrase would have no intrinsic force on its own: it works as an account through its placement.

In the above example, the speaker himself orientated to the lack of a proper answer to the shopkeeper's question and provided the appropriate account unprompted. It can also be the case that a speaker can be *made* to treat an utterance as accountable, even though it seems to have been structurally sound. In the following example reported by Heritage (1988), G and S are talking about an exam, which S has failed. We see how G signals a complaint that S's response is not full enough.

```
    G:   So yih gonna take it again?
    S:   nNo
         (0.5)
    G:   No?
    S:   No
         (0.3)
→   G:   Why not?
→   S:   .t.hhhh I don't rilly want to
    (Heritage, 1988: 134; transcription slightly simplified)
```

On the principle that people normally take their turns up rapidly, G's silence before taking up her turns means something. She is expressing dissatisfaction with S's responses. G's first question projected agreement, but S didn't echo that, as would have been the preferred thing to do – but she doesn't explain why not. G pursues her, eventually with an explicit question, and S ends up giving the grounds for her dispreferred response. Note that the explanation is required not necessarily because G is curious about S's activities (although that may be true), but because G is policing S's violation of a conversational norm, namely that of properly taking up the preceding turn. This is an important variant, at the base level, of why people engage in explanation-giving and in explanation-soliciting. Here is another example, again reported in Heritage (1988):

```
    A:   Well listen (.) tiz you tidyu phone yer vicar yet?
         (0.3)
    B:   No I ain't
    A:   Oh
         (0.3)
         Ah:::⌈::
→   B:        ⌊I w'z gonna wait 'ntil you found out about . . .
    (Heritage, 1988: 135; transcription simplified)
```

A gives B the opportunity of explaining why he hasn't phoned the vicar; or perhaps it is nearer the truth to say that A, by not taking up his turns quickly, is making it quite clear to B that explanation is required; it comes eventually. Silence, then, is an effective signal that something wants explaining. Conversely, a speaker may jump in with an intervention that tries to neutralize what seems to have been taken as an accusation.

```
    A:   How's your thesis going
    B:   eh I'm typing it up now (.) typing up the final
    A:   [hm]
    B:   Copy
    A:   When are you submitting it
```

```
      B:   e:h Well ⎡it
  →   A:          ⎣Next term
      B:   It would have been this autumn but eh I had to go to work . . .
      (LL S2.1, p. 372, 5)
```

A's question *when are you submitting it?* is responded to by B with a pause
and a prefacing hedge *well*. This signals a dispreferred, implying that B has
read A's preceding turn as an accusation. A nips in to intervene with a
candidate reply (*next term?*) which might neutralize the accusation, but the
slot is still open: B presses on to fill it with the exoneration (*it would have
been this autumn but eh I had to go to work . . .*).

Blame

In all the cases of utterance pairs we've seen so far, it looks as if the simple
rule at work is that the preferred response is some kind of agreement (the
taking up of an invitation, the agreement with an assessment, and so on).
This might suggest that 'preference' in a second-part utterance is merely a
matter of saying what the first person wants you to say – that 'preference'
means 'what the questioner prefers'. To see that it isn't, consider what
happens when somebody blames someone else. If preference was what the
blamer wants you to say, then, presumably, you should be quick to accept
and admit fault. But what happens here is that the quick, emphatic response
is a denial. For example:

```
      A:   I've heard from a number of sources (.) that you have said in a [3 to 4
           syllables unintelligible] that you think that you did not get the job here
           because of me
  →   B:   Oh no I have never said that (.) in fact I went to great pains I will be
           perfectly frank with you I went to great pains to (.) put it (.) about quite
           publicly that you were the one who in fact was supporting me in the
           interview
      (LL S2.1, p. 375, 141; transcription slightly simplified)
```

As Levinson (1983: 336) observes, this is compelling evidence that
'preference' is a normative matter of what is the usual case. Hence we see the
odd consequence that it will be someone who 'admits' blame who will mark
their utterance in some way. Here is an example from courtroom talk:

```
      J:   And having that in mind are you ready fer yer plea sir
           (pause)
  →   D:   Ahah, – guilty in part sir. With extenuating circumstances
      (Pollner, 1979: 233)
```

By introducing his plea with a pause and a preface (*ahah*) and giving a
qualification (*in part* and *with extenuating circumstances*) the defendant is
marking the plea as a dispreferred one, functionally equivalent (he may
hope) to 'not guilty'. It is rather like crossing your fingers while telling an
untruth.

Self-initiated second-pair parts

The section immediately above, on how people manage denial of blame, brings us near the end of the catalogue of ways in which speakers may set up slots for themselves in local pairs of utterances. Soon we shall get on to larger scale sequences, but there is one more class to record first. So far we have seen variations on the theme that a speaker will protect a dispreferred second part with some kind of account. This has the flavour of explanations being set up rather mechanically in responses to a first-pair part spoken by another person; yet they need not be. The speaker may offer an explanation for something that he or she has initiated; that is to say, if we think of the examples in the section above as being accounts given for 'omissions' (failures to respond adequately, to agree, and so on), then these are accounts offered to mark unexpected or controversial 'commissions'. There could be, in principle, counterparts to every point on the list we saw at length above – requests, assessments, answers to questions and denials of blame – but examples of only the first two seem to be easy to spot: initiated requests and initiated assessments.

Initiated requests and invitations   Where the speaker makes a request that may be interactionally unexpected, it may need accounting for, as in this example:

>   *A:*   m Thank you very much indeed – do you know anywhere which does . . .
>   sort of . . . service flats for people 'cos I've got, I . . . think I shall
>   probably have to come up to town . . . and stay for a few weeks in
>   October
>   (LL, reported in Antaki and Leudar, 1992: 191)

Really such cases are examples of 'pre-requests', in which the speaker gives notice that he or she is going to come up with some further demand. Pre-requests take many (usually interrogative) forms; the marks here are the use of 'do you know' and the provision of an account. The speaker is signalling that what comes next might be hearable as a costly demand – perhaps as a request for accommodation. (One can also think of this kind of case as an example of the speaker acknowledging that she or he needs to warrant certain assumptions, or 'felicity conditions' in what is said; we shall see more of this in Chapter 9).

A related case is what happens when the speaker initiates an 'invitation' which may require warranting; for example, as below, when it is an invitation to take the floor.

>   *A:*   What about you (.) cos you were there first (.)
>   *B:*   You er asked to come didn't you
>   *D:*   er er
>   *B:*   You applied to go didn't you
>   (LL S1.12, p. 303, 66; transcription slightly simplified)

The fractional pause after A's invitation shows trouble: D may not know that the invitation is directed at him, or may be deliberately marking some kind of resistance to the question; in any case, A quickly addresses the trouble with an account (*cos you were there first*), and B helps out twice when the uptake is still unforthcoming.

Initiated assessments   A speaker will set up both parts of the 'offence'– 'account' pair when the speaker him/herself initiates an 'assessment'. This is the single-person counterpart to the two-person statement–assessment pair we saw above. Now, rather than have to account for disagreeing with somebody's explicit statement, it falls to the speaker to account for making an assessment in the face of only implicit controversy:

```
      A:  (. . .) and I do think that these three portraits are ⎡very good
      C:                          ˙                              ⎣m (.) m
      A:  And this one here (.) this gay one (.) rather grows on you
      C:  Yeah (.)
  →   A:  That's the one I should have if I had any I think because er (.) it's jolly
          isn't it
      (LL S1.8, p. 210, 590)
```

It will be difficult to complete the set with examples of speaker-initiated question–answer or blame–admission pairs. To find a single-speaker counterpart to the question–answer pair, one would have to see speakers marking as unsatisfactory an answer to a question (as opposed to the interactional requests that we saw above) that they had posed themselves. Such cases will happen, but the convergence of the two unusual cases – asking oneself a question and providing an unsatisfactory answer – will be rare. The same holds for accusing oneself and providing an account-marked admission. So we stop here with this set of within-speaker explanations incomplete, and now leave the entire section on adjacency-pair explanation slots to go on to see how they appear in sequences of talk that span many conversational turns.

Explanation slots in larger-scale sequences

The preceding long section was devoted to showing how a speaker might open up an explanation slot for him or herself as a matter of marking, and palliating the effects of, a very local unexpected omission or commission. Here we stay with speakers' own openings but, knowing that conversations are organized at a more molar level than the adjacency pair, we look to see this marking also happening when there is a deviation from a step in a larger sequence.

Closing

Levinson (1983), summarizing conversation analytic work on the closings of speech events (shop encounters, telephone calls and so on), observes that they are accomplished by a well-structured series of identifiable features. Closing an interaction needs all this traffic management because the participants have to release each other from the normal turn-taking rules that force turn after turn in endless democratic alternation. To close down the system in an orderly way, participants typically display these signals: there will (often, but not always) first be an invitation to future joint activity or a reiteration of a topic from earlier in the conversation; then speakers will (virtually always) interchange passing turns like *OK, all right* and so on. Then they reach the normatively terminal exchange of *bye*, or its equivalent, which frees everyone from having to respond to the last speaker's turn, and participants can go off.

From our point of view, what is important is that if any of these steps go wrong then they will need to be bolstered by the provision of some kind of an account. One potentially tricky feature which may well need this support is what Button (1987) calls 'referencing': the revival of the topic which had signalled the start of the interaction. If this had occurred some way back, the speaker might need to do some explicit marking to jog other participants' memories; an account for raising the matter might do the trick. This is what happens in the following example. Dai is taking his leave of a group of friends.

	(Talk about pubs in the neighbourhood)	
	Dai:	((That reminds me)) I'm going
	Monica:	Well when I I
→	*Dai*:	Monica, I can't offer you any of Malcolm's sherry ((because)) he hasn't got much
	Monica:	No
	Dai:	But (.) would you get (.) one of them to bring you round and have a pint of beer with us just now ((if you've)) time
	Monica:	That would be lovely
		⌈that would be lovely yes, right that would be very ((nice))
	Dai:	⌊Yes (.) well I'm going to the Scarborough eh em I'll have it lined up for you dear
	Monica:	OK well I shall look forward to that
	Dai:	Good great
	Monica:	[*laughs*] Great
	Dai:	I don't want you to (.) to (.) I mean you ((can)) have their company (.) but I'll buy you a pint there
	Monica:	Yes (.) right (.) that'll be nice
	Malcolm:	Good see you Dai
	Monica:	Right bye bye thank you
	Dai:	[*coughs*] Thanks [*2 syllables unintelligible*]
	Malcolm:	Pardon
	Dai:	Thank you for the sherry
	(LL S1.9, p. 229, 512)	

There are various indications that this is a closing sequence. Dai calls for attention and signals he is leaving. He makes an invitation for future arrangements, there is a crossover of passing turns and a final flurry of goodbyes. In the middle of all this he makes what looks on the face of it a straightforward failure claim (*I can't offer you any of Malcolm's sherry*) and an exoneration (*because he hasn't got much*). On the face of it, this is a claim bolstered by an explanatory account, but why should Dai offer Malcolm's sherry at all, and why should *he hasn't got much* be chosen as the account?

The argument I'm pursuing is that what Dai is doing, and his account for it, can only be understood by reference to its place as part of a closing sequence; specifically, its role as a signpost pointing a long way back to the beginning of the larger interactional episode. If we look right back to the beginning of the interaction, we see that the topic 'shortage of sherry' had in fact been orientated to by Malcolm (the host) exactly as a matter of inducting Dai into the group:

> Malcolm: Hello hello Dai come and have a glass of sherry man
> [*8 turn sequence of greetings between Dai and Monica*]
> → Malcolm: Monica, er er ((meriander)) em th– the bottoms of a lot of bottles
> I'm afraid ((ordered from ⌈the window))
> Monica: ⌊I don't mind in what order I begin
> Malcolm
> Malcolm: Right well there's less of the Tio Pepe than anything else,
> Manzanilla
> Monica: erm Thank you
> (LL S1.9, p. 220, 18)

This talk of there being only the bottoms of a lot of bottles – in other words, not much wine – is what Dai is referring to, some 200 turns later. The claim that he can't offer Monica sherry sets up a slot for an account which, by referring to Malcolm not having much sherry, echoes early talk. By making this reference back to the start of the interaction he produces the closing bracket to match the opening one, neatly accomplishing one of the regular features of a leave taking. The reference also, we should perhaps note in admiration of Dai's ordinary ingenuity, does extra work besides. He uses the reference to alcohol as grounds for one more, clinching, leaving-sequence feature, that of orientating participants to future engagements: *but* (he says to Monica) *would you get one of them to bring you round and have a pint of beer with us* . . .

In making all these obervations we – or rather the participants, with us watching over their shoulders – can't understand what Dai has said either in a vacuum or even in the very local run of talk; what he says hooks back right to the beginning of the encounter, and the account is the handle of that hook.

Exonerations as filling 'explanation slots'

The point of this chapter has been to try to show that one can treat explanations as matters of interactional organization rather than worry over what they mean abstractly, in cognitive isolation. The specifics of the argument I've pursued are that conversationalists' contract forces them to mark some utterances as being unexpected, and that this marking is (at least sometimes) done by offering an explanatory account. Since there is an identifiable regularity (in, at least, the Western anglophone tradition in which most conversation analytic work is done) of what is expected and unexpected, we can make reasonable guesses as to when an explanation will be required, and we can speak of a 'slot' being opened up at short and long range. The speaker might do it for him or herself, might have it done on his/her behalf, or might force it on the other participant. It is in every case done regularly, and to a knowable mechanism; that frees the study of exonerations from reliance on less public linguistic categories like the speech acts we saw in Chapter 4.

Now, looking forward, it is at least arguable that the organizational scaffolding which supports the discrete explanations we've seen here also supports larger-scale ones as well. Throughout the rest of the book I shall return again and again to this scaffolding of conversational sequence. What it offers is a systematic way of analysing interactions which will prove useful, as we shall see, for very different kinds of account.

In the next chapter we shall be looking at accounts considered as integral wholes. I shall hold off the conversation analysis until the end of the chapter, devoting the first sections to treatments with a more literary inspiration. Then I shall come back to conversation analysis to see how those whole-story accounts might be interactionally accomplished.

Note

1 From the London–Lund corpus; for details see note on p. 42.

6

Storied Accounts

I made the decision to ah go into furniture, just in that I had an intuitive sense about woodworking, which I didn't about landscape architecture. uh Some landscape architects . . . they'd go into a nursery and select trees. Just the right kind of tree. And they'd bring it to the site, and they'd position it just in the right place, and have it rotated the right way. They had it – a real sense of – of how that should be. And I didn't. Whereas if – in – talking about woodworking, I – I knew exactly looking at a board whether it should be used for a table top or a table leg. I just knew that. Felt very comfortable with it.
(interview reported in Mishler, 1992: 28)

We could read the extract above as a straight piece of reportage, a simple explanation of why one man chose the profession that he did. For some purposes, that might be enough (we might be marketing people doing a survey of career choices, or job-placement officers checking a client's c.v.). But for other purposes we shall want to do a bit more than that; and in this chapter we shall take up the notion that an account like this does work in constructing social realities. We shall see what progress can be made by approaching accounts as if they were structured, first by taking them to be some kind of *narrative* – how, in the example above, the man's explanation worked as an integrated story moving from departure to destination – and then as if they might be organized around a central *metaphor* (which, here, might be the metaphor of 'seeing' for understanding). Then, returning to the methods of conversation analysis we saw in the last chapter, I shall finish off by turning to see how such idealizations might be achieved in actual performance.

Accounts and social constructionism

The kind of explanations we shall be looking at in this chapter are those that carry a substantial freight of description, strategy and definition. They are orientated not so much to very transient interactional goals and very specific requirements for explanation, but rather to freer exchanges of knowledge under less constraining circumstances. They respond to questions, or prompts, like *why did your relationship break up?* or *what were the 1970s like?* and, as is implicit in the example at the head of the chapter, *explain how you got involved in your job*.

Such questions are, of course, routinely asked in social psychology and in some other corners of the social sciences where there is a respectful interest in collecting and analysing, fairly literally, what people say about their lives; for examples see Burnett et al. (1987) and Harvey et al. (1990). Often, such accounts are solicited in order to diagnose the individual's, or group's, psychological make-up, and what is at issue is their motivation, their well-being and their relationships. A typical piece of research might be like this: separated heterosexual couples are asked for their accounts of their relationships and subsequent break-ups. The researcher codes their accounts and discovers (say) that the men in the sample gave reliably more recriminatory accounts than did the women. The researcher infers that the men are worse affected by the break-up. In corroboration, the researcher points to a separate questionnaire index, taken at the same time, which shows that the men do indeed report greater levels of stress and upset. As to the objective reality of the events in the respondents' explanations, the researcher concedes that this has not been measured, but reminds us that, if the aim of the study is to understand the respondents' feelings, then it is the psychological, not the objective, reality that is at issue – and that the proof of the pudding is in seeing an empirical correlation between the explanation and the respondents' well-being on some other index.

To do work like this (of which there is a great deal in the social psychological end of what is often called the 'accounts' literature) is to risk treating the account as two things at once. On the one hand, it is to respect its authority and endorse – implicitly – the notion that there is a knowable world which could be measured if the instruments were well enough calibrated. Had they believed this the researcher would have tried to find out, independently, what the events being explained 'really were', something which is rare in social psychological research. But neither is such a possibility explicitly rejected; correlating the account with some other index of mental life keeps open the realist hypothesis that there really is something material of which the account is the sign or symptom.

So the traditional social psychological treatment of accounts is rather equivocal. Were the researchers to go the whole way in accepting the contingency of the respondents' words, they would be chary of interpreting them in a cultural vacuum; but if they really did want to treat them as accurate reports, they would make some effort to check their veracity. In short, the social psychological treatment of accounts sets them in a sort of limbo, halfway between a reliable report and a wholly contingent construction.

This quiet middle ground disappoints relativist critics. Their objection is that to fence an account into such equivocal ground means that one can only ever come to it through the gate of the researcher's own culturally or personally idiosyncratic prejudices. A really committed relativism would ask rather different questions. It might start by asking where the analysts' *own* vocabulary of the account comes from: 'heterosexuals', 'partners', 'break-up' and 'recrimination' in the example above (a question which would perhaps be more obvious had the research been done using other, and more clearly contentious, descriptions – 'people with traditional sexuality', 'husbands and their wives', 'dissolution of the marriage contract' and 'guilt', say). It would avoid aggregating accounts together and treating every instance of (say) 'recrimination' as being identical; rather, it might search for variation in one person's account for recrimination sometimes used to do this job, sometimes that; and it would make some claim about the social reality that the deployment of such vocabulary constructs.

This kind of thinking is often referred to as *social constructionism*, and social constructionists are much happier with the notion that accounts are not so much aids to psychological diagnosis as means, in their own right, of constituting social reality; to describe something in a certain way is to make it truly so. This is a very crude formulation of social constructionism (more elegantly expressed in, for example, Gergen, 1985) but will do as a starting slogan. We shall be pressing on with that reading of accounts in this chapter, and leaving to one side the more content-orientated social psychological work which, although often sympathetic to the general idea of social constructionism, puts more of a premium on straightforward content analysis than it does on the kind of formal analysis that we shall be seeing here.

The formal description of accounts

Any description of an account which treats it as a unified piece will proclaim the primacy of language, and will draw heavily (though not always explicitly) on the bank of literary stylistics, the study of how the formal features of a text affect its interpretation by the reader. Stylistics insists that the choice of expressions in a text is not accidental, nor is one form of words reducible, without loss, to another form; the prose paraphrasis of a poem, though it might apparently be faithful to the state of affairs the poet describes, can never recapture its spirit and force.

The same can be claimed for two prose accounts, even at the level of the sentence. It is a commonplace to note that *my employment was terminated at short notice* gets across a message different from *I was sacked*. Just as a stylistic analysis will reveal how a poem or novel achieves its effects, the argument runs, a language-rich analysis of the kind championed by the constructionists will reveal how an account achieves its meaning. The principle that the exact expression of the account matters informs the general social constructionist enterprise, and here the principle draws explicitly on its literary inheritance to say something about the power of an account. It does so in two ways. One is to look for clues in the account's structure (usually though a consideration of its *narrative form*); the other is to look for its reliance on some key *metaphor*.

Social construction through narrative

People certainly tell narrative stories about themselves and their worlds, but before we look into how these might attract an analyst we need to spend a moment thinking what the word 'narrative' might mean. Considering narratives as linked events which play to some set of story-telling rules is a reasonable start. But that glosses an important question about what kind of rules we are interested in – crudely speaking, rules of comprehension on one hand or rules of production on the other.

Were we to be interested in cognitive rules this might suggest that story-telling was best considered a purely intellectual accomplishment. There is indeed a tradition in cognitive psychology which believes just this, and mines stories (or rather, the comprehension of stories) for what they have to tell us about people's mental powers (of dealing with implication, summarizing gist, keeping track of who did what and so on; see, for example, the collection edited by Britton and Pellegrini, 1990). That kind of work, however, is designed to reveal cognitive powers of information processing. While it has much to say about the rules by which the mind copes with various tests of coherence, it has little to say about why people produce stories, nor about the meaning of the stories' constituent parts or about the linguistic and pragmatic devices they use to bind them together in an acceptable performance.

I shall keep to a wider interpretation of narrative coherence and, in the sections below, we shall be looking at rules of cultural, rather than merely cognitive, structure, and rules of practical story-telling performance rather than of abstract story comprehension.

Literary structure

One principled way of analysing ordinary narrative is to fit it into classic literary form. This insight can be traced back, in modern times, to Kenneth Burke's *Grammar of Motives* (1945/69). Social psychologists who follow in Burke's wake find themselves somewhere below the very universal claims for the pervasiveness of narrative in human affairs (as proposed by, for example, Barthes, 1973, or more recently, Bourdieu, 1993) but above the ground-level of maps of plots, scripts and grammars (of interest to narratologists; for a review see Pavel, 1986). The social psychologist pulls down from above a general spirit of narratives as driving forces, and from below a vocabulary of terms with which to translate people's accounts as the working through of some structured, usually chronological, sequence of stages.

At first sight literary form seems rather an odd structure to impose on people's spontaneous first-person accounts since, after all, literary narratives tend to be in the third person, and tend to be polished and dramatic. Constructionists answer that, since the Russian formalist Propp (1968), it has been useful to think of narratives (especially folk narratives) as expressing a basic set of well-worn ingredients. Regularities in the mix of such ingredients, the reasoning goes, reveal prototype stories – meta-narratives – put together quite as rigorously as grammatically well-formed sentences. Constructionists claim that these regularities are not only rules for fictional story-making but also for personal biographies; that, in other words, the laws that bind the folk tale also bind our conceptions of ourselves. The meta-narrative is a happy gift from the culture to its analyst, making a formal offering of the vocabulary, the dramatis personae and the plot lines out of which that culture's individuals construct themselves.

Clearly, the traditional basis of such a claim – regularities in myth, folk tale, and so on – is far removed from any close definition of an 'explanation'. The bulk of its application has been, understandably, to larger-scale stories. Nevertheless, the case can be made for conceiving of explanatory accounts as formal structured narratives in and of themselves – accounts given (often in response to an interviewer's explicit probing) as a matter of making plain, or of warranting one's actions on a broad canvas. This is the guiding principle behind recent work in the social construction of identity through narrative.

There is a stream of work which surrounds this central formalist core, and leaks away into one-off exegesis of individual stories (as, for example, confessional autobiography, therapeutic exercise, or raw material for the oral historian) but we shall keep to the core concern for principled mapping.

The central line is well illustrated by Gergen and Gergen's (1987) proposal that any individual's story will be told as a well-formed narrative which can be fitted into the classical typology of narrative literary form. Invoking classic genres of drama, they argue that such a story might be 'comic' (in which, crudely speaking, the new vanquishes the old), 'tragic' (noble failure), 'romantic' (the restoration of the past) or 'ironic' (the rejection of any moral progress). They apply this robust strategy to people's stories as they 'explain themselves' by invoking these stylistically well-known story types. Each genre establishes some end point to which the explanation orientates itself; for example, the narrative may be orientated to explain *how I got to the top*, *how we first met* and so on. The end state keys a certain set of possible story elements and, in putting these together, the story-teller plays to appropriate norms of causation and chronology and brings the whole thing to a recognizable conclusion.

The researcher's job then becomes the quasi-anthropological one of documenting the realizations of the story-structure available to speakers in a culture, the culture 'speaking through' the individual (Shotter and Gergen, 1990). So, according to Gergen and Gergen (1987), people's relationships in Western cultures are driven by comedic 'unification myths', which chart progress from singlehood to union. These myths, it is claimed, are so powerful as to channel any culturally competent individual's relationship progress, and to specify in advance the kind of account she or he will give on its termination.

If the general principle is right, then one can collect spoken accounts and examine them for signs of approximation to the classic literary structures. A clever attempt at getting enough data to do the comparison is reported by Murray (1985). He reasons that, if the resources that people use to construct hypothetical lives are much the same as they use to construct their own, then one can read off personal identities from invented ones. He takes the transcript of groups of respondents' inventions as the manifestation of the culturally powerful stories that underlie our conception of ourselves. The extract below nicely shows how what probably feels to the participants like nonchalant invention can reasonably be read by the analyst as the clear invocation of literary form to channel meaning:

> (Speakers are inventing a fictional woman's biography)
> *F:*   I like the idea of her coming from [the suburbs] cos now she's . . . the struggle to overcome
> *P:*   It's the battler syndrome [*laughs*]
> *F:*   Well, otherwise, what's her struggle going to be? Let's say she comes from [a suburb] . . gone to the private school – whichever one it was – and she's gone through Uni and she's done all the obligatory things . . .
> *J:*   What's going to make her interesting?
> *F:*   Maybe she has no struggle? Everything . . her life goes extraordinarily smoothly
> *J:*   Do we want her to have a struggle?
>   (. .)
> *T:*   Okay [*pause*] I think she's got really pushy parents who have high aspirations, cos they had to work really hard
> (Murray, 1985: 189; slightly simplified)

We can see how the group cast around for a 'life' that fits not so much mundane reality as the demands of a 'well-formed narrative' – in this extract, the setting up of some conflict for later resolution. Otherwise the life lacks something – it is not 'interesting', as one of the speakers puts it. It may be that conflict with parents as a 'struggle' generator, and a life-story summary like 'battler syndrome', are peculiar to this (Australian) sample, but that does not invalidate the principle that such form is there to be read.

Murray's intention is now to hear echoes of this account in the respondents' own personal stories. He finds, for example, that the common thread of 'travel' in the groups' narratives (the character in the story above, for example, is sent to the US, to South America, to Italy and back again to Australia) appears in respondents' own life-histories. A vindication of the method, and the kind of grounds that one would need to draw out the personal conclusions the project was aimed towards: 'individuals must leave the familiar everyday world and not only engage in tests . . . but also find release from normal controls . . . And narrative is the means by which these departures are managed and inscribed in one's biography' (Murray, 1985: 201).

Inferred narrative structure

If the surface seems to be too troubled and changeable to support a classic analysis, some propose that one ought to delve down to what they claim will be the narrative's deep foundations. They read accounts as embodying a rule-bound sequence of given narrative steps. This takes us from the identification of story types or genres onto a specification of the sequence through which they unfold. Here the social scientist has a wide range of models to follow (described pithily by Wales, 1989: 356–7), but the favourite among social scientists seems to be the identification of functional rather than propositional steps. That is to say, the researcher is keen on identifying what various parts of the account do, rather than what they are; this bypasses the laborious and probably impossible task of defining sequence steps in terms of their categorical content.

Labov (most famously in *Language in the Inner City*, 1972) had used narrative complexity as grounds on which to respect a low-status language variant like inner-city North American Black English. Narrative was thereafter in the sociolinguist's toolbox, and available for more technical purposes. Applying approximations of formalist Russian literary system (see, for example, Todorov, 1984) to narrative, they could then strip narratives down to this kind of sequence: orientation to a problem; abstract of the entire story; starting event; complications; ultimate resolution. Sociolinguists of this persuasion mean this to apply explicitly to spontaneous conversational accounts given in interviews, data which get their meaning precisely from being set out as a sequence. Marrying this up to the idea that somewhere in what the speaker says is a 'key', the analyst is on the lookout for what might be the speaker's 'core narrative' (though, now, not a classical one in the sense of literary comedy or tragedy) which somehow colours or captures their life and experience.

To see this principle in operation, consider this extract from Mishler (1986), which embeds the analyst's interpretation into the respondent's talk:

> They weren't troubles in the ordinary sense or real troubles no, but they were en– en– enforced *lean* times. [*initial orientation*]
> Yet we always *did* what we had to do some*how* we did it. We got through it. [*abstract of entire story*]
> Ah, Danny got severely burned and uh, had to have skins – a skin graft and uh, surgery and was in the hospital for 45 days and it was expensive. His clothing caught fire and he lost all of his skin up here [*complicating action*]
> from the top of his ankle all up t'here. And they did a graft on him down t'here. The whole bill came to fifteen hundred dollars. Everything. Anyhow he [*the doctor*] called me up one day and he said 'Jim, would it help you at all if I considered – if I' he said 'if I reduced my bill.' Well I almost fell to the floor. And when he said that to me I – I almost – I think I did get a little bit dewy round the eyes. And I said 'no, I won't consider it' his reducing this bill at all. I said 'I was about to call you up and here you are calling me up on the telephone.' And I said 'believe it or not, you're next up at the bat.' 'n I said 'Bill, if you can just hang in there I'll get your – I'll mail a check in about three or four days and that will start a run on this thing and we'll *stamp* the *life* out of it.' And that's what we did. [*resolution*]
> (Mishler, 1986: 237)

This extract, which the analyst pulls from a longer interview, is chopped up into a given sequence of elements which form the speaker's 'core narrative' to be interpreted in contemporary terms – in this case, as the speaker presenting as a man who meets his obligations against the odds (Mishler, 1986: 243). The analyst's motivation is to get a handle on other things the speaker might say, and an interpretative frame against which to set whatever other data he might have on him – his record, his biography, and so on.

What clues is the analyst relying on in chopping up the story? Unlike a stricter conversation analyst who will identify very particular sequences of words and phrases (which we saw in the last chapter, and shall see again below) the kind of analysis exemplified here relies on a more impressionistic sense of what counts as the 'complicating action' and so on. Like Goffman's notion of a social 'move', an important subsidiary source of inspiration for this way of thinking about talk, we are not being persuaded by (what might be considered to be) merely mechanical utterance-level traces in the text. The analyst here is interested in the text's coherence as a social story, and believes that this can be charted by its topical shifts; when one has them catalogued and laid out, then one can stand back and ask what social identity the whole story promotes. The fact that the analysis has taken the trouble to keep the account in the story form in which it was offered adds weight to the claims it makes. In that sense it can be said to exploit the notion of narrative structure; but the analyst's molar interests mean that, like the work done in the literary spirit, unambiguous connection between what the respondent says and the analyst's interpretation remains elusive. The analyst's motivation is to uncover inner mental life and the subject's biography, but both are highly resistant to an outsider's interpretation.

Culturally available narratives

We remarked back in Chapter 2 that it is a simple matter (or would be, if it was attempted more often) to see differences in lists of explanatory concepts used by respondents in different cultures. But we also observed that the differences in the list would be unintelligible without some sense of the meaning of the terms *in situ*. It would be unsafe to infer cultural difference simply from the appearance of apparently different categories of explanation, suggestive though these might be; nor is it enough to guess at the cultural significance of the categories without ethnographic or anthropological work which triangulates them against other indices of cultural practice.

This means that properly to redress the Western-centred balance of familiar theories of explanation (say, by discovering new causal attribution categories) can't simply be done by adding to the existing list. Suppose, for example, one found more use of 'contextual' explanations among a sample of Indian respondents than among American ones (as did Miller, 1984). The interpretation might be that the American explanations 'appeared based, in part, on the culturally derived premiss that agents possess enduring generalized dispositions and constitute the primary locus of moral responsibility', while the Indian explanations 'appeared informed by a culturally derived view of persons as highly vulnerable to situational influences and of the social role as a basic normative unit' (Shweder and Miller, 1985: 55–6). This interpretation courts circularity, since the evidence that the two cultures believe that individuals have 'enduring personality dispositions' or are 'highly vulnerable to situational influences' is the very fact that respondents use just these explanatory categories. A more satisfactory account would brace the explanation categories against something else: the respondents' own behaviour, perhaps, or cultural practices in their society at large.

This kind of support is common in ethnographic work. Let us take the example of the relation between accounts, myth and experience (Hutchins, 1987). In a culture foreign to him (the Trobriand Islands) the ethnographer takes care to articulate those of his respondents' background beliefs which are likely to infuse their narratives but which in one's own culture would remain unarticulated. Hutchins then has a triad of data: what the members of that society do; how they report it; and what beliefs they draw on to make the reports and the actions make sense. The particular set that is relevant to this example is the following. The Trobriand villagers believe that the spirits of the dead visit the living, but are nearly always invisible. On one occasion one of Hutchins' respondents had a troubling encounter with a visible spirit: a recently dead villager who came to her in a series of night-time visitations, each time appearing more decomposed and revolting. This unusual circumstance occasioned a lengthy search for an explanation. Her explanation was couched in the terms of a rich, complex and normally taken-for-granted narrative myth to do with a certain prototypical relation between a mother and her pregnant daughter – a narrative which would seem, at first sight, to have little to do with the actual encounter which troubled her. Hutchins then has everything in place to pursue his particular anthropological interest in the cognitive universals which he takes to underlie the myth, the behaviour and the experience. But we need not follow him down that trail. It is enough to see that he makes a case for taking the three components together – the reported event, its explanation and the cultural narrative that underlies it. We can get away without that triangulation in cultures that are familiar to us, but at the risk of a comparatively superficial account.

One might go further and follow Quinn and Holland (1987) in saying that cultural narratives inform the understanding of any episode whatever; that the description and explanation of even the most apparently mundane activity is already circumscribed and constrained by the expectations about its proper sequential unfolding. Thus to say I am 'buying' something is to mobilize a 'frame' or 'script' involving a purchaser, a seller, merchandise, price and so on, all tied together by a fairly inflexible chronological series of steps. The anthropologist Lutz (1987) gives a persuasive example of cultural infusion of action and narrative. She sees a young Ifaluk child happily, if carelessly, at play, and responds with a smile; for this she is reprimanded by an adult. That her response was a mistake only makes sense once one has teased out the Ifaluk narrative of emotion, the general principle of which is that emotions are readable from situations (not, as Western habit would have it, from internal promptings) and lead to determinate actions. The fragment of the Ifaluk emotion model which was operative in this case is this: the child's happiness would lead to misbehaviour; this would elicit justifiable anger in the observer, prompting a reprimand; this would have the effect of generating fear or anxiety in the child and a recognition of the error of her ways. The anthropologist had violated the sequence by ethnocentrically responding positively to the child's display of pleasure; in the Ifaluk sequence, she had demonstrated her ignorance of what narrative of emotions was in operation.

Metaphor

Looking for narrative structure in people's explanatory descriptions has the attraction of being able to identify something fairly specific about the linkages and sequence of what they say, but the commitment to seeing an account as laid out along a central spine does have certain difficulties, which we shall expand on at the end of the chapter. A broader alternative is to read an explanation as spreading out from a central key 'metaphor', or a 'model'. These terms are sometimes interchangeable, occasionally without loss. Of the two, 'model' is perhaps the less easy to define, encompassing as it does a range from prescriptive blueprint to suggestive analogy (see, for example, the range of meaning in Holland and Quinn, 1987). 'Metaphor' seems preferable because, although quite how it works is not completely clear (see Levinson, 1983: 146 ff for a discussion), there does at least seem to be a consensus about certain of its features. A metaphor will map one domain onto another (for example, 'emotion' onto 'containment') and, by mobilizing our analogical abilities, generate an indefinitely large number of revealing substitutions of concrete images for abstract ones (thus *it was all bottled up inside, it all came out in a rush, he kept his feelings hidden*, and so on).

The indeterminacy of the substitutions that metaphors allow will frustrate precise prediction, but it will allow generous play to the invention of the explainer. To say that, for example, a person's relationship account relies (at least in part) on the culturally powerful metaphor of love-as-a-substance is not to be able to predict exactly what images he or she will invoke, but rather the class of images that cluster round 'substance': mass, portability, exhaustibility and so on. Hence one might see the respondent say *I had no love left for him, she has a lot of love inside her* and so on; we read this partly as the manifestations (in our culture) of the metaphor of love as a 'thing' which can be weighed, contained, given, and so on.

Occasionally, perhaps, this metaphor might drive an entire account, from description to explanation. For example, it might be that using a certain metaphor has unlooked-for implications: talking of the stock market as a sentient, volatile being (it climbs, it is jittery, it reacts sharply, it is unsettled, and so on) might have the effect of occluding the 'real' agency at work, exempting the activities of stockbrokers and speculators from any responsibility for those financial transactions we call 'the stock market's behaviour'.

One could go further and say that the use of one metaphor rather than another represents a certain party's interests. Hence it could be claimed that (for example) the use of pacific-sounding names for weapons promotes not only one view of arms at the expense of another, but also promotes one (pacific) explanation of their deployment over another.

Metaphor and explanations

More globally, it might be the case that certain systematic metaphors infuse the entire meaning system of a language, in which case whole explanatory frames will be privileged at the expense of others. Perhaps the most linguistically fundamental of such accounts of metaphor in English is Reddy's (1979) account of speakers sustaining a certain image of English itself, as a 'conduit' of expression, carrying meaning as it is despatched from speaker to hearer. This generates such statements as

I tried to get my thoughts *across*
He *put down* his ideas on paper
We *poured out* our troubles
I *gave* him some idea of the problem

Reddy convincingly shows not only that such expressions are extremely numerous in English, but that it is hard to express the same sentiments in other metaphors. The upshot of all this, he argues, is that it puts the burden of successful expression on the sender of the message, rather than the recipient. Imagine that a communication has failed, and one has to turn the above statements into advice – all of them would be addressed to the sender, none to the receiver. Equally, criticisms of a failed communication would be of this sort:

That sentence is just *empty*
There is nothing *in* what you're saying
It just doesn't *come over*

The importance of this example is that Reddy has shown the working through of a metaphor (language as a conduit) which is systematic, unconscious and disinterested and yet has potent effects on the way that success and failure in that domain is explained. It approximates a cognitive account yet has the appeal of a linguistic one.

Lakoff and Johnson (1980) expand on Reddy's linguistic case about English to make the more general social scientific claim that any and all domains of discourse can be infused by metaphors which are pregnant with explanations and justifications. They take the very constructionist position that the way people talk about social objects fosters a certain kind of understanding of what that object *is*. Take the concept of 'argument'. We know that argument can be talked about as if it were war. Lakoff and Johnson make the claim that this is what argument *is*; the metaphor has filled out to cover all the ground that the 'meaning' of argument covers. This subverts any prim pretension that argument is, or ought to be, resolvable by non-belligerent means. The traditional case, of course, is that argument is not war, and that it can be resolved by the exchange of rational propositions. But behind each of these propositions, Lakoff and Johnson claim, is the operation of the war metaphor. Thus typical formulations such as *clearly* imply intimidation; *as Plato argued* is an appeal to authority; and so on.

The objection to this from the classicist would be that there is no place in formal argument for such phrases, which are merely human commentaries which help make the austerity of proper argument more accessible. But Lakoff and Johnson could reasonably reply, with the informal logicians we shall come cross in Chapter 8, that this is simply to insist that formal logic does not very well capture what ordinary people mean by argument, and that it is questionable to call one part of the whole a commentary and the other the real event. In any case, such commentaries are what people do, and how they decide reasonableness; they can't be ignored by an account of reasoning.

These metaphors might be 'deep', informing all our sense of meaning, yet they need not (according to Lakoff and Johnson) be the same in different languages. There is no simple one-to-one correspondence with a metaphor and a domain of experience. A given experience, as Lakoff and Johnson themselves demonstrate, can be talked about by any number of metaphors – thus 'argument', for example, can be talked about as 'war' (*she shot me down in flames*), but also, in more fundamental registers, as 'moving' (*I never got to the next step*), 'building' (*you've constructed a neat case*) or in the miscellaneous metaphors of inviolability (*a watertight/airtight/fireproof case*) and so on. Two things follow from this. The first is that we should not expect to read explanations off a catalogue of metaphors, though we can still make connections among the constituent parts of the same metaphor as it appears to be used in one explanation. The second is that the speaker's use of one or other alternative metaphor is significant, though we shall have to see what else is going on in the speech situation to know what that significance is.

Clearly, metaphors sweep through the language (as is persuasively documented by Paprotte and Dirven, 1985; Lakoff, 1987), and we are only considering here how they might show up in explanations of things closely involved in people's constructions of their everyday lives.

The deployment of metaphor in explanatory reasoning

A good example of metaphors in explanations of everyday activities is Lakoff's examination of the metaphor of sexual attraction as a physical force (Lakoff, 1987). He takes this extract from a set of interviews with men in the United States (collected by Beneke, 1982):

Let's say I see a woman and she looks really pretty, and really clean and sexy, and she's giving off very feminine, sexy vibes. I think 'wow, I would love to make love to her', but I know she's not really interested. It's a tease. A lot of times a woman knows that she's looking good and she'll use that and flaunt it, and it makes me feel like she's laughing at me and I feel *degraded*. I also feel dehumanized, because when I'm being teased I just turn off, I cease to be human. Because if I go with my human emotions I'm going to want to put my arms round her and kiss her, and to do that would be unacceptable. I don't like the feeling that I'm supposed to stand there and take it, and not be able to hug her and kiss her; so I just turn off my emotions. It's a feeling of humiliation, because the woman has forced me to turn off my feelings and react in a way that I don't really want to. If I were actually desperate enough to rape somebody, it would be from wanting that person, but also it would be a very spiteful thing, just being able to say, 'I have power over you and I can do anything I want with you'; because really I feel that *they* have power over *me* just by their presence. Just the fact that they can come up to me and just melt me and make me feel like a dummy makes me want revenge. They have power over me so I want power over them. (Lakoff and Johnson, 1987: 74)

The key metaphor in this man's description is that the woman's sexuality is a physical force (she 'melts' him; she 'gives off vibes'). What is perhaps more important is that the metaphor is crucial to his 'reasoning', which goes in outline as follows: (a) a woman is responsible for her physical appearance; (b) physical appearance is a physical force (exerted on others); so (c) a woman is responsible for the physical force she exerts on men.

Step (b) in the argument is essential, yet there are two queer things about it. One is that the man nowhere defends the claim; it is taken for granted that it is a perfectly legitimate thing to say. The other is that it is indefensible on any formal reading of logic. The closest one could come to a logically acceptable proposition would be the weaker simile 'physical appearance is *like* a physical force' but a simile doesn't support the full range of implications that a metaphor does. Just because physical appearance is *like* a physical force isn't enough to guarantee that it produces causal effects in the world. But if it *is* a physical force then that implication, and any others that are true about physical force, is inescapable. That's why a metaphor is rhetorically more powerful than a simile. It allows the man to claim, among other things, that *they have power over me just by their presence*. So the man's argument depends on an unquestioned claim whose implications are manifold, but logically indefensible.

The man's use of a metaphorical step which is outside the strict bounds of logic is not abnormal or perverse; metaphorical reasoning, as Lakoff and Johnson (1980) observe, is quite normal. But we can make a judgement of the desirability of the particular use of any one metaphor, and it may be that, in a case like this, we might be alarmed at the effects that it has.

Metaphorical explanation and practice

Lakoff and Johnson's demonstrations are compelling enough, but one can always search for still more cut-and-dried evidence that metaphorical explanations have impact on ordinary behaviour and experience. This is a counterpart to the extra search we made in the section above on narrative, where we looked outside traditional social psychology for a triangulation of culturally specific narratives with behavioural practices. Here we are looking for some aspect of our lives that might be fairly unambiguously controlled by our metaphorical account. An attractive possibility is the domain of ordinary models of the physical world, where we can make reasonably straightforward observations of our respondents' behaviour.

A nice example is given by Kempton (1987) who discovered that his Mid-West American respondents would talk in two ways about the thermostats that controlled the heating in their homes. Either they believed that they were like 'gas pedals', which, when depressed, increased the output; or they believed that they were like 'persons with feeling' who switched themselves on when they felt too cold and off when they felt too hot.

Now if you believe in the gas pedal analogy then you should also believe (falsely) that your house will heat up and cool down more quickly the more extravagantly the thermostat dial is turned. Kempton had had recording devices installed in the people's homes, and was able to match their operation of the thermostats with the theories they held; and, indeed, those who talked of the thermostat as a gas pedal tended to turn it up 'to make it produce heat quickly' and then turn it off after a while.

Explanations in narrative and metaphor

The notion that there might be some cultural structure informing an explanatory account – either linearly as a narrative or centrally as a metaphor – has a heuristic power. It gives the academic researcher leave to press the respondents' talk against the grid of a previously worked-out system of meaning, forcing previously camouflaged parts to stand out and making the whole intelligible as more than a free-standing, individual tale. What is less obvious is the criterion by which such pressing and such interpretation is to be judged.

The situation is less dangerous for metaphor analysts, as they can at least draw on their – comparatively public – resources as native language speakers as grounds for their claims and arguments (and they may even turn to the apparatus of experimental psychology to test its predictions about how the use of metaphor might affect how a hearer or reader dealt with a text). The danger is greater for narrative analysts, especially those who want to apply strong narrative form. To say that this explanatory account draws on that previously existing cultural structure is plausible, first, to the degree that the structure is securely knowable independently of the individual stories to which it is applied, and then, secondly, to the degree that any particular story fits it, or can be made to fit it. The choice of classic Western linear narrative does offer a fairly clear set of known elements whose use can reasonably be charted, so the first criterion seems on the face of it to be secure. The problem is that not many analysts seem to follow it very closely.

Partly this is because the rules turn out to be optimistically strict: although the original formalist claim (that there is a great deal of similarity among myths and folk tales) is plausible and illuminating for a certain set of material, it under-emphasizes differences among instances and can't account for idiosyncrasy except by multiplying, as folklorist catalogues are prone to do, an unprincipled taxonomy of varieties. It seems to be accepted in literary stylistics that not too much reliance can be put on genre as an analytical notion. As Wales (1989) points out, each genre is a broad type ('tragedy', for example, will cover both *King Lear* and, say, *Batman*) and the variation within its boundaries may, for certain analytical reasons (say, a concern for metrical style), be more significant than its categorical difference from some other genre. Nor is genre membership fixed; at the borders, genres mix to produce either ambivalent examples, or ones whose mixture (the mock-epic, the tragi-comedy) presents something genuinely unlike either. Moreover, only some genres have a fully fledged checklist of classificatory features: what counts as a sonnet, say, is much better worked out than what counts as a detective story. To cap it all, genres develop and change, throwing into confusion any analysis that claims to decode a candidate text by the rules obtaining at one frozen moment. So social scientists' claims to identify narrative structures, and, from their identification, to read off significant social messages, may be less well founded than might appear.

One could go further and say that the degree that the narratologist is committed to any recognizable literary form (classical or otherwise) is the degree to which he or she might be criticized for drawing attention away from ways in which the respondents' lives are inscribed elsewhere, and out of the individual's control: lives can be 'narrated' by medical records, prison logs, school examination achievements, credit ratings, and all sorts of public and private traces. Each has its own idiosyncratic structure, which may have little in common with others or with idealized literary forms. Although (say) medical records might be turned into a tragedy (in the technical, if not the ordinary, sense), that is to impose a literary reading on the series of dates, diagnoses and medical marginalia.

Doubts about the utility of formal features may be one part of the reason why not many researchers work at the formalist core. The other, perhaps more positive, reason is that researchers want respectfully to say something about the idiosyncrasies and individuality of their respondents'. lives. Although (in some cases) the analyst might look to have confidently identified classic plots or personae, the commitment to formalism is sometimes, at least, no deeper than a conventional use of its vocabulary as a means to get into a sympathetic personal contract with respondents, and a vehicle for local interpretation of the content of their accounts. Such analysts of the narratives of personal lives are much more likely to do a kind of bespoke content analysis than they are to press the account into the more rigorous – but less yielding – frame of formal theory.

Yet to move away from the reassuring cradle of formal structure is to stray into territory that demands that one be knowledgeable about the cultural history of one's respondents (and that might extend widely, and far back) and be able to manage a mass of historical and anthropological data outside the stricter confines of the talk and its local context. Such demands, though perhaps not unfamiliar to many social scientists, are (and perhaps ought to be) daunting; to meet them is to draw on reserves of cultural capital which not all of us can properly claim to possess, if we are trained in the mono-disciplines of psychology, sociology, linguistics or communication studies. In other words, to do narrative or metaphor analysis of storied accounts is likely to be very revealing but, since that will mean doing it as a form of cultural interpretation, it is also likely to be exceptionally demanding. Is there something in the actual performance of stories in real exchanges that we can fall back on as a more robust alternative?

The conversational organization of storied accounts

It is, I think, in the organized exchange of storied accounts that we can find firm ground for our claims. In the rest of the chapter we approach accounts from the conversation analytic perspective, looking for the sequential rules which might be applied to the giving and receiving of account 'chunks'. We shall find these rules have something helpful to say about the telling of tales which are called up by the interactional demands of the moment, and whose force is measurable within the interaction itself.

Sequential organization: traffic management

Sacks (1972, 1974) engaged theoretical attention by observing that the long stretch of a story (of which an explanatory story is a subspecies) managed to keep at bay something that everywhere else was rampant in conversation: rapid turn-taking. What was it that the speaker was doing to manage to hold the floor for so long? After all, accounts are full of small stops and starts and, in principle, any of these offers the other participants the chance to jump in and take the floor.

This observation – already familiar to us from Chapter 5 – allowed Sacks to probe just what was going on in the management of stories, and by doing so to advance his thesis that the management was an integral part of its meaning. Sacks observed that the typical story-telling was organized into three segments: the preface, the telling and the response. The point to stress is that Sacks was offering us a very principled reason for the sequence being as it was: that it had to be that way so that the traffic management could proceed in an orderly fashion. This kind of thinking was revolutionary because the alternative (as we saw in many of the narrative analysis examples in the early part of this chapter) is to have something invisible – the speaker's personality, mental apparatus or desire – motivating the sequence of words. Here, on the contrary, the insistence on talk as traffic untied the analysis from the words of the account: the literal words would *by themselves* be an insufficient guide to what part of the story-telling episode they signified. That would only be specified by where, and how, the participants in the talk exchange placed them.

Prefacing an account

If a speaker wants to give an account which will cross a point at which another speaker can take the floor, then they have to warn that they are claiming the right to suspend the normal rules of turn-exchange. 'Pre-sequences' like, for example, *did I tell you what happened to Annie?* allow the listener to grant the speaker permission to start off on the rule-suspension. They also give an early warning to the hearers what kind of utterance will signal the end of the tale – a punchline, a moral and so on; and what kind of response will be appropriate to it – laughter, sympathetic murmurs and so on.

The prefaces, though, will not spring from nowhere. The principle that Sacks was at pains to establish was that no form of words was so innately powerful as to dominate its local terrain. To say that a phrase had a conventional meaning (as a preface or any other meaning) was to say that the phrase *when set into a certain sequence* had that meaning. In Sacks' example, two identical-sounding cases of *hello?* in a telephone call will mean different things when they are revealed to be at the beginning (as a greeting) and in the middle (as a check that the caller is still there).

Example of a preface: 'oh'

Thus a preface would get its force from its local context. Prefaces will be related to, or made to relate to, whatever is already happening in the talk exchange. Look at these uses of the preface '*oh*':

> *Roger*:   The *cops* don't do that, don't gimme that shit I live in the Valley
> (0.5)
> *Ken*:   The cops, *over* the hill. There's a place up in Mul*holl*and where
> they've – where they're building those hous⌈ing projects?
> → *Roger*:   ⌊*Oh* have you ever taken
> them Mulhollan' time trials? 'hh You go up there wid a girl. A
> buncha guys'r up there an' [*story*]
> (Jefferson, 1978: 220; transcription slightly simplified)

and in the visible world

> (Three people walking together: someone passes them wearing a photograph
> teeshirt)
> → *Nettie*:   *Oh* that *tee*shirt reminded me [*story*]
> (Jefferson, 1978: 222)

Just to make the point about sequential placement being important, look at the *oh* in the second example. In general, the particle *oh* marks something, what Heritage (1984) calls a signal of a speaker's 'change of state'. What purpose that signal is put to depends on the context; it is not always used to signal a story. Here are two examples of such other uses of *oh*: as responses to 'informings' and 'repair' (Heritage, 1984).

> *I:*   Yeh. 'h uh:m (0.2) I've jis' rung tih teh- eh tell you (0.3) uh the things 'av
>   arrived from Barker 'n Stone'ou⌈:se
> → *J:*   ⌊Oh:::::
>   (Heritage, 1984: 316; transcription slightly simplified)

> *A:*   Well who'r you working for
> *B:*   'hhh well I'm working through the Amfat Corporation
> *A:*   The *who*?
> *B:*   Amfah corpora⌈tion. 'T's a holding company
> → *A:*   ⌊Oh
> *A:*   Yeah
>   (Heritage, 1984: 316; transcription slightly simplified)

In the former example, the *oh*'s placement is a signal that the message has been received and understood as a piece of news. In the latter example, the placement of the *oh* signals that A, who has prompted B to offer a correction, is now satisfied.

To return to *oh* as a preface: in the hands of a hearer, *oh* can be used to indicate that the hearer is in a state of uncertainty, and ready to be given an explanation; its placement invites an account.

> *N:*   My face hurts =
> → *H:*   = W't (.) *Oh* what'd'e *do* tih you
>   (Heritage, 1984: 303; transcription slightly simplified)

There are, of course, many other ways of prefacing: tokens of *speaking of* . . .; *by the way* . . .; *now* . . .; *it's like* . . .; *as a matter of fact* . . . and the equivalents of *once upon a time* . . . will all, in suitable contexts, do the job (Jefferson, 1978). Such forms of words might perhaps, as Jefferson tentatively suggests, be complemented by such paralinguistics as intakes of breath or other 'perturbations'.

Telling

The agreed frame of the story-telling episode will suspend certain standing orders for the middle section. It will give special meaning to moves that, outside such a frame, might be construed as challenging for the floor. If someone comes in with an appreciation of the account's termination prematurely – at a point which, for example, where what has ended is just a segment of the account – then the teller has the right to re-establish the storyline. Sacks suggests a still more economical rule: within an agreed story-telling frame, an interruption is to be treated as a signal of 'understanding problems'. In the following two examples from Sacks the understanding is cleared up right away:

> *Ken*:   No. To stun me she says uh there was these three girls an' they jus'
>   got married?
> *Roger*: ehh hehh hhh hhh
> *Ken*:   An' uh–

```
  →  Roger:    ⌈Hey waita se(h)cond
     Ken:      ⌊[unintelligible]
     Al:       heh!
     Roger:    Drag th(h)t by agai(h)n hehh hehh
               [6 turns omitted]
     Ken:      And uh . . so . .
  →  Al:       The brothers of these sisters
     Ken:      No they're different – mhh/hh
     Al:       heh
     Ken:      You know different families
     (Sacks, 1974: 338)
```

But it might be the case that the 'understanding problem' generates its own subroutine which embeds a number of turns into the main account, as in this example (arrows show the embedded structure):

```
     Phyl:     Mike siz there wz a big fight down there las' night
     Curt:     Oh rilly?
               (0.5)
     Phyl:     With Keegan en, what. Paul ⌈de Wa::ld?
  →  Mike:                                ⌊Paul de Wald. Guy out of =
  →  Curt:     = De Wa:ld yeah I ⌈((know'm))
  →  Mike:                       ⌊Tiffen. D'you know him?
  →  Curt:     uhhuh I know who 'e is
               (1.8)
     Mike:     Evidently Keegan musta bumped him . . .
     (Goodwin, 1984: 311; transcription slightly simplified)
```

This signal of an 'understanding problem' can be turned to the hearer's advantage; the hearer can use it to register her or his attention or to underscore certain segments as being specially newsworthy. The *oh* particle can come into play here:

```
     M:    'hhh (.) Um: 'Ow is yih mother by: the way (.)
     J:    We:ll she's a:, bit better:
     M:    mm ⌈::
     J:        ⌊She came: do:wn on Satidee :eveni⌈ng
     M:                                          ⌊Oh: did she:
     (Heritage, 1984: 303; transcription slightly simplified)
```

Responding to account chunks

At the end of the tale the speaker needs to signal the resumption of normal turn-taking rules. There is an equal obligation on the audience to display that they have understood and appreciated the story, and to signal that the story was appropriate to the speech event in which everyone is engaged. In fact, the talk is prolonged until these responsibilities are taken up; dilatory or unsatisfactory responses from the audience will produce a sequence like this:

```
     Maggie:   [story] a:::n uh: I guess once wz enough
     Gene:     Yeah (.) yeah
     Maggie:   'tlk But as far as I'm concerned he [ex-husband] has shown his true
               colours to the point where 'hhh nobody in his right mind who's ever
```

got a *de*cent breath left *in* them 'hhh would think that he was
                   accep*t*able
Gene: Yeah
                   (0.7)
Maggie: 't 'en it's a sure damn thing that whenever:: this *kid* [*her son*] grows
                   up he'll have n:*no*body to thank for *any*thing 'hh uh: of *that* family
                   [*her ex-husband's*]
Gene: Yeah (.) Yeah
                   (1.0)
Maggie: I wouldn't spit on the best side of'm en I've yet t' see the best *si*:de
Gene: hhhehh heh-heh-heh 'hhh Well now *about* the rest of the
                   fam'ly . . .
(Jefferson, 1978: 232; simplified)

The teller is looking for the hearer to confirm that he has heard, understood and appreciated the end of the story; her prompts eventually take effect, but only after the story's end point has been twice ratcheted up to a new height of outrage.

The response sequence allows the listeners to show that they have understood not only what the story 'meant' but also the speaker's right, or felicity, in telling it. This latter appreciation can be accomplished by an explicit account, as in this example:

(An academic and three secretaries are talking. This extract concludes a story about a senior academic, Hart, introduced earlier as 'and Hart you've got to stand up to, haven't you?')
Secretary: I must say I rang up on Thursday because I had a letter an official
                   letter ages ago from Miss Baker saying come at ten o'clock so I
                   rang up saying I'm terribly sorry but I shan't be with you until
                   five past ten (.) well the immediate reaction I got which rather
                   tied me was *why* [*laughs*] I said I've I'd just ex*plained* in a full
                   long sentence why I was going to be there at five past ten just to
                   get [*3 or 4 syllables unintelligible*] *why* (. . .) I don't mind *sarcasm*
                   I get *on* with *sarcasm*
→   Academic: *That's* all right cos the *trouble is* he'll be there *himself* soon after
                   nine isn't he (.) and he expects everybody to do likewise
(LL S1.5, p. 130, 172; transcription edited and substantially simplified)

The secretary has told a story hearable as being a jokey complaint about Hart's pedantic insistence on timekeeping. The academic orientates to the story and sets up a slot for an account (*that's right, cos* . . .). The account not only confirms the general complaining note of what the secretary said (by being explicitly cast as a formulation of 'what the trouble is'), but also homes in on exactly the same area of Hart's behaviour (his self-centred expectations about punctuality). In other words, the account makes clear to all participants that the secretary's story was heard, understood and appreciated.

Non-verbal signals to sequential organization

It is a commonplace of conversation analytic commentators to look forward to a day when their work will be properly rounded out by a description of the non-verbal signals that accompany talk. The technological and conceptual difficulties of recording and transcribing such signals – for which we have no ready language – have hindered quick progress. Nevertheless, there does exist a fair literature on the general features of non-verbal signals (see, for example, treatments of gaze, body position and gesture by Kendon, 1982; Heath, 1988; Schegloff, 1988). We can follow Goodwin (1984) in picking out certain things that can tell us something specifically about account organization.

Let us just follow Goodwin's analysis of an anecdote about a gaffe. John and Beth are entertaining Ann and Don to dinner. We pick up the talk just after the point where Ann offers a suggestion that something unusual, or tellable, happened to her that weekend. Beth solicits the account with the formula *what happened?*

> *Beth*: What h⌈appened
> *Ann*: ⌊Karen has this new *hou*:se en it's got all this like (0.2)
> ssilvery:: g–gol:ld wwa:llpaper, 'hh (h)en D(h)o(h)n sa(h)ys, y'know
> this's th'firs' time we've seen this house fifty-five thousand dollars in
> Cherry Hill. Right?
> (0.4)
> *Beth*: Uh hu:h?
> *Ann*: Do(h)n said (0.3) dih–did they ma:ke you take this
> ⌈wa(h)llpa(h)p(h)er? er (h) di =
> *Beth*: ⌊hh!
> *Ann*: = ⌈dju pi(h)ck i(h)t ou(h)t
> *Beth*: ⌊Ahh huh huh huh huh huh h⌈h
> *Don*: ⌊Uhh hih huh huh
> (Goodwin, 1984; transcription slightly simplified; '(h)', as in 'Do(h)n', is a
> laughter token)

The story has a simple preface (the advertisement that it was a tellable tale, not shown), sanction (Beth's *what happened?*), background (Karen's new house and the ostentation of the decor) and climax (Don's conscious or unconscious gaffe in querying the wallpaper) with an extra bit of background (that this was the first time that they had seen Karen's expensive house) bracketed in. Purely as a story it seems quite straightforward, but Goodwin reveals interesting twists in the physical circumstances of its telling. The teller and the audience don't, as one can imagine, sit deadpan through its telling. Their physical orientation to it helps 'structure' the account and signal two socially vital messages: who the tale is being told *to* – who is the addressee and who the recipient (an echo of the 'footing' problems we came across earlier); and how the talk is received by the candidates for these roles.

All these things happen at once, and the resulting torrent of data on gaze, facial expression and gesture make it impossible to do anything here other than give a flavour of some parts of Goodwin's analysis. Ann, the teller, emphasizes the verbal separation of preface from story by a complementary shift in body movement and position. For the preface she sits up, adjusts her hair and glasses and rearranges the glass on the table in front of her. At the start of the tale proper, she clasps her hands together, puts both elbows on the table, and leans forward, gazing at Beth. Her elbows reach the table on the beginning of the phrase *new house* (second line in the extract above) and stay there until the end of the phrase *pick it out* which terminates the story. All this helps the audience know what is going on, and where to make their appropriate responses.

In the middle of it, though, there is a complication: Ann breaks off her trajectory towards the punchline to introduce two pieces of new information. This requires some management by teller and audience, and once again the physical channel provides a complement to the verbal medium. Ann has signalled that she is reaching the climax by her use of laughter tokens (the aspirations in *(h)en D(h)o(h)n sa(h)ys*), and Beth is reciprocating by leaning forward just at that point. Now Ann introduces (with *y'know*) the information that this is the first time they've seen the house; Beth keeps up the recipient posture, but when Ann starts to introduce a second item (*fifty-five thousand dollars . . .*) she lets it drop. A lost audience presents a problem to the speaker; Ann has to solicit attention explicitly (*right?*) and closes the parenthesis once Beth (after a pause) brings her gaze back. All this choreographs the straightforward talk and turns it into the performance of what is recognizably a story with story-teller, protagonists and audience.

Narratives, then, can be marshalled not only according to the pattern of words in their conversational structure, but also by the paralinguistic features which accompany them. Recording and transcribing such things as gaze, intonation and gesture is, however, notoriously difficult, and the small instance that served as the example above hints at the labour cost of doing a full-blooded analysis. What conversational organization would promise, though, would be a more complete description of account-giving to set alongside (and possibly to be a channel for) the narrative and metaphorical structures that a different sort of analyst could provide.

Explanatory accounts

This chapter has been about explanations considered as integrated wholes, but ranged across two rather different ways of looking at them. First we saw that one could, if one felt confident enough, try to apply culturally identifiable structures so as to reduce people's accounts to some principled simpler form. To do so meant that one had some idealized sense of a deeper, hidden narrative or metaphor that moulded the talk; that the dips and hollows of the surface followed the course of a subterranean story down below. The promise of such analysis is enormous but, I argued, makes equivalently enormous demands on the analyst's cultural capital.

On the other hand, the talk can be examined with no attempt at reduction. Here the analyst will stand by and watch what it is that the speakers do to set the talk up as an explanatory account; to make it count as an acceptable one; and to return thereafter to the interaction from which it sprang. The analyst is proceeding from an *anti*-reductionist principle: that everything in the sequencing of an account matters, or may matter. Sequencing a story is a matter of traffic management, but such management, far from being an insignificantly mundane matter, actually organizes the meaning of what is said. To study it is to move away from the analyst's cultural exegesis and onto the more public ground of the behaviour of the speakers themselves. Nevertheless, it is at first sight silent about the greater issues of the cultural content that informs the accounts, whether as narrative substance or as metaphorical inspiration. It may be, though, that the two kinds of enterprise could operate in partnership, even though they do seem to work to very different criteria of assessment; in the next chapter, we shall see how one might try to make the partnership work in various kinds of discourse analysis.

7
Explanatory Discourse

Marie: Well I think that men have less potential to do work that women do because women have more potential to do work that men do in general
Peter: Why?
Marie: Because men don't have the sensitivity in general that women have. Like the nurturing faculty which is necessary in caring for people
Cathy: I think it depends on the individual don't you?
(Billig et al., 1988: 133; transcription slightly simplified)

Our starting example of an explanation comes from an investigation into the way that ordinary people weigh the pros and cons of social issues. The investigators (Billig et al., 1988) watch Marie, Peter and Cathy juggle with explanations of women's and men's abilities, and they ask: where does the vocabulary of such accounts come from? What images of society do the accounts perpetuate? Who gains by them?

These questions reprise themes that we introduced at the end of Chapter 3. There we saw how Edwards and Potter's discursive action model (Edwards and Potter, 1992) showed up the partiality of explanations and the importance of seeing them in context. We followed up the line of an explanation's 'interestedness' in Chapter 4, and by the end of it came round to insisting on seeing interestedness by inspecting the talk in some detail. That pushed us, in Chapter 5 and the end of Chapter 6, into conversation analysis' close grapple with the structure of talk. Now, before we swing into the detail of this chapter, we should pause a moment and reflect on the general principle that has taken us this far from the cognitive understanding of explanations in Chapter 1.

The claim has been that explanations, like other forms of talk, 'do' things – specifically, that the exchange of explanations helps regulate that complex of human ambitions and frustrations that Goffman calls the 'moral order'. We have seen how one could get a handle on that regulation by inspecting the way that talk sets up and sorts out the problems that emerge in interactions, and, separately, by asking what cultural themes it invokes in doing so. In this chapter we shall try to knit the two together.

Look again at the extract above: one can certainly read the talk as a question–answer exchange in which Marie justifies to Peter her earlier claim about men and women. But we might want to go further than that, and read something less interactionally bound into the exchange. We might, recalling the social constructionism of Chapter 6, want to speculate about the *very constitution* of men and women through the interplay of accounts like Marie's and Cathy's; in other words, we might want to take their talk as locking together to make up (one of many) polarities and dimensions on which men and women are set by society at large. Marie is not to blame for the fact that her society allows, and perhaps insists, that one can explain the difference between men and women according to 'sensitivity' and 'nurturance'. But her explanation is a common one, and its deployment by Marie and a thousand others (and its challenge by Cathy and a thousand more) not only demonstrates how men and women are explained, but goes significantly towards defining what men and women 'are'.

That gives us the theme for the relation between explanations and the moral order that we shall explore in this chapter. Explanations, we shall see, can lock together as a means of constituting the social world (and, some would say, the physical world too) and constituting the people who navigate through it. To understand the accounts properly, one has to dismantle them to show their inner assembly and the points at which they latch onto the outer world.

That is a high claim to make about what might be learnt from accounts; and the prospect of dismantling them, rather than taking them as unitary narratives and metaphors, requires a bit of scene setting. So I shall spend the early part of the chapter describing a bit more of the sociological foundation that supports the claim, then I shall go on to describe that part of modern discourse analysis it gives rise to that bears most directly on explanations and accounts.

Discourse analysis

Choosing where to start unravelling an intellectual history is always an arbitrary matter, decided by a trade between completeness and one's immediate purposes. For less-curtailed accounts of discourse and discourse analysis, one should look elsewhere (in, for example, van Dijk, 1985; Potter and Wetherell, 1987; Parker, 1992; McHoul, in press); here we can take just a brief moment to discriminate among the various senses of the word 'discourse' then go on down the line that interests us most.

The common starting point is to take discourse to be some stretch of connected sentences or utterances, a mass noun – discourse as stuff that can be cut and shaped like dough. Thereafter discourse analysts differ. As McHoul (in press) divides it up, there are those who treat the material linguistically, as text which has discoverable rules of coherence; then there are those who treat it sociologically, as conversational interaction which works as social glue; and lastly (and most abstractly) there are those who treat it as fuel for critical theory, interested in it as the manifestation of cultural ways of thinking and doing. Of course, any one analyst probably shuttles between each station as they go about their job, but the three stations are at different points on a line between the abstract and the concrete, or perhaps it is better to say between the grand and the minute: critical theorists would want to deal only in wholesale rolls of language, while the linguistically minded insist on the weave of small swatches, and the sociologically inclined do their tailoring somewhere in the middle.

Since our purpose is to get a grip on the kind of discourse analysis which has something to say about ordinary explanation – in manageable lengths of talk – we shall be staying around the central station, and if we travel up and down the line it will only be to trade in empirical, talk-based analysis.

Accounts are variable, interested and constructive

A good place for us to start is at the point where Gilbert and Mulkay, in the fittingly titled *Opening Pandora's Box* (1984), alerted researchers to the possibility that there was something empirically interesting going on inside the explanations and accounts their respondents were giving them. They resisted the temptation to boil the accounts down until only the bones which appeared in all respondents' stories were left and idiosyncrasies and contradictions had evaporated out. Rather, they identified what they called different 'linguistic repertoires' in their scientists' talk. These would be mobilized tactically according to the local terrain. In public texts the vocabulary (the 'empiricist repertoire') would paint a picture of an empirically knowable real world populated by equally knowable and secure facts. In private, however, the words would change to a 'contingent repertoire' which described a shifting world where things could have been otherwise and where facts were humanly constructed. Up to a point all this is uncontroversial; the scientists in their sample were happy themselves to volunteer the observation that the buttoned-down language of the journal was not the jocular loose talk of the laboratory. Where Gilbert and Mulkay went further was to show that the contingent repertoire was used *perfectly seriously* by the scientists, when it suited them to do so; as seriously as the empiricist repertoire and without qualification.

Much of the variation was in accounting for error. Gilbert and Mulkay found that their scientists' talk was so thoroughly soaked in worry about error that it alerted them to the possibility that error might be, as they put it, 'the fundamental principle of social accounting in science' (1984: 64). Error seemed undemocratic: it was overwhelmingly the case that it was *other* scientists who were wrong. Others' errors were usually attributed to intrusions into the scientific project: these would often be, for rhetorical reasons, underspecified and variable, but ambition, incompetence and closedmindedness would be typical examples. Speakers' own positions, in contrast, were impeccably based on secure data: their relation to the knowable world was frank and impartial. The speakers were willing to press these claims even though there was (on reflection, and to the researcher) a fairly obvious asymmetry in the rigour of the two explanations. The account of a fellow scientist's work as being 'stupid' – imprecise, merely insulting, and prima facie wrong in the case of the typical highly qualified scientist –

would appear in the same breath as a description in some detail of the speaker's own empirical base. Schoolyard name-calling and journal-standard factual report would share space in the same account, equally seriously.

Do we dismiss all this as merely showing that petty human interests can corrupt even scientific reasoning? If so, then Gilbert and Mulkay would only have done the journalistic job of revealing that scientists, like the rest of us, are vain and uncharitable. But there is more to it than that. Gilbert and Mulkay show that the claim that another scientist's fact is 'humanly' mistaken is to exonerate science itself, and to keep inviolate the principle that there is a knowable objective world. The scientists are not being (merely) self-interested in the petty sense; they are defending their constitution of science.

Just to make the point that this is not something specially wicked about scientists, or a curiosity of the 'actor–observer difference' in attributions (see Chapter 2), it is worth putting it in its anthropological perspective. Communities, Lévi-Strauss observed, act to preserve not just facts, but the way that facts are arrived at. The Azande interpretation of fact makes sense out of what would be, to a Western observer, the oddity of relying on animal sacrifice as a basis of prediction. Should the prediction fail, the Azande would invoke the interference of external agencies, the incompetence of the human interpreter, the subtlety of the original prediction, and so on. The Azande believe that the oracle never makes a mistake; their accounting practices ensure that nothing it does counts as a mistake; so the circle is unbroken. In any culture, Pollner (1974) goes on to say, care is taken that disagreements over what is the case are resolved in ways that do not trouble the socially untouchable assumption that we all have a single shared experience. On the contrary: a disagreement about what happened, or what is the case, is resolved precisely by seeking reasons why the two 'accounts' differ, while reality stays the same. It is inconceivable to us that a court could be satisfied that the accounts of both the defendant and the plaintiff were correct and that reality should be variable. Gilbert and Mulkay's scientists' accounting preserves the face of the individual scientist, it is true; but, probably unconsciously, and certainly more importantly, it preserves the foundational belief in a world knowable by scientific means.

There are a number of possible morals here for the study of accounts, and they have been most forcefully drawn by Potter and Wetherell's *Discourse and Social Psychology* (1987); we have already seen, in discussing Edwards and Potter's (1992) discursive action model (p. 39), a particular development and application to the study of causal explanation. For our purposes, we can extract three particular morals that, through Potter and Wetherell's work, social psychologists have benefited from. First, that we should avoid looking too insistently for statistical consensus in beliefs and explanations (as our traditional social psychological instincts might tempt us to), since the important work might be being done by variation rather than uniformity. That is, that we should acknowledge that explanations are not fixed scripts applied to every likely object in the explanation domain, but rather are forces to be deployed for strategic (though, of course, not necessarily conscious) ends. Secondly, a demonstration like Gilbert and Mulkay's shows that accounts work by judicious choice of available cultural explanations ('repertoires'): that means that in at least some accounts, the analyst might productively ask where the vocabulary comes from, as well as what the speaker is doing with it. Thirdly, it energizes the now familiar claim that people's accounts can construct (or be used in the construction of) large objects in the world – even, in the case of the scientists we saw above, as large as 'science' itself.

These three morals prompt analysts to go further down the track of treating accounts with the respect due to things which achieve a great deal more than merely reporting, as it were cold-bloodedly, the straight answer to a straight question. If they have the power to choose among available ways of thinking strategically to 'construct reality' then they need an analysis fuelled by the kinds of things which have something to say about culturally available accounts, strategic choice and the construction of social reality by 'talk in action'. This is what discourse analysis claims to be.

'Talk in action'

A word more is in order about 'talk in action', which means different things at the various stations of discourse analysis we mentioned above. At the furthest outpost of critical theory, this 'action' shades into abstract relations between cultural meanings and practices, not necessarily locatable in any one person's talk and behaviour at any one place or time, but infusing the general understanding of some institution like government, madness or sexuality. Such profound relations between discourse and action are addressed most famously by that combination of philosophy and history associated with the name of Michel Foucault; some reference to his work is, indeed, beginning to be made even in the middle range of discourse analysis that is our concern, but perhaps too tentatively to give us enough purchase on his work to apply securely here. So when we say 'talk in action', we need to come down the line a bit.

If we swing down to the other end of the line, 'talk in action' can mean what is achieved in the very local organization of talk: how teachers, say, pattern their interactions with schoolchildren to produce a cooperative lesson or how a speaker will pattern her or his talk to produce what is recognizable as a story-telling sequence. Discourse analysts of this stripe are committed to a fairly flat, utterance-level analysis which means to tease out some regularities in the way that people use various speech acts in their alternating turns at speaking. For them, the 'action' that talk does can be fairly described as what is done by the uttering of discourse in certain ways and in certain circumstances – the classroom will feature speech acts of asking, prompting, interrupting, questioning and accepting, collectable together into an 'action' described at one level up: 'taking a class', perhaps, or 'telling a story' and so on.

The sense of 'action' which informs the kind of middle-range discourse analysis described in the rest of this chapter does include something of both its neighbours. It is certainly aware that some meaningful work is achieved in the local organization of talk, but reaches up to bring in culturally charged content: themes, repertoires, concepts and other chunks of talk, not necessarily all in the same spot in the transcript, and not all necessarily spoken by the same person. So the 'action' that this talk does is almost automatically (and certainly by preference) 'action' of a rather metaphorical kind: the use of themes, repertoires and so on to do some work on the setting up or knocking down of social realities – to promote this version of sexuality, to exercise that power of authority, to institute such-and-such a change in the law. 'Action' here is, as it was for the more formal work we saw in Chapter 4, the social construction of meaning, and language is its primary medium.

We shall see something of the variety among these discourse analysts as we follow Fairclough (1992) and Burman and Parker (1993) in distinguishing content-based analysts from their organization-based colleagues (though I should say that this is to coarsen both Fairclough and Burman and Parker's finer-grained classification). Those who use the 'content' of the material identify coherent themes (sometimes called, after Gilbert and Mulkay, 'repertoires') in their respondents' accounts; the others rely as much, or more, on the material's linguistic 'organization' (or, as Fairclough, 1992, more broadly has it, its 'texture'). In the sections below, I shall give some examples of each type, but we should remember that the groupings are rough, and that even the content-orientated analysts are sensitive to the landscape of the text, and the difference is a matter of degree and explicitness.

To remind us of our interests: we shall be looking at discourse analysis of these various types to see what they have to say about the accounts people give when some issue is made problematical or worthy of explanation; we shall be on the lookout for what discourse analysis can reveal that other analyses might miss. I shall describe the territory along the line by pointing out examples of illustrative research work, liberally dotted with extracts of data to help show what kind of claims the discourse analysts are making. As we travel from predominantly content-based to organizationally sensitive work, we shall log a variety of ways in which accounts might be analysed, but, I should say in a spirit of caution, also accumulate a set of obligations which will weigh heavily on the analyst.

Predominantly content-based analyses

The principle at work here is that people's accounts are (necessarily, because this is the way language, as a shared system of meanings, works) shot through with references and allusions; and that an account's particular orchestration of these allusions makes its own particular 'discourse' for its own particular purposes. So the, or an, explanation of (say) 'debt' would be the orchestration of certain identifiable cultural themes of (to invent some examples) balance, greed, misfortune and mismanagement; these would be arranged in the explainer's account to promote some conscious or unconscious position in the context of the talk – to (say) justify a certain piece of legislation, or to sustain a social identity and so on (just as Gilbert and Mulkay's scientists promoted the inviolability of science by using 'error' in the way they did).

In introducing content-based analysis this way I realize that I am specifying little or nothing about the word 'content', but that is a general complaint whenever discourse analytic work is being reviewed. For some (but not many) the content is little more than the lexicon of the words used, though of course this can yield a fair haul of information. I shan't be giving any examples of that strictly lexical kind of work, if only because vocabulary is a resource that discourse analysts share with explanation analysts in everything from social cognition (which spots differences in, for example, the way events are explained according to the verbs that are used to describe them; see, for example, Semin and Fiedler, 1988) to communication research (which charts, for example, news broadcasters' use of things like euphemisms and loaded words; see, for example, Gastil, 1992). For those who are more properly discourse analysts, content is some more complex constellation of cultural theme (variously called 'repertoires', 'practices', and even, rather confusingly, 'discourses', this time as a count noun), and this would cover the majority of analysts we would be interested in; for others still it is not only the theme but the variety of genre or medium in which it is expressed, and perhaps even its physical representation. It is tempting to say that the only thread which binds the variety is the negative one that none of these notions of 'content' explicitly calls on the way the traffic of the material is regulated – its cohesion, its turn-taking, its rhetorical devices and so on. This is, admittedly, a dangerous way of thinking about it, since it partitions out two aspects of meaning – form and content – which have no business being separated, but it will do as a rule of thumb so long as we remember it is just that.

Culturally informed reading of content

The idea here is that the analyst must acknowledge, and make a virtue of, their own reading of the text so as to go beyond its superficial content. Suppose you were interested in seeing whether the educated elites who write and control news reports acknowledged or denied racism in society. A plain content analysis would be happy to make a category list of predefined things which would count as 'acknowledgements' and 'denials', specifying perhaps certain combinations of words and phrases, and then scour the material to count how often each type appears. But a discourse analyst would say that this is to rely too much on mechanical recognition of just when something *is* an acceptance or a denial, and wouldn't capture the subtleties which are arguably still more significant than what is obvious. Take, for example, the following extract from a British newspaper editorial, which appears at first sight to be unexceptionable:

> No one would deny the fragile nature of race relations in Britain today or that there is misunderstanding and distrust between parts of the community. (*Daily Telegraph*, 1 August 1985, quoted in van Dijk, 1992: 106)

It may look plain enough, but van Dijk calls our attention to the discursive work that the concessionary form of the piece is doing: it sets the tone as being one of judicious objectivity (there *is* a problem) but, he argues, smuggles in a prejudicial definition of the problem under its cloak of evenhandedness. To define racism as *the fragile nature of race relations* is to strip it of any implication of inequality of power in society, and to call the parties involved *parts of the community* is to imply that they are equal, and equally to blame. Van Dijk's reading uses his analysis of society (that 'races' have unequal power) to spot the discursive work done by linguistic devices (here, implication and presupposition) which play tricks with the surface content. The net effect is to unearth the kind of semi-hidden message that a word-level count would miss or misinterpret.

We can take the notion of culturally informed reading further, and add to it the discursive maxim (explicit in Edwards and Potter's discursive action model which we saw back in Chapter 3, and implicit in the example above) that accounts are 'interested'. Discourse analysts can use their cultural resources not only to spot hidden messages, but also to make a prediction about what kind of message it is from diagnosing the context in which it is given. That is to say, discourse analysts are happy to use their cultural antennae to feel out the context in which the text appears, and read off the force of the account their respondents give at least partly from a knowledge of who they are and who they're talking to.

A good example comes in the accounts given by employers when asked why women are under-represented in their workforce. Of course, that bare formulation has to be qualified; it doesn't work if the answer is 'obvious' (as the employer might consider it to be in the mining industry, perhaps) or if the question is culturally unfamiliar (as it would be if you had been asking the same question fifty years ago, and so on); but if you are asking an employer in an industry which 'society' has identified as not inappropriate for women, at a time when there is a debate about women's access to employment, and about a job which some women, but not many, do perform, then it is hard not to read the likely explanations as being pretty well necessarily justificatory. Let us see what Gill (1993) makes of just such a situation: radio stations' accounts of why they don't employ women disc jockeys.

Plainly, one could do a simple content analysis of the explanations that come up – so many of this kind, so many of that. But Gill goes beyond that static exercise. She asks us to wonder what each of the explanations draws on to make it work as an explanation; and what further work the explanations might also be doing to promote a certain view of women.

Take the explanation that 'no women apply'. This, apparently, is the first and most commonly offered explanation. It would do as a final word so long as one agreed with the implicit argument that it is not the employers' job to do something about it; clearly the broadcasters themselves don't expect 'us' (or, more accurately, the constituency the female interviewer might represent) to believe that, since, Gill observes, they go on to offer still further accounts which cover more justificatory ground. One of the most interesting of such further warrants is the idea that women just don't want to be DJs:

PC: And it's where people come from (.) so in hospital radio there aren't
       many women DJs (.) there aren't many women DJs in pubs. (.) there
       aren't many female DJs (.) especially teenage age which is when we're
       looking to bring people like (.) who are interested in doing it
(Gill, 1993: 78; PC means programme controller)

The punchline is the business of women not really being 'interested'. Gill points out that there is a cultural loop being sent out here to draw in the commonplace that if someone has a problem then it is of their own making. Women, the implicit argument runs, could be DJs but choose not to; a polite way of exonerating the station itself from responsibility. A hint that the broadcasters themselves are aware that this is not the whole story leaks out from another programme controller's account for the lack of applications from women:

PC: It's also very much a man's world so they're picked on if they are here
       (.) you know a woman has got to assert herself pretty definitely if she's
       working in radio
(Gill, 1993: 79)

This does suggest that the broadcaster is aware that women might realize that they are in for a tough time if they apply, and get, a job in radio. But the way he sets up the problem is to cast it, once again, as the woman's own problem, to be resolved on her own: she's got to *assert herself pretty definitely*.

The fact that the explanations are not just static reports of some fixed belief is brought out by Gill's spotting contradictions (or 'variability', as Gilbert and Mulkay, 1984, would have it) in what the broadcasters say. As we mentioned before, in describing Gilbert and Mulkay's work on scientists' discourses of error, a straight account of beliefs and values would have strongly suggested that they should be at least reasonably consistent; but in talk, when tactics demand a flexible response to the interviewer's questions, contradictions can indeed arise. The broadcasters seemed to be willing to say that few or no women apply to be DJs, but also that women would in any case be objectively, and irremediably, poor at the job:

PC: (. . .) Presenters have to have a number of skills. They've got to have
       . . . they've got to be very very dextrous (.) they've got to be very

familiar with technical equipment (.) they've got to have a personality
they are used to expressing and they've got to have a good knowledge of
music as well as having a good personality (.) and those things are *not* as
advanced in my view as far as women are concerned as with men
(Gill, 1993: 82–3; emphasis in original)

Repertoires

The kind of research that we are making Gill represent might look like a
straightforward content analysis. What makes it qualify as some kind of
discourse analysis is the interpretative connections it makes among the
elements of the text as a whole (where content analysis might be more
cautiously satisfied with identifying the elements and letting them quanti-
tatively speak for themselves). But discourse analysis can do more than just
making connections between parts of the text: it can say something more
substantial about the cultural givens that the explainer is deploying. In
Wetherell and Potter's analysis of racist talk, for example (Wetherell and
Potter, 1988, 1992), such repertoires are explicitly identified and their
variation plotted. In the following extracts, the speakers (white New
Zealanders) seem to be expressing rather warm attitudes towards Maoris:

I think the sort of Maori renaissance, the Maoritanga, is important like I was
explaining about being at that party on Saturday night, I suddenly didn't know
where I was, I had lost my identity . . . I think it's necessary for people to get it
[Maori identity] back because it's something deep rooted inside you. (Reed)

I'm certainly in favour of a bit of Maoritanga it is something uniquely New
Zealand. I guess I'm very conservation minded and in the same way that I don't
like seeing a species going out of existence I don't like seeing a culture and a
language and everything else fade out. (Shell) (Wetherell and Potter, 1988: 179)

Wetherell and Potter cast these two as being in some senses contradictions, or at least inconsistencies; on the one hand, new emphasis on
Maori culture is valued because everyone should have one's roots for the
sake of securing their identity: the implication is that the current generation
of Maoris have 'lost' it, possibly through their own negligence. On the other
hand, the second extract promotes Maori culture as being positively
unmistakable: it is as vivid and unique as a rare species. This contradiction
(or inconsistency) suggests to the watching analyst, as scientists' variable use
of error suggested to Gilbert and Mulkay (1984), that there is some
important work going on.

Wetherell and Potter interpret it as being the manifestation of what they
call the repertoire of 'cultural fostering', the idea that Maori culture is a rare
bloom that can only survive by the sympathetic attention that any exotic
specimen would demand. In other words, the Maoris need the patronage
and sympathetic husbandry of the whites to survive; otherwise, unable to
meet the demands their own exoticism makes on them, they will 'lose their
identity' and die out. This sentiment is much more clearly racist than either

of its two constituent parts which, on their own and without being set against each other, might pass muster.

Once one is aware of the possibility of contradictions, one can see the cultural fostering repertoire as itself in conflict with other material in the text. Here, the concern again seems to be sympathetic:

> I actually object to um them bringing um massive Maori culture curricula into schools etcetera . . . because I do feel this doesn't equip them for the modern world at all. Because what's the use of being able to speak Maori if you can only speak it to a limited number of people in a limited area and it has no use in the actual, you know, in the real world as it were, if you'll pardon the expression. (Wetherell and Potter, 1988: 180)

The concern is for Maoris being able to get on in the real world, yet it demotes their language to the status of a useless eccentricity (not even dignified, now, as being 'uniquely New Zealand'). The speaker's brand of realism is almost certainly not intentionally mischievous but, as Wetherell and Potter say, 'there is a depressing irony about the members of a group who have done their best in the past to suppress an indigenous culture, arguing at this stage that the success of their oppression is good grounds for continuing to suppress it' (1988: 180). Just as with van Dijk's analysis of racist denial and Gill's analysis of sexist justifications, Wetherell and Potter's analysis makes a linguistic exercise do discursive work by fuelling it with an appreciation of cultural meaning. But they are perhaps clearer in their insistence on engaging the reader's cultural, or perhaps it would be better to say 'political', understanding of the issue at hand; for some (especially those who want to trade up to critical theory; for example, Henriques et al., 1986; Parker, 1992), this is not only an inevitable but a desirable feature of discourse analysis.

What, though, of the very local context in which the talk was exchanged? Condor (1990) has objected that to read culturally thick meanings into empirically thin slices of talk can be dangerous. To crop extracts from transcripts may be to alter significantly the meaning that they had at the time; and certainly what we have seen so far has shown us the respondents' words only through a narrow window. For our last example of 'repertoire' identification we can turn to a piece of work that uses more of the available transcript, cropping the extracts less severely.

The scene is a British public inquiry, a legal hearing in which some issue of public policy is decided by the weighing of evidence from interested parties. McNaghten (1993) shows how a discourse analysis in the culturally explicit sense, but now paying greater respect to the ebb and flow of contextualized exchanges, can illuminate the justificatory accounting that must inevitably go on. In this case, the issue is whether planning permission should be granted to a private company to develop a piece of land on the outskirts of a city as a 'landfill site' or rubbish tip. The local council's objection is that the site would significantly alter the landscape; the developer's case is that it would not. To defend either position seems just a matter of fact. At one point, for example, the issue turns on the apparently factual question as to whether the site was in 'green hills'. One can certainly set out the argument we shall see below as if it were a formal exercise in claim, rebuttal and support, but there is more to it than that. (The cross-examination in this and the following extracts is from McNaghten, 1993: 65–6; C is a council official and D is a developer.)

C: The site contributes to the integrity of the range of green hills to the west and the south-west of the city
D: It depends whether you refer to the 'green hills' as a planning area or 'green hills' as I understand them

Although the developer's response looks petty, its immediate context, and the fact that he is speaking as a party with enough legitimacy to have a voice in legal proceedings, shows that he is raising an important issue: that what counts as the definition of the countryside can be a matter of debate. The developer challenges the council officer's bureaucratic classification – *'green hills' as a planning area*, with all its implication of arbitrariness and officiousness – with his own common-sense *'green hills' as I understand them*. If the developer can persuade the inquiry not only that the meaning of 'the countryside' is debatable, but also that his version of it is more common-sensical than the planners', then he will have won an important battle. The council officer, perhaps sensing this, manages at the end of this next response to switch away from officialese and into the same common-sense language:

C: However it is characterised in policy terms: the area comprises green gently undulating hills

The developer needs to counteract the visual persuasiveness of the 'gently undulating hills':

D: They are not always green. If I may finish, I would say that the colours change. As I said in my statement, so they are not always green. They are multicoloured
C: They are predominantly green, aren't they?
D: Well, I accept that they are predominantly green
C: And pastureland tends to remain green throughout the year, does it not?
D: Pastureland does or can remain green. I suppose it can go yellow

The council official seems to have recovered a lot of ground, and it is hard to see the developer winning back the audience with this argument about he colour of the hills. Why is he so insistent? McNaghten cleverly shows that promoting nature as changeable and varied is an important feature of the developer's entire argument in favour of the waste-tip. In this 'discourse of nature', as McNaghten calls it, nature is never static; existing human artefacts have already changed it; so a new landfill site is simply a further stage in nature's everchanging cycle. From elsewhere in the transcript:

D: Well, you see me smiling because, er, any landscape in Britain, especially in lowland Britain is not natural at all; it's man-made. I mean, for example that valley had naturally a small seasonal stream . . . So to say it's natural – it's not natural
(McNaghten, 1993: 69–70)

D: Such major features as the concrete interchange, the deep cuttings and embankments to the north and south of the interchange now dominate the local landscape . . . These structures have already left a permanent artificial or man-made landscape; the *natural* landscape of the valley has been dramatically disturbed

(McNaghten, 1993: 59)

What McNaghten does is to pick out those passages in the stream of talk and written evidence that hint most strongly at the discourse which informs what the participants are saying. It's not the case that there are certain key phrases that one could identify, or even that one could count up every instance of a set of candidate words or phrases and take the biggest totals to be the most significant categories. McNaghten shows that the sense of what is being said is best understood as a constellation of terms, phrases, references, metaphors and allusions that all act together. The 'argument' between the participants, then, is not so much a straight reading down from premises to inevitable conclusion, but rather a battle between one discourse and another, and knowing the context in which it all happens is an essential part of making sense of it.

Enriched notions of content: 'intertextuality' and 'footing'

The notion of 'repertoire' among the analysts we have used to represent discourse analysis so far varies from being nearly intuitive to being closely defined. There is sometimes a sense that what makes the discourse more than the sum of its parts might be more profitably left unspecified (or, it would be better to say, unrestricted) so as not to cramp the analyst's room for interpretative manoeuvre. Other analysts are more willing to put a name to the extra ingredient, and I shall just mention two.

Fairclough (1992) backs the notion of 'intertextuality', the notion of the text being inhabited by various kinds of 'genre' or styles of talk. (The definition of 'genre' turns out to be just as slippery as 'discourse'; Fairclough means 'linguistic activity with specified positions for subjects (e.g. interview, television news)', 1992: 215.) It's up to the speaker to arrange those genres to suit, and the resulting pattern will be significant. For example, were a student to ask her tutor to explain why the student's essay had not yet been marked and returned, it would be significant that the tutor used a markedly formal register (a frosty *marking shall be at the discretion of the tutor*) or a markedly informal one (*well, it's all down to when I get round to doing it, really*). Even though the 'content' in some sense is the same, the formulation in the style of the official handbook gives a different message from the one in the genre of the coffee-room chatter.

To take an empirical rather than a hypothetical example: in the following exchanges between patients and their nurses, one could apparently read the straight content of the account the nurse supplies as suggesting that she is supporting the patient – that the nurse is 'legitimizing her experience' as Fisher (1991) puts it:

> *P*:   You know, just the normal things that I've always been doing. I don't know, I'm just tired. I don't know if I need vitamins or what?
> *N*:   And then you fall face forward on the floor

and, in another exchange

> *P*:   He thinks his sex life is crazy. He thinks 'what do you want to read books', when you know it . .
> *N*:   When you could be having sex
> (both originally from Fisher, 1991, reproduced in Fairclough, 1992: 197; P means patient, N means nurse)

What Fairclough argues is that what has force in the 'content' in each case is the nurse's mobilization of a genre outside the medical consultation that is taking place – namely, the homely seeming genre of the counsellor or therapist. Seen in that light, of course, the sense of support is now tinged with the element of control and distance which comes along with the therapist's role; so we have a rather more equivocal reading of 'support' than might at first have been suggested.

Another example: in the following extract, an interviewee gives a view about news broadcasters being influenced by the commercial concerns of their parent companies:

> *Interviewee*:   Well they would have to, there probably'd be some relation-ship between the two because they have a responsibility to the companies that are backing them. And if something's going on with a company in another country, you know it, you can't, they wouldn't be able to show a bad side. I wouldn't think. Because that company'd yell, like loud. You know, pull away their backing
> *Interviewer*:   So you think there could be some sort of relationship there
> *Interviewee*:   mmmm hmmm
> (Hacker et al., 1991, reproduced in Fairclough, 1992: 202)

The genre shift happens, according to Fairclough, at the point where the interviewee says *you can't, they wouldn't be able to show a bad side*, a formulation whose style comes from the genre of interpersonal chat. The interviewee goes on to use the expressions *because that company'd yell, like loud*, setting herself still more concretely into the loose, gossipy, laconic genre of ordinary social experience. The net result is that we read what she says as being much more 'authentic' than we would have done had she stuck to the formal register which her interviewer seems to favour.

The two examples from Fairclough's reworking of data which other analysts have read for their 'straight' content does suggest that content-based analysis can usefully broaden what it takes as being analysable content; even if 'genre' looks difficult to specify with great precision, it does look as if one can identify 'content' that comes from a distinguishably different speech situation, and read something off its use in unfamiliar territory.

The other ingredient in content that is coming into view in discourse analysis is 'footing', or 'participant status' (Levinson, 1988), a crossover from the linguistic tradition we shall see more of in the next chapter. The notion here is that we shan't make the right sense of an account unless we know who is giving it; not in the biographical sense of the individual and their personal psychology (the sense that would make us reject the account of a known liar and so on) but rather the more formal sense of what position or footing the speaker must be adopting for what they say to be intelligible. For example, it is typical for narrated stories to work only because the listeners can decode who is meant to be speaking at any one time; the story-teller doesn't have to continually be signalling *he said . . . and then she said . . .* Or, to take another example (from Levinson, 1988: 196), there is a convention in Barbadian speech which allows you to have a dig at someone present without explicitly addressing them; a Barbadian can (in the example Levinson gives) say to someone close by *oh, I thought your mouth was burst*, meaning it not as news to them, but rather a dig at the vivid lipstick of a third party who is within hearing distance, and whose ears are intended to burn.

This notion is Levinson's revitalization of Erving Goffman's observation that people have different speaking and listening roles (or, more transiently, footings) in encounters; Levinson shows that the sense of what anyone says is (partly, at least) dependent on which of these footings (or statuses) they are adopting. Let us see his analysis at work in an example of a justificatory account. In the following, Sharon, Mark, Ruthie and Karen are all present, and we join at the point where Sharon directs a question at Mark:

1 *Sharon*: You didn't come tuh talk to Karen?
2 *Mark*: No, Karen – Karen' I're having a fight (0.4) after she went out with Keith and not with (me?)
3 *Ruthie*: Hah hah hah hah
→ 4 *Karen*: Well, Mark, you never asked me out
(from Sacks et al., 1978; reproduced in Levinson, 1988: 166)

How do we understand Karen's utterance in line 4? It looks apropos of nothing, since no one had, apparently, questioned her or even addressed her – on the contrary, Mark's answer to Sharon in line 2 seems to be explicitly designed *not* to address Karen. But look how the participant statuses are being used. By naming Karen, Mark makes her the indirect target of the utterance and thereby picks her out as an appropriate next speaker. This has the conversational effect of turning the state of affairs that Mark describes (*Karen and I are having a fight*) into an accusation, which means that we must read what she says as being set up as a justificatory reply. In other words, the sequence hinges on the participant status of 'target' that Karen is cast into by Mark. Otherwise, we would have missed the significance of what Karen says as an account and coded it perhaps as a non-sequitur or a change of topic.

This is getting us perhaps too close to issues of organization and conversational analysis, which we deal with more directly elsewhere in the book. But it does show that, like the interposition of different genres into an account, there can be something 'there' which benefits from specifying rather more tightly than is often done by content-based discourse analysts.

Analyses sensitive to text organization

The content-based discourse analysis we saw above can be a good demonstration of the identification of cultural repertoires, or the more ghostly presence of other genres and voices, in a text, but it usually avoids making explicit call on the way the text is organized. There are, of course, many principles of such organization. One catalogue breaks down the main varieties used among discourse analysts at large into: pragmatic (including speech acts, implicature, syntax, pronouns and naming conventions); rhetoric (including various devices of persuasion) and conversational tactics (including turn-taking and other forms of regulation) (after Gastil, 1992). We shall see examples of all of these.

I should say in parenthesis that some discourse analysts would include the organizing principles of narrative and metaphor. But there is some reason to resist that, as I tried to show in the previous chapter; there is a sense that too strong a reliance on prefigured form rather ties the hands of the analyst, and that one would be distilling important things out of the data. Better to keep narrative and metaphor separate and deal with them as formal structures on their own (see Chapter 6).

Pragmatic, rhetorical and conversational organization

Staying with pragmatic, rhetorical and conversational organization, then, let us have a look at the analysis of an account which, like those we have seen so far, is 'placed' by the analyst's cultural understanding.

The account comes from a young man who has been asked to talk about the way he dresses. Widdicombe (1993) gives us the time (the late 1980s), the place (a rock concert) and the young man's choice of clothes (distinctive even within the subculture of late 1980s rock fans) to help locate the kind of account we shall be seeing; likely, as she observes, to be orientated to questions of justification and choice. Widdicombe uses the talk to specify just what it is about the young man's identity that he sees as a problem, and how he resolves it.

Note that this sensitivity to the context setting the speaker up is the same as Gill's choice of male employers for discourses of female under-representation in the workplace: the context itself – or rather the analyst's culturally informed reading of it – sets up the encounter as being 'accountable' or justificatory without the need for any special challenge. In reading the resulting accounts, Gill attends to the content, whereas Widdicombe is willing also to read clues from the way they are organized. In the following extract the respondent is explaining his reasons for changing to a 'Gothic' clothes style:

> I mean ever since I started wearing clothes which I chose then they may be conventional clothes but I probably wear them in a strange way you know in a strange mixture so they always so I always you know look strange to people anyway even if I was wearing conventional clothes and it went on really cos feeling different to everybody else and what I'm wearing is a way of expressing the isolation you know if if you felt isolated from everybody else then once you get to the age where you can choose for yourself then I would choose to wear clothes where I I could show that I felt differently to everybody else around me so that's how I started doing it. (Widdicombe, 1993: 104–5)

If one merely attended to the words and phrases, and one wanted to reduce the explanation to one of a number of countable categories, then one might say that the young man's reasons were 'to look different', and pass on to the next account. By paying attention to the exact way he expresses himself, however, Widdicombe spots some odd things about the description, which may or may not be significant. The first is that he shifts from past to present tense, and from statement to concession, in the opening remark:

> Ever since I started wearing clothes which I chose then they may be conventional clothes but I probably wear them in a strange way

Widdicombe reads the shift as indeed significant. It signals that the speaker is dissatisfied with the first account he's launched – that the change of clothes could be accounted as being due merely to simple choice; it would put his clothes on the same footing as the straight world of high street, or shopping mall, fashion shops. This reading is helped by his immediate shift to a concessionary form of words (*they may be . . . but . . .*) which acknowledges that the listener might have picked up that reading, and explicitly corrects it. Even if we were to go no further, all this activity in and around the straightforward content of the words already suggests something rather different from the flat coding of the reasons as being 'to look different': it suggests that, on the contrary, the interviewee cares about not being mistaken for a mere follower of fashion.

There is another piece of organization that bolsters this reading. He says

> If you felt isolated from everybody else then once you get to the age where you can choose for yourself then . . .

What conclusion might follow what he has set up as a driving argument? One plausible possibility is that the person who felt isolated might try to 'pass' in the outside world, and perhaps make some contact with it, by buying conventional clothes. But he goes on, in what Widdicombe points out is a significant shift from the general 'you' (*if you felt isolated. . .*) to the specific 'I':

> I would choose to wear clothes where I I could show that I felt differently to everybody else around me so that's how I started doing it

What this does is mark him out as being different from those who would have been bound by the plausible logic of trying to pass as normal; *his* choice is to stay true to his isolation, and choose clothes that celebrate it. As he says starkly: *what I'm wearing is a way of expressing the isolation really*.

Widdicombe shows that even in a fairly short passage there is enough organizational activity going on to subvert any easy coding of its content. A casual classification of the young man as accounting for himself merely as 'wanting to look strange' (for whatever perverse reason to do somehow with 'isolation') is overturned by attending to the devices in his talk. They signal that he is implicitly contrasting himself with, and distancing himself from, exactly those people who merely 'want' to look strange: his own 'strange-ness' is not a matter of choice, but as Widdicombe puts it, of authenticity.

Conversational exchange

This kind of analysis can go still further and attend to the structure of the conversational exchange; so far, we have seen examples here and in the section on 'content' above, most of which have stuck to stretches of monologue talk, to the extent even of eliminating the researcher's own part in its production (a queer failing from people who are otherwise so respectful of the power of words, as Condor, 1990, points out).

Edwards and Potter (1990, and in their discursive action model, 1992) are much more strongly committed to the analytical significance of the conversational byplay. In this analysis of an exchange between a politician and a television interviewer, they pull out not only the interior structure of the monologue turn, but draw inferences from its place in the dialogic interchange. Margaret Thatcher, the British Prime Minister at the time, is being interviewed about (among other things) the resignation of her Chancellor of the Exchequer (the British minister of finance). In this extract, the interviewer (Brian Walden) and the Prime Minister pit their different versions of what happened against each other, knowing that each version suggests its own more- or less-damaging explanation of the Chancellor's fall:

> W: .tch Let's look though at what he sa:ys you see (.) he: is making the (.) claim (.) here that (.) successful conduct of economic policy is possible only if there is *seen* to be full agreement between the Prime Minister and the Chancellor of the Exchequer .hh now he's right about that isn't he?
>
> T: Yes .hh and I am right about the successful six ye:ars he's had in the Treasury (.) *very* successful the economy of Britain has made great strides under his Chancellorship .h (.) and we have worked together those are the facts
>
> W: But y–
>
> T: And no one can get round them .hh it has been ex*treme*ly successful
>
> W: But you are not claiming Prime Minister (.) it may or may not have been extremely successful (.) but you are not claiming that there *was* seen to be full agreement between yourself and the Chancellor are you?
>
> T: .hhh I am claiming that I *fully* backed and supported the Chancellor (.) of course we discuss things we discuss things in Cabinet we discuss things in the economic committee .hh we discuss things with *ma*ny advisers there is not only one adviser there are many advisers in the Treasury .hh

we have *ma*ny advisers and we *hamm*ered out a policy and on that policy
and on that policy we were *to*tally agreed

W: tch–
T: Totally and it was implemented and it was implemented *very* successfully
and the success *mat*ters

(Edwards and Potter, 1992: 143; transcription slightly simplified; W is the
interviewer, T is the Prime Minister)

The interviewer is keen to establish that the Prime Minister disagreed with
the Chancellor's policies; the Prime Minister resists it, since it would suggest
that she sacked him and that there was disunity at the top of the government.
What Edwards and Potter do is show how this is achieved partly by the
content and partly by the organization of the talk.

A lot goes on in the Prime Minister's third turn. She reworks the
interviewer's suggestion of a hostile 'disagreement' between her and her
Chancellor with 'discussion', not simply by substituting the word, but by
placing it in the rhetorically forceful device of a three-part list:

Of course we discuss things
(1) we discuss things in Cabinet
(2) we discuss things in the economic committee
(3) .hh we discuss things with *ma*ny advisers

This three-part listing is a useful device when a speaker wants to make a
special point. Atkinson (1984), who identified it as a powerful tool of the
orator, catalogues it as a signal of the special comprehensiveness of what the
speaker is claiming (*I will fight, fight and fight again: I have nothing to give
you but blood, sweat and tears; so much has been owed by so many to so few*).
By three-part repetition, the Prime Minister makes her claim of thoroughgoing consensus undeclared but unmistakable. The 'we' in that consensus-
seeking also dissolves the interviewer's setting up of an argument by putting
the two antagonists on the same side; moreover, they discuss not only among
themselves but also with a number of advisers, defusing in advance any
further suggestion the interviewer might make that there is some special
adviser that the Prime Minister favoured over the Chancellor (as was indeed
an accusation at the time of the affair).

What Edwards and Potter are up to is trying to persuade us of the strategic
use of rhetorical devices somewhere at the level of (the organization of)
words and phrases, but which can only make sense when one knows (as they,
and most of their British readers, do) something of the political issues at
stake; their reading, to be fully persuasive, must assume a shared
understanding, if not of the particular characters involved, then at least
some generalized notion of cabinet-style government, the workings of the
press, the status of a minister of finance and so on. That allows them to
concentrate on the detailed mechanisms of the Prime Minister's management of her talk, and show how they serve her interests in conjuring a
version of events, without having to be too laborious in calling up the
cultural milieu.

Discourse analysis, then, is always balanced on three legs: two are the content and the organizational structures that the researchers have explicitly identified; the third is the less evident cultural homework they've done to make the other two stand up. We can finish off the chapter with a look at an example of discourse analysis in which this third leg bears a little less weight, and the conversation-analytic organization does more work than in any discourse analysis we have seen so far.

Markings in monologue

To introduce the example, we just need to note something about narrative style. As conversation analysts have observed, the use of a narrative style of account rather than flat description seems to be a feature of accounts of events whose truth, appropriateness or plausibility is in question. In exchanges between callers and emergency service telephone operators, for example, there is quite a difference between the marked and unmarked case of descriptions of the motivation for the call. In the unmarked case, the exchange would go something like this:

> *CT*: Mid-City Emergency
> *C*: 'hh Um: yeah (.) Somebody jus' vandalized my car
> (Zimmerman, 1992: 438; transcription slightly simplified; CT means call-taker, C means caller)

Whereas, in the following case, the description is marked with a prefix, pauses and an account:

> *CT*: Mid-City Police an' Fire
> *C*: Hi um (.) I'm uh (.) I work at thuh University Hospital and I was riding my bike home tanight from (.) work
> *CT*: mm
> *C*: 'bout (.) ten minutes ago, 'hh As I was riding past Mercy hospital (.) which is a few blocks from there 'hh ( ) um I *think* uh couple vans full uh kids pulled up (.) an started um (.) they went down thuh trail and are *beating* up people down there I'm not sure (.) but it sounded like (something) 'hh
> (Zimmerman, 1992: 438–9; transcription slightly simplified)

Zimmerman makes the point that the narrative style allows the caller to cast himself as ordinary (through specifying his place of work), disinterested (by making clear his own non-appearance as an actor in the story he is telling) and responsible (by combining specificity about facts he can reasonably know about with uncertainty about those he can't). All this hedges his account with just enough ambiguity to allow the emergency operator to display her greater authority in determining from this evidence whether or not an emergency is in progress.

This sets up the possibility then that monologue descriptions may call on the same devices in order to bolster the truth of the events they are presenting, even when such events are of a very dubious provenance. This gives a discourse analyst interested in how people deal with 'facts' a powerful set of analytical tools at the very local conversation-analytic level. Let us see how those tools are used in Wooffitt's (1992) analysis of how someone gives an account of a paranormal experience.

In the extract below the informant is describing the experience of a paranormal event. The very way this extract starts off (*It's very interesting because . . .*) keys the subsequent story as being a justification in the sense we discussed in the last chapter. It is organized externally as a story; the analyst shows that its internal organization can tell us something about the speaker's discursive concerns.

> It's very interesting because 'hh (0.5) something like this happened to me hhh a few years ago (.) when I was living in Edinburgh (.) Every time I walked into the sitting room (0.3) er:m right by the window (0.3) and the same place always I heard a lovely (0.3) s:ound like de dede dedededededah just a happy little t:une (0.5) a:nd of course I tore apart ma window I tore apart the window frame I did everything to find out what the hell's causing that cos nobody else ever heard it 'hhh (0.2) y'know (.) there could be ten people in the room nobody'd hear it but me (0.7) er:m: and I wanted to know what was the: (.) material cause of this.
> (Wooffitt, 1992: 73–4; transcription slightly simplified).

Let us see how Wooffitt strips down the narrative to locate the ways in which the speaker conventionalizes the unconventional. The speaker starts by avoiding forensic dating of the event, but by placing it in the continuous past and in a certain physical location (*every time I walked into the sitting room*) granting it a historical reality; as Wooffitt observes, the fact that she is not talking about a particular occurrence implies that she had had enough similar experiences to justify referring to the event in the abstract. The paranormal stimulus itself, the sound, is described by a three-part list (*a lovely sound*; *like de dede dedededededah*; *just a happy little tune*) common to productions of other lists for more conspicuously rhetorical purposes (*Labour will spend and spend, borrow and borrow, tax and tax*). Two peculiarities of such lists are interesting. One is that once it has been embarked on, the speaker is normally given time to finish it; it is thus a way of holding the floor. Another is that the placing together of distinct characteristics into a list implies that the speaker has already done some analytic work to find a way of organizing the list: in that sense, it promotes the speaker's claim to be an authority on what is being listed.

An omission also bears mentioning: nowhere does the speaker mark the noise as supernatural at the outset, although she does mark its puzzlingness (with *of course*) as a prompt for her search for its whereabouts. This asymmetry, as Wooffitt observes, casts her in the role of the puzzled and sceptical observer; in fact, just like one of her potentially disbelieving audience. The search is then described by another three-part list (*I tore apart ma window* / *I tore apart the window frame* / *I did everything*). This marks the search as a normatively correct one; it would have risked oddness had the list stopped at two. In that sense the speaker is being careful to preserve the 'ordinariness' of her behaviour and her status as an impartial or common-sensical observer. The generalized third part could have been something along the lines of *and that*, or *and so on*, but the speaker chooses *I did everything* – an extreme case formulation (Pomerantz, 1986) which marks the search as meticulous and thoroughgoing, further enhancing the speaker's authority.

The window frame is rather an odd place to look for something that might produce a sound, especially a 'tune'. This turns out to be another device. Casting the first alternative as an unusual one allows the ultimate solution to be even more unusual. Wooffitt quotes a vivid example of this device from Sacks (1984):

> I was walking up towards the front of the airplane and I saw by the cabin, the stewardess standing facing the cabin, and a fellow standing with a gun in her back. And my first thought was he's showing her the gun, and then I realised it can't be and then it turned out he was hijacking the plane. (Sacks, 1984, quoted in Wooffitt, 1992: 78)

In the hijacking example, the speaker is mobilizing the contrast between appearance and reality in an *at first I thought . . . then I realised* contrast pair. As Coulter (1979) says, thinking something the case and knowing it are disjunctions one of which always implies a rejection of the other, hence to say that you (initially) 'thought' something is to automatically set up, semantically as well as temporally, its (later) correction. In Wooffitt's informant's story the disjunction operates less explicitly, and in the part I have extracted we only see the initial *at first I thought* phase. It is enough, though, to give us the strong expectation that a second part will follow and that the second part is the truth, just as it was true that the plane was being hijacked. The very next lines of the 'supernatural noise' story are:

> 'hh well (0.4) I never could figure it out and it didn't (.) upset me in fact it was quite a lovely little happy sound un:d so I just let it go (1.7) one night however a friend was with me (.) and we're just watching the telly . . . [*story*]

The speaker introduces the concluding phase of the story with a description of a new scene, but the use of the word 'however' is weighty. It is the realization of the implicit promise that, in fact, the original mistaken perception (that it was a noise with a 'material cause') would be recognized as such and corrected.

An aspect of the conventionalization of the motive for the search we could also note is the insertion of a little passage which casts it as intended to reassure us that the speaker reacted to it in a normal way. *I did everything to find out what the hell's causing that cos nobody else ever heard it 'hhh (0.2) y'know (.) there could be ten people in the room nobody'd hear it but me.* She uses an extreme case formulation (what *the hell* was causing the sound) and what we saw Pomerantz call an 'official' description (the *ten people in the room* who do not hear what she is hearing). Both of these promote the implication that it weighed on her as a normal person. Had she been a fanatical spiritualist then, the implication goes, such abnormality would not have bothered her. Once more the speaker has used a device which casts her in the same role as the sceptical listener, preparing the ground for the sensibleness of the conclusion when it comes. That conclusion is brought nearer in a non-neutral way by the speaker saying that she *wanted to know what was the material cause*. This, as Wooffitt observes, keys into a way of describing events that strongly imply failure; one doesn't normally include *I wanted to arrive on time* in a story in which one did indeed easily arrive on time.

Wooffitt shows us that the speaker has accomplished a number of things in these comparatively few lines, all of which prepare the ground for the conclusion that the event was indeed paranormal. First, an external stimulus is established. Then a 'search' is reported, implying the speaker's common-sensical wish to locate the ordinary cause of the event. The search is conventionalized and the speaker presents it and herself as ordinary and meticulous. The very fact that the search is given so much weight in the account is a signal that it was unsuccessful, leading to the implied conclusion that the sound was non-material all along. Thus we are borne along with the speaker's tale and unconsciously half-expect the denouement before it comes.

Wooffitt's discursive analysis profits more than any other we have seen in this chapter from the uncovering of conversational devices. Wooffitt's position is that one can identify devices in monologues because people produce them from the same linguistic resources that they produce conversational turns; and, moreover, he could say that the speaker herself provides internal evidence that she 'orientates to' the devices she herself is using. The idea is an attractive one, but it is further than a strict conversation analyst would go, as it does import motivations and 'interestedness' as an explanatory device. It is a good example of work at the border between conversation analysis and the kind of discourse analysis we have seen in this chapter so far.

Explanations and discourse analysis

I started off the chapter by discriminating between three kinds of discourse analysis and the sense of 'talk in action' that belonged to each one. Most of the work I've described has been at the middle station, where what pulls in for analytic service is some reasonably manageable stretch of discourse (a few turns of talk, some extracts from an interview, a tranche of monologue), and where the action that it does is thought of as some kind of social construction – constituting, perpetuating or (less often) challenging social realities.

What does all this tell us about accounts? If we accept the general starting point that the way people explain things to each other can (under appropriate circumstances) actually constitute what those things *are*, then we can take the work we've surveyed in this chapter to do two things: to catalogue a number of devices through which accounts do their constitutive work, and to show, by example, the kind of orientation that analysts ought to take to their data.

First, accounts do discursive work in a more or less public way: by explicitly mobilizing chosen cultural themes and by implicitly making reference to others; by deploying those themes in sequences, possibly with some degree of variation and inconsistency up to outright contradiction; and by denying weight to rival themes and voices. So far this is at the level of content, but it is not simply a matter of the analyst reading ingredients off the label attached to a bundle of talk; the analyst has to parcel the material off from its surroundings and do the labelling him or herself. This is more obvious when it comes to the less visible features of accounts that discourse analysis orientate us to: the genre, or style of the talk; the positions (established or transient) of the speaker and audience; the pragmatic implications of the talk; and the way it exploits the expectations of conversational structure. It can never be the case (as it sometimes is with cruder forms of content analysis) that a nugget of talk will appear before the reader and supposedly prompt the analyst to say 'here: this clearly shows that such-and-such a thing is happening in this explanation'; in discourse analysis the hand of the analyst is already needed.

The obligations this places on an analyst are enormous. If analysts are to persuade us of the effects of genre, positioning and the effect of conversational sequencing then they are obliged to do homework in stylistics, pragmatics and conversation analysis and find some way of making consistent their sometimes contradictory demands. If they are conscientiously to prepare themselves to identify and catalogue speakers' overt and covert use of repertoires then they are committing themselves to a wide, and demanding, cultural training. Discourse analysts face the persuasive task of any interpretative commentator: unless their claims are grounded in structural properties of the talk, a certain fraction of the analytic impact of what they say will be delivered by mobilizing the cultural, social and perhaps political assumptions they share with their audience.

8

Making Claims in Logic and Rhetoric

> But you see one of the things that happens if you're a stockbroker is that you tend to act too quickly. You see if for the sake of argument you had some shares in DeBeers: now, at the end of February, if you'd bought some DeBeers, let's say about twenty-seven pounds a share (you don't pay much commission because you work with the firms), and you – your dealing expenses are very small – and you'd try to get into DeBeer at twenty-seven pounds you see, thinking you were, er, most, taking the most frightful risk, erm, and then a, a fortnight later they were at thirty-four – ah 'We must get out!' well they subsequently went to fifty-five, and they're still over forty-nine or something . . . Well now the person who . . like yourself would be *in* them . . . 'cos you'd have thought 'Oh no, they might go up I'll stake my profit'.
> (LL S2.2, p. 433, 997; transcription greatly simplified and punctuation added)

In the book so far we have ranged over various readings of explanation: explanation as the identification of cause, as the exoneration from blame, as part of the construction of social reality and as part of the regulation of the traffic of talk. In this chapter, we turn to explanation's close cousin, argument. Where the last chapter was devoted to explanations as discursive accounts, this chapter and the next are devoted to explanations like the one above – an insurance broker's account of why it is fair to say that one of the things that happens if you're a stockbroker is that you tend to act too quickly. There are cases where explainers show their reasoning that something is as they claim it to be; and, like all the explanations we have seen so far they, too, help police and challenge the moral order.

In the early part of this chapter I shall introduce some of the background of argument in its more abstract form; then, in the second half, go on to a consideration of recent movements which acknowledge argument's rhetorical nature. The theme that links informal logic and rhetoric is that both offer (though, as we shall see, to different degrees) to tell us something about the way people warrant the claims they make in ordinary talk.

Backing one's claims: explanation, argument and quarrel

Ordinary talk is full of claims being made and defended, positions being put, evidence being adduced, and support being offered. Quarrels break out and arguments are made; people explain what they say and why they say it. We have already seen (in Chapters 4 and 5) how psychologists and others go about analysing the kind of claims one makes when one is exonerating oneself at various grains of fineness; but what about claims made rather more impersonally, when what is at stake is not so much (or so directly) one's moral standing but rather (so far as it is separable) one's position on this issue or that, and when it is contrasted with some rival claim?

Explanation shades into argument, and argument shades into quarrel, so we shall have to see if we can make some early discriminations between the terms before we look further into the story. The confusion over quarrel and argument comes about merely because we casually use the word 'argument' in two senses: we say things like *I had an argument with so-and-so* and, in the same breath *my argument was such-and-such*. The first use means a quarrel, and the second means the piece of reasoning you used within it. There is no particular reason to choose one or the other senses of the word 'argument' as being right or wrong, but just for the sake of convenience in this chapter I shall keep 'quarrel' back for disputes and squabbles and make 'argument' just refer to the offering of justifications for claims. More on that later.

The puzzle over explanation and argument is harder. On the face of it, 'explanation' (varied as it is) has no particular commitment to leading from one statement to another, while 'argument' (in the sense I described above) means the positive setting up of some set of statements so that they lead to a conclusion. There is, we feel, something inevitable about an argument – it has a momentum towards a conclusion which a mere explanation can't have. Surely, then, argument is quite different from explanation and has nothing to say about it? But we do occasionally use the words interchangeably: if I ask you to do the washing up because it's your turn, then (crudely speaking) that is both the explanation of why you should do it and also an argument in favour of you doing it. We shall have to tread carefully here, because we are in danger of confusing people's justification for the *way* they put something and the actual proposition itself (a consideration we shall come on to in the next chapter), but let us stay with it for a moment.

The position being advocated (most cogently by Thomas, 1986) is that when what is being said looks like a claim (*you should do the washing up*), then there is a case for handling any explanatory backing (*because it's your turn*) with the apparatus of argument analysis of the kind we shall see in the first half of this chapter. If this turns out to be correct, then we have a very powerful ally on our side: we can go to explanations (or at least some explanations, those that justify a claim) and, rather than wonder about their content or their literary form, take them apart as premises that lead to conclusions.

There are, as Thomas says, at least two grounds for doing so. The first is that to explain something is to show what would have led you to have been justified in predicting it; in other words, that it is to argue for it. For example, if I explain why Sydney was chosen for the Olympic Games in the year 2000, I am revealing what it was about the decision (for example, that only the Australian government offered to pay all athletes' travel expenses; that Sydney had the best guarantee of weather; that more of the sports could be accommodated within a short distance from the athletes' village; and so on) which, had you known in advance, would have allowed you to predict that (or argue that) Sydney would indeed be chosen. The second reason Thomas gives for equating explanation and argument is that the explanation for a certain event can also count as grounds for asserting it. Suppose I claim that the light will come on if I press the switch; my grounds are that the room is wired up in a certain way, the electricity is on at the mains, and the switch is not faulty. Exactly these same propositions will do as my explanation for why the light came on when I pressed the switch.

So far, the grounds for treating explanations as equivalent to arguments look good. But Scriven (1976) reminds us that we have really been talking about only a very limited notion of explanation. Only 'hard determinists' would equate explaining something with arguing that it is the case. Hard determinists are those who say that once you know what brought something about, you know that that is the only set of circumstances that *could* have brought it about. In other words, Scriven argues that explanations will be equivalent to arguments only in the reduced case of deductive explanations. But, he points out, not all explanations are deductive:

> The form of words '*q*, because *p*' is often an indication that *q* is the conclusion for which *p* is the reason – but not always. Sometimes it's just telling you what the cause of a particular event was. For example, 'I got wet because the top of the car is leaking' isn't telling you about a premise from which you can infer a conclusion; it's telling you about a physical cause for a physical effect. (Scriven, 1976: 65)

Scriven is particularly keen to distinguish explanations from arguments on the grounds that an explanation can never give conclusive support to a statement. You may explain someone's good mood by saying that they had just got a letter from an old friend, but getting a letter would hardly be conclusive, or perhaps even normal, grounds for claiming that someone was in a good mood – after all, letters from some old friends are unwelcome, and might even bear bad news.

Scriven is right to complain that (as we saw in Chapter 1) there are many kinds of explanations which can't really be read as leading deductively from premiss to conclusion: explanations define, resolve puzzlement, elucidate, paraphrase, make clear, fill in detail, supply stages, reclassify and re-interpret, and none of these can really be read, in a formal way, for their 'conclusiveness'. Moreover, just to keep up the barrier along the road leading the other way, there are things that are clearly arguments from premiss to conclusion which, though they might be used *in* an explanation, don't constitute one on their own. So the more extreme position that we should equate all explanations with deductive arguments, and vice versa, is probably wrong. On the other hand, perhaps we don't need the argument to be fully deductive before we can benefit from the techniques of argument decomposition and analysis that the informal logicians offer. If not, then we should be able to apply the techniques of argument analysis to cases of claim-making whether or not they are indeed deductive.

It might in any case be impossible to separate the two: we saw that in a statement like *you should do the washing up because I did it yesterday* the explanation of the claim is also an argument in its favour. Govier (1985) gives us a hint that we might distinguish pragmatically between two cases in ordinary speech. An utterance of the 'because' type will be likely to be an explanation when what is being explained or argued for is already given, and will be an argument when it is not. So if I say *the room is hot because of the central heating*, it will be construed as a causal explanation by someone who is there already, and knows that the room is indeed hot (and doesn't have to be persuaded that is so). But it will be understood as an argument by someone who hasn't gone into the room yet, and who might be expected to follow the reasoning that since the house is centrally heated the room is indeed likely to be hot. The difficulty about applying a test like this in empirical work – as we would like to do – is that it involves the analyst in a great deal of inference and guesswork about the various parties' knowledge, and, although something tentative can be done, one risks overinterpreting the data; fortunately, the scale of the problem is manageable since only a comparatively few cases of explanation seem to be even-handedly readable as either cause or justification (see Antaki and Leudar, 1992).

Proponents of treating argument and explanation as both being essentially activities of claim-backing acknowledge, then, that although they are conceptually distinct at the extremes, they are not easily separable in the grey area in the centre. Let us see what argument analysis can do in that large central ground where the safest thing to say about what people are up to is that they are at least potentially backing their claims, though what they might be saying might, in a few cases, turn out to be making some causal statement.

Can logic help us understand ordinary argument?

How do people know what counts as good backing for a claim in an argument? At first sight, dry 'logic' would not seem to have much to tell us. It conjures up syllogisms, archaic terminology and the ideal of geometric proof. We may admire its rigour, but we are put off by what seems to be an unbridgeable gap between the strictness of what we remember of the logician's procedures and the messiness of our own reasoning. With the image of the arid syllogism in mind, we are unlikely to be very enthusiastic about the relevance of what logicians have to say to ordinary reasoning and argument.

But while it is certainly true that deductive logic is alive and well (and we might note in passing that it serves as a model for a good deal of work in the cognitive psychology of reasoning, none of whch we shall be mentioning here), it is not now the *only* logic; perhaps it has never been so, although certainly, for one reason or another, it amassed the prestige of being the only one with a body of necessary truths. Moreover, there is nothing incompatible between logic and argument – classical scholars would have been quite happy with the notion that they were arguing, or setting out arguments, as we shall see later in the chapter. The historical point at which formal logic eliminated the very notion of argument from its vocabulary in favour of the stricter notion of 'proof' is rather closer than we might have imagined. In any case, modern logicians take for granted that there is more than just one logic and one kind of proof.

Now, it is true that much of the new range of modern logics, devoted to increasingly sophisticated elaborations of deductive, mathematical and scientific reasoning, is, as Fisher (1988b), says, not relevant to our concerns with natural argument. But one particular corner is highly relevant, and that is 'informal logic' which is directly and explicitly geared to argument in natural language.

Logic and informal logic

A logical argument is one in which a conclusion is drawn from propositions (premisses) which are asserted or supposed. The conclusion is validly drawn if the argument is such that the conclusion *must* be true if the premisses are true. The rules against which this can be assessed are such that the content of the propositions is irrelevant to the validity of the argument: validity is purely a matter of the form in which the propositions are related to each other and to the conclusion.

Informal logic naturally bears a very strong family resemblance to logic as such. It is committed to the notion that conclusions follow from premisses, and that there are ways of assessing whether those conclusions follow truly or not, without reference to the content of the propositions that embody them. These family traits are unmistakable (and, as we shall see later, they distinguish informal logic from the adjacent fields of rhetoric and argumentation theory). Where informal logic finds its own identity, though, is in its insistence that although the standard of validity in formal logic is appealingly clear and unequivocal (or at least seems so), it is difficult to apply to real arguments – that is, to arguments that we come across in ordinary life, and not the ones invented at the logician's desk. Experience and theory have shown that slavish application of the rules of formal logic is impossible. Although some arguments may be valid in the same way and by appeal to the same formal rules as deductive arguments, others have quite different criteria of validity – induction, analogy and so on (the list is not endless, but it is reasonably long, although different informal logicians endorse different items on it). Still other arguments, in spite of being perfectly clear and convincing to the ordinary person, are simply too opaque to yield any image under the logician's microscope.

There are two reasons for formal logic's disappointingly poor application to ordinary-language arguments. One is the conflict between the meaning of logical relations (or rather, the terms which denote them) in ordinary and in formal language; the other is the very common existence in ordinary language of arguments which are vulnerable to disconfirmation through the revelation of new information.

Conflicts in the meaning of logical relation terms   An argument in formal logic depends for its validity on its structure. The structure of an argument is the disposition of its elements (sentences, for example) according to terms such as *and, or, not, if . . ., then . . ., therefore, implies* and so on. These terms have clear and recognized meanings in logic, but the meanings are not the same as those in ordinary language. Conversely, there are terms in ordinary language which are well understood by language users, but which have obscure meanings, or perhaps no meaning, in logic.

In ordinary language the relationship *if p then q* seems unambiguous. I can say *if the battery's dead, the car won't start* and expect it to be verified or disconfirmed straightforwardly. If the battery is dead and the car won't start, that confirms the claim. If the battery's dead but, to my surprise, the car does start, then the claim is false. So far intuition accords with logic. But, as we mentioned above, logic is blind to the 'content' of the elements of the argument. So, according to formal logic, what is true about the argument *if p then q* is as true about any two propositions as it is about the battery and the car. We can replace *if the battery is dead* with *if the pyramids are in Cairo* and the truth-value (as it is called) of the if–then relation remains identical. If my car again fails to start, both the propositions are true, then the whole argument is true – and we have to accept that the assertion that *if the pyramids are in Cairo, then my car won't start* is a true one. To pursue the paradox, it is also true in formal logic that the *if p then q* argument is true when *p* is false and *q* is either true or false; so that would allow me to say truly that (for example) *if the pyramids are in Norway then my car has square wheels*, and also that *if the pyramids are in Norway then my car has round wheels*. Both of these statements, though absurd to our ears, are perfectly true in the terms of deductive logic. The crucial difference is that for us, an if–then relation must have a sensible relation between the two propositions, preferably a causal one (as in the case of the car battery); otherwise, we should be very unlikely to link them together and very unlikely to think that the link was a 'true' one even if both propositions were unambiguously correct.

Just to return the compliment, very ordinary terms like 'although' and 'in spite of', which are well understood and convey often essential subtleties of meaning in ordinary language, have no meaning in formal logic, in which they would both be glossed as the relationship 'and'. So a sentence like *Sandra went out without a coat even though it was snowing heavily* would reduce logically to *Sandra went out without a coat and it was snowing heavily*, losing the implication that her action was unusual, a fact that might be crucial in understanding what the speaker was trying to get across. The validity of an argument, then, cannot be assessed in quite the same way in formal logic as it is in everyday argument, since there is a mutual unintelligibility in the working of at least some of the terms in which the arguments are constructed, and on which their validity depends.

Defeasibility   There is a further gap between the two sorts of argument, again to do with validity. Once an argument has been shown to be deductively valid then, by definition, nothing can alter its validity. But this is not the case with other forms of argument. Induction is perhaps the best known case of an argument which is profoundly liable to disconfirmation by extra information. I may say that I have never known my local bus to run after 10.30 at night on a Sunday, but even as I say it I know that I am easily liable to be wrong next Sunday, perhaps because the new summer timetable will have come into force, or because my initial observations were based on too small a sample, or whatever. An inductive conclusion is in principle liable to rebuttal. A similar thing can be said for arguments by analogy, which are liable to be undercut: I may argue that there will be a revolution in Cuba on the analogy with the events in Eastern Europe, but I am again liable to all sorts of objection from extra information that would reduce the relevance of the analogy: you may reveal that Cubans enjoy a high standard of living compared to other Caribbeans and Central Americans, that their leader is popular, that the communist revolution of 1959 was a genuine liberation from dictatorship, and so on.

Such 'defeasible' arguments, as they are called, have been the poor relation of philosophical interest in argumentation (Pollock, 1987, dates the first philosophical interest to the 1950s). Yet many ordinary language arguments are like this, whereas no deductive argument can be so. Fisher (1988b) expresses the informal logician's point of view when he gives up the Cartesian standards of conclusive proof as inappropriate for the assessment of ordinary arguments; only the purest of deductive arguments are invulnerable to the complete sceptic, and such a person's life would hardly be humanly possible.

With these objections to the rigidity of the language and standards of formal logic in mind, informal logicians have turned to reshaping and reorientating argument forms; and this reshaping is always, necessarily, in the direction of making clearer their psychological assumptions. It is important to remember, however, that it is only the most radical informal logician who would want completely to break the family tie with formal logic; the basic faith in rationality is still strong among informal logicians, and the difference is in how they identify that rationality in ordinary reasoning.

The pedagogical background of informal logic

Informal logic is sometimes subsumed under the educational exercise of teaching students to think clearly – the 'critical thinking' tradition, more current perhaps in North America than in Europe. At one end of the continuum are those who model argument on something like formal deductive logic, and at the other are those who want to go far beyond the confines of 'argument' and into the realm of any kind of thinking whatsoever; the mainstream runs somewhere in the middle.

Taking deductive logic as a model   The claimed advantage of teaching argument analysis through the rules of deductive logic is that the cost of learning these abstract rules is more than compensated by their rigour and well-tested power. The balance of opinion among informal logicians has swung against this view. They tend to think now that the abstractness of specialist deductive language and notation is not compensated by transferable skill; moreover, informal logicians claim that in any case deductive logic has lost the privilege of being the only guarantor of valid argument, and what the student might learn is only some part of the criteria for validity. This criticism also applies to the method of teaching argument through the analysis of 'informal fallacies'. It is less abstract than working with the deductive rules as such (there is a full catalogue of fallacies dating from the Greeks, and topped up with examples by, it seems, the publication of virtually every newspaper editorial). But it is a rather negative programme, and its underlying model of argument is still that of formal logic. It is, however, popular (spilling over from the academic world into books for the general public), and apart from the critical thinking literature there is some corollary work on cognitive accounts of people's liabilities to fallacy and error.

Discipline-based modelling   The claim here is that it is most productive to concentrate on the kind of argument appropriate to each student's own particular field: legal argument for lawyers, engineering argument for engineers, and so on. This is, in fact, rather a minority position, and most formal critical thinking teaching is of a deliberately non-disciplinary kind. The mainstream objection is well articulated in this list given by Govier (which incidentally forms an illustrative catalogue of the kinds of argument forms which interest the informal logician):

> Syllogistic arguments, appeals to testimony, appeals to authority, analogies, inferences-to-explanations, question-begging arguments, and so on appear in a wide variety of contexts and it is just not plausible to think that there are no common standards for argumentation at all. A question-begging argument is as wrong in history as it is in physics, and for the same reasons. (Govier, 1988: 3)

Modelling argument as general 'critical thinking'   Some educators take the view that the student should be encouraged to consider the validity and soundness of any kind of claim whatsoever, not simply those which fall within the recognizable areas of argumentation. Their conception of argument includes assertions, opinion in matters of taste, estimation, and so on. The most ambitious version of this is in the 'strong critical thinking' approach of Richard Paul. Paul objects to critical thinking which does not involve the students' understanding of their social and moral environment: 'it is possible to use the traditional argumentative skills as tools for rationalisation and self-deception . . . a person who can think critically only in this restricted sense has little hope of becoming a genuinely open- or fair-minded person, little hope, in other words, of becoming a rational person' (1987: 379). The obstacle to rationality is that we are 'deeply resistant to recognising our fundamental contradictions' (1987: 381). Paul's insistence on what, to the informal logician, must seem like an alien vocabulary of personal psychology, virtually guarantees that his programme will not command much interest. He is criticized for requiring too much to be taught to the student: history, politics and 'heaven knows what else' (Govier, 1988: 37). One critic goes so far as to foresee that his project could 'have the undesirable reverse effect of founding a Critical Thinking Church heaven for the happy few . . . and scaring others away to the non-argumentative hell of the established and non-established churches' (van Eemeren, 1988: 41).

Mainstream modelling of natural argument The mainstream of informal logic work is perhaps easiest to introduce by contrasting it with the methods above. Rather than teach the student how to avoid specific errors, or how to argue within specific domains, or how to think critically for personal enlightenment, the common practice is to teach the student how to decompose *any* argument, and how to evaluate it according to a given model of assessment. What is heavily emphasized is the identification of argument in natural situations (editorials, magazine articles, politicians' speeches, and so on), the location of the key operators (the 'inference indicators') and the filleting of the premises and the conclusions accordingly, often by way of a diagram. This is not to say that every informal logician will recommend the same filleting or diagram; as many writers point out, even though informal logicians agree on the *general* procedure of how to get their students to approach an argument, there is no one single model of argument with which they would all be satisfied.

What is an argument, and how should it be assessed?

Probably everyone in informal logic would agree with the proposition that argument is 'a more or less complicated set of premises supporting a conclusion' (Blair, 1987: 16). From that point on, there is less consensus. On one side are those who, coming from a North American tradition of orthodox logic, are more sympathetic to the idea that the 'set of premises' that Blair describes form, and should be assessed as, a single coherent piece of reasoning. On the other side, there is a 'European' tradition more sympathetic to the idea of argument as a dialectical process, for which the criteria must be sensitive to the context of the argument, its audience and the language in which it is conducted.

Internal coherence This definition, from Thomas (1986), is a general exposition of the 'coherence' case:

> An argument is a sentence or series of sentences containing statements some of which are set forth as supporting, making probable, or explaining others. That is, an argument is a discourse in which certain claims or alleged facts are given as

justification or explanation for others. In other words an argument contains reasoning and any discourse that contains reasoning is an argument. (1986: 11)

Thomas's definition is widely shared in informal logic circles: it emphasizes the internal relationship of the parts of the argument at the expense of the context in which it is given and its relation to the giver's motives, audience and conversational role.

The external context Perhaps the best known of the proponents of a contextualized, situation-specific index of validity is Toulmin's call to conceive of argument as an entire social act:

> The term *argumentation* will be used to refer to the whole activity of making claims, challenging them, backing them up by producing reasons, criticizing those reasons, rebutting those criticisms, and so on. (Toulmin et al., 1979: 13)

Toulmin's is a more functional account of language than the mainstream; it emphasizes persuasion and convincingness over dry validity; and is especially insistent that the model include niches for qualifications and rebuttals, as well as for positive supports for the conclusion. In his model, the arguer will offer some data which support the claim. If necessary, she or he will make the case why the data are relevant by warranting it; and may also need to back up this warrant if it is not sufficiently convincing. An opponent may rebut all this somehow, in which case the claimer might qualify the original claim.

Suppose, for example, that I claim that swimming is a particularly good form of exercise. As an argument for (or, of course, an explanation of) what I say, I might offer you the evidence that it activates the whole body without unduly stressing any one part. You would be entitled to ask me why this meant it was a particularly good form of exercise. I would reply with the warrant that avoiding local stress is a good thing, and to back it up I would say that this is what the experts say. You might rebut this by pointing out that some kinds of swimming (like the butterfly stroke) develop one particular set of muscles and do nothing for others; in which case I would concede this exception, and qualify my claim by limiting it to most, but not all, forms of swimming.

You can see that this is different from the general case in informal logic, where all the premisses have the uniform function of supporting the conclusion. Toulmin claims that this identification of specialist premisses better captures what actually happens in argument. Moreover, he explicitly leaves room for doubt and less than perfect conclusiveness in his model: Toulmin's model insists that the validity of ordinary argument is not a mechanical matter. In ordinary argument, the persuasiveness of the conclusion depends on new information; in fact, the point of an ordinary argument is to buttress a claim about which we are unsure with new information – data, warrants or backings – about which we are perfectly sure. In deductive arguments, in contrast, this is not the case, since everything is already there in the conclusion and the undifferentiated premisses add nothing new.

To make that last point clearer: suppose I claim *this bread is stale* and, when challenged, say that I deduce this from the fact that we bought it two days ago and that any bread that's two days old is stale. Toulmin would object that this form of words hides two very different arguments, one analytic (and very unusual in ordinary talk), the other substantial (and much more common). The analytic argument is the one we have come across already under the title deductive, or formal: the conclusion is true if the form of the argument is such that if the premisses are true then the conclusion must be so. Here the form being invoked is *if p, then q; p; so q*. The version of the bread argument which fits this pattern goes as follows: *if this bread is two days old, it's stale; it's two days old; so it's stale*. If by the statement *if this bread is two days old, it's stale* I mean that I've tried and tested every loaf of bread that's two days old, and they are all stale, then perforce I will have also tested this particular loaf. So it follows that this loaf is stale. Toulmin objects that this form of argument is a bit of a trick: if I've tested every loaf in the world, then I've tested this loaf, so really there's no need for an argument of any sort (I can just report on the staleness or otherwise of this loaf). People in ordinary logic can't simply be reproducing their conclusion as a repeat of one of their premisses, so that can't be the way they assess the bread argument.

Compare it with this version of the story: the bread is stale because it is two days old and two-day-old bread is *generally* stale. This is, of course, not as conclusive as the deductive logic argument (after all, this bread could be that supermarket kind that keeps for a week, or I might have bought it fresh and put it straight into the freezer, and so on), but, according to Toulmin, it is really what people actually mean. In other words, Toulmin is invoking the general point we made above – that ordinary arguments are defeasible, as is this particular inductive argument about bread.

The question of reasonableness is at the centre of this illustration. The proper study of argumentation starts with tackling at a general philosophical level the question of what it means for a rational judge to be reasonable. Argumentative discourse should be measured against a certain standard of reasonableness, but which? The illustration shows that perhaps even an informal logic measure would be inflexibly normative, prescribing standards against which there would be no appeal. Toulmin prefers rationality to be the rationality of social consensus. This takes on a different colouring in the law court, the case conference, on the shopfloor and in the classroom; each has its own proper standards, always historically shifting, and only the broadest rules of procedures are recognizable across them. It is legitimate to make comparisons of argument within an area of practice so long as you are careful about setting the proper boundaries – for example, it is fair to ask whether in (say) the Napoleonic Code as it obtained in France in the nineteenth century, this legal argument was better than that one; but it would be unfair, and scarcely sensible, to make comparisons between arguments across boundaries of discipline or historical era. Under Toulmin's influence, informal logic has gone a long way towards the contextual, and perhaps most modern informal logicians would agree with Fisher's formulation: 'Could the premises be true and the conclusion false *judging by appropriate standards of evidence or appropriate standards of what is possible?*' (Fisher, 1988b: 27, emphasis added).

That permissive formulation also has the happy effect of opening up the study of argumentation to systems of reasoning about which typical Western ideals have little to say. We touched on the anthropological approach to argument in Chapter 7 where we saw that there might be reason to compare, or perhaps it would be better to say equate, Western scientists' discourses of error with those of the Azande. The formulation of validity we have arrived at here is consistent with this relativism, and is crystallized by Miller's (1987) call for the study of what he calls 'collective argumentation', that is to say a still more culture- and context-bound version of Toulmin's domain-specific model of argument. We shall be seeing more of cultural bounds in the next chapter; the moral to be drawn for the moment is that one can come away from a review of informal logic quite some way out along a relativist line. If there is a universal in argumentation, it is the very openness to argument itself; everything else is relative.

Can we apply the structures of informal logic to real arguments?

If we do hitch our flag to a more contextualized informal logic model, how readily can we apply its analytical breakdown to the range of more or less articulate and messy arguments that we find in talk? Two warning notes are sounded by Morton (1988). One is his observation that, after much teaching, many intelligent university students still do not get the grasp of informal logic techniques. They can understand the arguments they are given to decompose, and they can make good sense of them, but they have difficulty in doing so with the paraphernalia of diagram and breakdown that informal logicians teach. This, by itself, would be of little consequence, since different intelligent students have trouble with different things, and it might be that skills like these – though they are meant to be the most general intellectual skills possible – are no different from the skills of operating a microscope or handling a paintbrush. But Morton makes a second, and more alarming, observation: when looking for examples to use in class, he has to reject the great majority of arguments that he finds in his trawls of newspapers and magazines: 'I reject at least 90% even of the clear, straightforward, unproblematic argumentative prose that I consider' (1988: 65).

This is rather like revealing that textbook grammar is all but absent from ordinary speech. It makes extrapolation from any theory of competence dubious. Why might there be so little ordinary argument that approaches that of the informal logicians? Or, to put it another way, why is it that the informal logicians – who claim explicitly to be concerned with ordinary language argument – are unable to give a conscientious practitioner tools with which to analyse the great majority of written-down, explicit arguments?

The answer lies partly in the nature of the arguments that informal logicians set themselves as problems to analyse. True to their origins in academic discourse, and concerned about their students' ability to cope with formal documents, they look for specimen examples of argument only in the restricted domain of text. This has the disadvantage of disqualifying arguments that are either 'practical' – that is, arguments including some element of recommendation or moral judgement – or what Morton calls 'argument by analysis' in which there are no premises as such, but the conclusion comes after a series of reinterpretations of a given case. A newspaper editorial may, on the face of it, promise reduction to a series of factual statements leading to a conclusion, but inspection may reveal moral or practical recommendations impossible to encompass within informal logic.

Application

If informal logic stumbles on application to written arguments, it might be still more unhappy with verbal ones. Informal logicians are interested not so much in the unfolding process of argument or reasoning – that is to say, its progress from launch to arrival, its destination and its deviations along the way – as they are in its form as a finished product, when it can be pinned down and its parts exposed to view. Setting the argument or explanation out in this rather dead way distracts attention from the context and the audience in which it was dynamically given, and certain crucial features of explanation and argument slip away even from Toulmin's liberal model.

If validity can be specified as being no more than the consistency or coherence of the argument, then a lot will turn on those stylistic things that bind talk together, and which might be outside even the flexible formalization of informal logic. Fisher puts the informal logic criterion of validity like this: 'in general the right answers are determined by how we learn and use language and this is what anyone knows who understands the language' (1988b: 136). If that is the case, then we have to attend to 'language' in more than just the sense of words and phrases that can be tidied up and paraphrased by the analyst looking to reduce the messiness and clarify the obscurity of the printed argument. Latent in what Fisher says is the recommendation that instead of trying to see ideal shapes in the mist, we should attend to the mist itself to break it down into its components: all the literary, stylistic and persuasive devices which speakers use to win over their listeners, with or without recourse to the hard coupling of formalizable premiss and conclusion. In other words, we shall need to bolster informal logic with rhetoric.

Argument and rhetoric

In the first half of this chapter we saw that certain, fairly formal, ordinary arguments and explanations could be filleted by the informal logician's tools. At its most contextualized, a model like Toulmin's would hand over the determination of the validity of arguments to specialist experts. Nevertheless, there is a certain insistence in staying close to a definable, rather abstract rationality; arguers are taken to be working to a fairly solid programme of examinable progress from premiss to conclusion. In this half of the chapter we shall be looking at the arguments as they might appear less straitened by appeal to logic, informal or otherwise.

Persuasive argument in politics and the law was the summit of achievement for the educated man (women were excluded) in ancient Greece. Rhetoric, as the study of persuasive argument, was immensely respected. It was an intellectual industry probably on a par with modern-day information science and, for the elite who were able to use it, it probably held out the same promise of profitable application. By the Middle Ages rhetoric had lost some of its lustre. It found itself taught, alongside grammar, not at university level, but at what would pass today for elementary or junior school. It had had its driving motor – the study of arguments and their arrangement – ripped out and set down in the separate study of logic; the purely stylistic apparatus that was left was put into the service of praising and blaming, and did not hold on to its prestige for long. Nowadays, to our ears, 'rhetoric' means empty and fraudulent floweriness.

But rhetoric is reappearing. It is being reintroduced not as an academic throwback, but as part of the 'linguistic turn' which the human sciences have taken – not in step, and not all round to quite the same angle – in the past generation (and has been informing the content of this book so far). Since rhetoric in its broadest general sense is the stimulation of 'feeling' (as Vickers, 1988, has it), one can co-opt its analyses to tell us how a text achieves anything from excitement and suspense to sympathy and fellow-feeling, or how it manages to crowd out certain voices at the expense of others; how it raises up one vision of reality and defeats its rival; and so on. The literary-inspired work on accounts we saw in Chapter 6 came down that intellectual line. But we shall take 'feeling' to be the rather narrower range of persuasion and conviction, and stay with rhetoric in its stricter sense of persuasive argumentation.

Rhetoric and the 'invention' of arguments

In classical rhetoric, the 'argument' that we have been discussing here in the chapter is involved in just the first two of rhetoric's five stages of an oratorical performance:

> Invention is the discovery of valid or seemingly valid arguments to render one's case plausible. Arrangement is the distribution of arguments thus discovered in the proper order. Expression is the fitting of the proper language to the invented

matter. Memory is the firm mental grasp of matter and words. Delivery is the control of voice and body in a manner suitable to the dignity of the subject matter and the style. (Cicero, *De Oratore*, cited in Vickers, 1988: 62)

It was 'invention', Ong (1958) records, that received the lion's share of attention from the start. While it was within the protective walls of rhetoric 'invention' was never reducible to logic; although, in the end, logic snatched it, leaving rhetoric with what seemed merely to be its more decorative parts. Invention, according to Ong (1958) and Vickers (1988), went through as bad a time as any other rhetorical division after its creative surge in classical times; it became rigidified and systematized into huge manuals of examples designed to be copied out by young boys at school. It lost any sense of starting on a path that would lead to a performance, and it stopped being very inventive.

The informal logicians and argumentation theorists we have seen are solely interested in the invention and the form of argument. But a rhetorician would say that to get the best out of argument, we ought to put *inventio* where it belongs, in among the series of steps towards persuasion; otherwise we shan't make sense of it or of the rest of the series. Just to give a sense of what a full-blown rhetorical analysis could do with a persuasive argument, take this example from Cockcroft and Cockcroft's (1992) review of rhetoric and persuasion. To illustrate rhetoric's arsenal of argument-types, they confect a wholly plausible-looking argument (in the style of the long-suffering newspaper editorials so often the butt of informal logicians), each sentence of which is an example of a certain rhetorical form. (The term in brackets should be fairly self-explanatory, each referring to a type of argument; thus the first sentence is an example of argument by definition, the second argument by appeal to genus and species, or generalizations and particulars; and so on).

> The National Health Service should be a completely adequate system for the health-care of the nation, provided at the public expense (Definition). It means precisely that: not some kind of nationally available system you can pay for, or a nationally available but second-rate service if you're poor and ill and can't afford anything better (Genus/Species). Today it is under threat from forces opposing these public ideals and wishing to promote private care for the sick (Contrary). The result is demoralisation for those who work in the NHS, and confusion for those who use it (Cause–Effect; Whole–Part).
>
> Building up a structure of legislation to 'improve' the Health Service, which in fact damages it, is like asking the fireman to put petrol on the fire instead of putting it out (Analogy). Only in this instance the fire is being lit across the country! (Degree). If you doubt this, ask anyone who has recently been in hospital or who works in the NHS (Witness). What do we mean, we might ask ourselves, by the terms *National Health Service*? Surely 'National' implies the good of the whole nation, not just those able to pay? Health means 'wholeness', not division; and 'service' means caring and protecting, not destroying (Argument from Root Meaning). (Cockcroft and Cockcroft, 1992: 77)

This is exactly the kind of text which, though perfectly sensible, defeats the rationality of informal logic. As Morton said, informal logic would have been poorly equipped in getting from premise to conclusion (or even, indeed, to identify which is which); but rhetoric allows one to name the parts and get a grip on what persuasive, if technically inconclusive, work is going on.

There is, of course, a large literature on the technicalities of rhetoric, cataloguing the forest of devices that can be used to cover the persuasive landscape; we shan't not see much of those, as it will get in the way of a clear view of the particular species of claim-backing that we are interested in.

There is also a large literature on 'persuasive communication' in traditional social psychology, but we shall not be alluding to much of it. The reasons will become clearer as the chapter progresses, but can be easily summarized: most of the research that informs it is based on the solicitation of examination-type responses from subjects presented with brief, fixed messages under laboratory conditions, and varying in rather a narrow selection of rhetorical 'variables' – principally the credibility of the source, the order and complexity of the arguments, the presence of counter-arguments, and so on. Theory is limited in its analysis of just what an argument *is*, and the methods used in research reduce the essential manoeuvrability of ordinary quarrelling, so critics do find it hard to see what conclusions can be drawn about the cut and thrust of everyday argument.

But this is to get ahead of ourselves. To make the link from informal logic to rhetoric we shall use the work of the philosopher Chaim Perelman, then move on to a recent application of rhetoric to explanation and argument in the very heart of social psychology.

Perelman and Olbrechts-Tyteca's 'new rhetoric'

Rhetoric became influential in the study of ordinary arguments through the 'new rhetoric' of Perelman and Olbrechts-Tyteca (1969). Its broad contours are these. First, Perelman and Olbrechts-Tyteca weren't satisfied with the mere listing of stylistic devices, nor did they mean to preach a set of recipes for successful orators; both these were dismissed as modern distortions. Rather, the mission was to bring rhetoric back into its proper realm of everyday, rather than set-piece, argumentative strategies, and to give it some of the prestige that scientific discourse had stolen. This was only marginally an empirical programme; much more attention was given to theoretical analysis of what it means to persuade.

What is interesting to the psychologist, and what links Perelman and Olbrechts-Tyteca to at least one strand of informal logic, was that they were keen to turn the spotlight away from the arguer and towards the audience whose approval the arguer would be looking for – or rather, the arguer's own mental representation of such an audience. An argument has to have an antagonist, and one has to want to persuade them; otherwise, there is no argument (just as Toulmin had been telling his colleagues in informal logic). Moreover, these two sides of the dispute wer not inferior and superior, and telling between them was not always purely a disinterested examination of the rational merits of the two cases. The values they mobilized would enter into such an assessment, and different audiences will bow to different ultimate values; it will be no easy matter to predict which argument will win, but it will be certain that even if it wins on this occasion there is no guarantee that it will win all the time and in all places.

The arguer will maximize the chances of success by making his or her representation of peculiarities of the audience as accurate as possible; in any case, even if there isn't a particular audience to persuade, the arguer has to keep some ideal audience in mind if she or he wants to sound convincing. Note the difference with informal logic, in which there would be no question of choosing your best argument; the procedure of analysing given texts of others' arguments in any case obviates any such choice in informal logic as practised in the classroom. Even in principle, if the need arose for you to make an argument, your only guiding principle would be to make a valid one; if there were more than one valid one, there would be no strategy to help you choose among them.

We shall not list the catalogue of argument types that Perelman and Olbrechts-Tyteca list, but it is worth looking at one of these to see how little they value logic as a model of ordinary argument. They only allow logical form to feature in what they call 'quasi-logical' argument: such an argument will present itself as having recognizable logical form while in fact failing any strict test of logical conclusiveness. Take the argument *you do the washing up tonight because you said you'd do it if I was busy, and I've got a lot to do for tomorrow*. It draws its power from the everyday feeling that it's a watertight 'logical' argument, but in fact it relies on several dubious missing premises and is easily defeasible. There are, of course, many possible such arguments, corresponding to the range of valid logical forms; but in every case it is the appearance of logic, and not the thing itself, that is being relied on to be persuasive.

Perelman and Olbrechts-Tyteca were influential in bringing the context into focus. However, posterity has been as hard on their theory and the possibility of its operationalization as it has been on Toulmin's and for the same reasons. Where Toulmin's case rests on the distinction between different sorts of premises, Perelman and Olbrechts-Tyteca's rests on the distinction between different sorts of argument; but it is no easier to make than is Toulmin's. There are four types of argument, according to the new rhetoric (we saw one of them, quasi-logical arguments, above) but there is no sure way of unambiguously deciding whether any given argument is one or the other; certainly, since Perelman and Olbrechts-Tyteca did not write in that mode, there is no set of instructions that would make the job operationally easy. Again, as was the case with Toulmin, the new rhetoric does not give generalizable rules of argument assessment, and this naturally disappoints theorists who want to be able to evaluate arguments themselves, or teach others to do so. Yet Perelman and Olbrechts-Tyteca insist that, ultimately, it is the audience that can be the only arbiter of whether an argument is good or bad – and audiences change with the occasion.

Arguing as social fabric

If we are to dispense with foolproof measures of argument and follow rhetoric and argument down to its use in very specific context, then we shall be entering into the arena of social interaction where the social psychologist will have something to say. In the section that follows, we shall be guided by Mick Billig (1987), whose recent enthusiastic championing of rhetoric makes him unique among social psychologists. He promotes his interest as being that of the antiquarian, searching for illuminating artefacts; but what he intends to illuminate is human thinking itself. His project is to show how the psychology of human affairs as they involve thinking – and that means much of social, cognitive and developmental psychology – are to profit from the insights of rhetoric. Put simply, Billig says that people are argumentative. They take issue with each other, and this taking issue happens not only with other people, but also, privately, inside the head.

Billig, as we shall see, argues that the craft of rhetoric and the affairs of the social world are lashed together by a double loop. Many human exchanges can progress only through persuasion, challenge and the defence of opinions. But these rhetorical devices are not empty shells, used mechanically: people use them because they have social and psychological meaning. If, for example, you 'have an opinion', you are pretty well committed to defending your case, and so necessarily using the craft of rhetoric. Those devices work because they trade in currency which has the authority of society's stamp of approval.

Argument and quarrelling

The Greek Protagoras is credited with the maxim that for every stand which could be taken on an issue, there was an exactly opposite stand which contradicted it. Billig draws out from Protagoras' maxim the implication that, since there are two opposite stands, that means that to express one stand is to do so in the (visible or invisible) presence of the other, and so to admit the possibility of a confrontation. To present one side of a case is, necessarily, to enter into a quarrel. So you can't have an argument (in the sense of a 'case') without having an argument (in the sense of a 'dispute' launched by the proponent of the opposite case). This means that the two senses of 'argument' which I separated at the start of this chapter cannot in practice, and should not in principle, be pulled away from each other. The central question of the validity of any argument, or case, is not resolvable by the internal coherence of the argument as such. Contrary to what an informal logician would say (centred on the form and arrangement of the argument, and ignoring the rest of its rhetorical performance) validity is, in fact, never establishable by 'argument' itself; for an argument to come to an end, some external force, or the human weakness of the arguers, must be the deciding factor. In other words, the argument lives and dies in dialogue.

Another corollary that Billig draws from Protagoras' maxim is that the two sides to a case may not be equally welcome to the audience. In the social world the clash is not simply between ideal cases but between people who hold real positions, and who are sufficiently disturbed by likely unfavourable evaluation to be spurred on to do something about it. Bringing argumentation down out of the clouds, Billig uses examples from both textual and conversational arguing. The textual examples are largely from self-consciously expository sources – the Talmud, Greek philosophical texts and so on – which means that the rhetorician's job is pretty well half-done; the original writers have already structured and selected the text so that the rhetorical force of the story has the greatest impact. The other account Billig gives is based on real-life conversation, and is perhaps harder work, promising greater application to our concerns in this book. To get a sense of what goes on in a rhetorical reading of argument, let us see first what one can make of an antiquarian text.

'Witcraft' and logic

Billig's book is full of entertaining examples, but the set piece that suits us best is the dispute between the Jewish elders and some Roman heretics who worship idols. Both put forward what an informal logician would be happy to call straightforward arguments. But this is the rhetorical case as Billig puts it:

> The debate starts with the Romans challenging the Elders with the reasonable, but tricky, question: Why, if God so disapproves of idolatry, does He not destroy all the idols? The Elders reply that He would certainly do so, if the idolators only worshipped useless objects. The problem was that idolators worshipped necessary objects such as the sun, moon, stars and planets. Destruction of these would entail God destroying His whole Creation: 'Shall He then make an end of His world because of fools?' The Romans are not satisfied with this answer, but they counter it with a further, and more difficult, challenge: If God does not want to destroy the world, then let Him destroy only the useless idols. Back comes the reply of the Elders. If God destroyed your useless idols, but kept the sun, moon, stars and planets, what would you say? You would, of course, say that these were the true deities, because they had been untouched by the destruction of idols. (Billig, 1987: 100–1)

What Billig wants to get out of this well-told story is the strong claim that logic is irrelevant, or worse, as a guide to what is going on in the argument. The arguments 'could be recast into syllogisms, but nothing is gained by doing so, and much is lost' (1987: 102). On his reading, the elders and the idolators are in no disagreement about logic. Neither side says, or implies, that what the other has said doesn't follow, or is a fallacy, or is badly derived. They both agree that premises can support conclusions, and that these premises do support these conclusions. What they disagree on is the 'choice' of premises in the first place (the 'argument by definition' we saw in Cockcroft and Cockcroft's list, above). The elders' first argument is that God hasn't destroyed the idols because He needs to keep them going so that the world can carry on normally. The Romans don't express any question about whether the implicit syllogism is valid or not. They are, Billig presumes, angry about their idols' material importance being brought into the discussion as a premiss, not what follows from it. The elders' next argument is that God would do nothing that encouraged the idolators in their beliefs; if he destroyed all the useless idols but left the sun and so on in place, this would encourage them; so He won't. Again, Billig claims that this doesn't rouse the Romans to any complaint about the form of the argument. Rather, they object to the premisses once again. And again Billig doesn't say which or why, but we might presume that the Romans are angry about the premisses the elders have chosen. Billig doesn't spell this out, but we presume he means that the Romans objected to the guess about their behaviour were only the useless idols to vanish.

Why does Billig insist that both sides agree on the form of the argument but disagree on the truth, or the relevance, of the premisses? We shall get to this in a moment, but let us first see whether he really can make such a claim based on this particular example. It would have been better for his argument had the Romans explicitly expressed themselves happy with the validity (in the logical sense) of the elders' reasoning, but they do not; we shall just have to go along with Billig that, in fact, they didn't raise any such objection. But if we look at the elders' arguments again, it might be the case that there was in fact nothing logically wrong with them at all; so there was nothing for the Romans to complain about. Suppose the elders' second argument was as I laid it out above.

(1) God would do nothing that encouraged the idolators in their beliefs;
(2) To destroy all the useless idols but leave the useful ones in place would encourage them; so
(Conclusion) He won't destroy all the useless idols but leave the useful ones.

This is a perfectly acceptable example of a syllogism. The Romans would have had no cause to complain about the logic, so we can't say whether their lack of complaint was because they just didn't care about logical form, or whether they cared and let this one pass. It would have been better for Billig to have had the elders slip a fallacy past the Romans, and the Romans to have swallowed it: if the elders had said *if the sun is unnecessary, God will destroy it. The sun isn't unnecessary, so God won't destroy it*. Even assuming that the first premiss was true, this is logically wrong. If the Romans hadn't complained loudly about it, then Billig would indeed have had a case that logical form wasn't important.

Why, then, this insistence? Partly it is because Billig wants to claim that rhetoric is 'democratic' in the sense that anyone can do it. In the story, neither side used purely technical expertise, and Billig concludes that anyone with cheek can do 'witcraft': 'For a courageous moment when wits are the only weapons, subjects can triumph over their rulers' (1987: 103). This torpedo is aimed at those stern reductionists (he is particularly disappointed with cognitive psychologists) who measure people against the standards of deductive logic and deny the skill of argumentation. There is

more to it than that, though. It is important in Billig's model of argument that the points at issue are substantive, not formal. That is to say, that people disagree about issues and statements: that to allow them to disagree about the form in which they reason would be to weaken the message. In fact, he goes out of his way to say that people's logical abilities are given, in the same way as their grammatical abilities are given: 'logic is assumed, just as grammar might be. In order to phrase one's arguments, one needs both grammar and logic, but the arguments are not necessarily about grammar or logic' (1987: 101). Let us see where his concentration on substantive differences of opinion takes us.

Arguing over differences of opinion

People argue over topics; the choice of which topics to argue over is partly individual, but must be limited by the stock of things that society at any one moment determines to be controversial. It would be idle nowadays to argue over whether one's soul was or was not lighter than a feather; but it would have been sensible, and perhaps urgent, in ancient Egypt. By identifying topics (rather than form) as the trigger of arguments, Billig has made it easier for us to see how the study of argument can reach right in to social psychology, and say something about people's understandings of the issues of the day. Let us see how he makes it in his analysis of a real-life argument.

This comes from an ordinary British family, tape-recorded in their own home while talking to a researcher who was asking them about their views on the British royal family. The views of the father are very pronounced; in fact, he is notorious in the family for having strong attitudes about the royals. A traditional attitude theorist would predict that a man with strong views would express himself pretty consistently. So, if we can see some rhetorical activity here – if we can catch the man chopping and changing what he says in response to the rhetorical demands of the moment – then we shall have tested rhetoric in the best case that a strong attitude theorist could wish for.

In this extract, the father is talking about whether he reads about the royals in the newspapers.

Father:	(. . .) I do read it, but I'm not interested, ha–ha, now if you can read between, I do read it anyway
Son:	He reads it to get wound up
Father:	No, I don't read it to get wound up, but I will read it but to be quite honest I'm not, I'm not that interested, no, I just like to know what's going off and what's happening
Mother:	So you're interested
Father:	No I'm interested in what's happening
Son:	You *are* interested

(Billig, 1987: 182–3; transcription slightly simplified)

There is clearly a quarrel going on, but if there is a single claim being disputed then it's something like the son's assertion that the father reads about the royals in order to disparage them. The argument proceeds very differently from the reasoned cut and thrust of the Talmudic story. In fact, it looks like mere contradiction.

The way that Billig makes his account richer than this is significant. He calls attention to the 'content' of the contradictions: the son, for example, insists that the father reads the stories so as to get 'wound up'. This 'psychologizes away' the father's views: by attributing them to a perverse pleasure in contrariness, the son doesn't have to confront the father's actual views themselves. He is using a stock device, one that all the speakers recognize – a 'commonplace'. He does so because the view that he is defending is unpopular, committing him to extra persuasive and justificatory effort, as Perelman had predicted.

Billig insists on content at the expense of form because he wants to tie arguing to social life. Social life is argumentative; and what moves an argument along is social: the topics people argue over, the content of the challenges and rebuttals, and so on. People argue about categories and particulars – what something *is*, and what implications you can draw from it; they argue over definitions, terms and usages. All of these are on the cusp of the semantic and the social. If Billig pointed us to valid form he would distract our attention from these meatier social issues. The debate in the extracts above is as much about society and the monarchy as it is about the father's psychology – it circles around just what is reasonable to say about political life. The content of what is being said shows that what is going on is not just the argument, but also a parade of social representations of society.

The conversational form of analysis of witcraft here is very different from the textual witcraft of the elders. The shifting sands of conversational allegiance, and the free movement of the participants in and out of the debate, allow Billig to make claims about larger-scale strategy as well as the tactics of claim and counter-claim, pulling back into the frame what was missing from the elders' story. Thus, for example, at one point the father counts himself as a member of his class (*we're the working people of the country*) who do not trust 'them' to distribute resources fairly; at another, he expresses himself as a citizen (*we've got a system in this country*) who doesn't mind there being some rich people (*we've got to have our businesses*). In the first voice he is radical; in the second, cautious. In another example of mobility, the mother at one point (in the extract we saw above) joins the son in directly challenging the father about why he reads stories about the royals, but later sides with the father in disapproving of the number of houses they own; and, immediately thereafter, shifts to join with her daughter in attacking the father's insistence on a financial account of the royal family's activities. None of this would have been possible with the fixed telling of the elders' dispute, let alone the stately progress of rational argument in informal logic. It shows how the tactics of disagreement saturate the talk, bolstering enormously Billig's claim that rhetoric is at the heart of human exchanges.

Rhetoric and routine quarrelling

The delight in ordinary people's perversity encourages Billig to go so far as to say that conversation analysis is badly wrong about what is normal in talk. Conversation analysis is, as we have seen repeatedly in this book, fixed onto the firm ground that people in conversation mark and resolve upsets so that the conversation can get back to a regular course. Billig's discovery of disagreement seems to weaken this foundation. He observes that his interactants disagree with gusto: there are none of the typical hedges, hesitations and so on that usually precede what the conversation analysts call 'dispreferred turns'. For Billig, the rhetorical frame fixed around social interactions means that people don't want to resolve their differences, but, on the contrary, actively want to maintain them. Even in a different discussion, between members of a family much more united in their support for the royal family, Billig argues, there is still plenty of to-ing and fro-ing: rather than consensus suppressing argumentation, it encourages debate and disagreement (Billig, 1989).

The conversational convention of agreement (and the Gricean cooperative contract) should not, we might object, be dismissed too easily. It may be the case that the rules of conduct are tacitly put to one side for certain speech events (like his respondents' family quarrels, and similar ones reported by Schiffrin, 1984 – both sets, of course, in the presence of an interviewer), but that does not affect the general background expectation that they are – normally – in operation. On the contrary, the family members' enthusiastic clamour of disagreement is given special point by its very unusualness: were disagreement to be the typical thing, it would be ineffective and colourless as a rhetorical device.

Billig's promotion of argumentativeness and the importance of the 'content' of argument – its social topics – should also be seen against the background of that large class of cases where claims are made and backed in the blind run of mundane talk. We saw in Chapter 5 how ordinary talk is laced with slots which require filling with explanations that make sense of speakers' unexpected utterances; what is unexpected about the utterance need have no great tactical or strategic importance, and would not bear the weight of a full rhetorical analysis.

The worry about Billig's orientation to the regularities of talk rears up again when we reflect on his use of data. Although it is a bit strong to say that he 'never has anything to say about the linguistic details of a text' (Myers, 1989), which is true only in the sense that he is unconcerned with the ums and ahs of talk unless they have specifically rhetorical effect, it is nevertheless the case that his style of analysis favours the intentional and particular at the expense of the routine and generalizable. It is here perhaps that we might be most cautious about applying a rhetorical analysis to ephemeral talk. To make claims about the rhetorical effects of what people are up to in their conversations, one needs to make inferences which necessarily take some steps away from the information given. Such interpretation of the content of people's arguments – the strength and promise of a rhetorical analysis, as it is of discursive and narrative analyses (as we saw in Chapters 6 and 7) – is best done on a certain range of material, and with a certain schooling in the social and cultural vocabulary at the speaker's disposal.

Billig's reply would be that it is no bad thing to find oneself up against the rails of interpretation, because that is where the understanding of human interaction will be. He has explicitly argued against 'methodology' as a straitjacket on interpretation, and a brake on scholarly understanding. For Billig, part of the scholar's skill is not to follow a pre-set programme, set down by a specialist methodologist, but to gather up clues which can nudge the search one revealing way or another. The analyst must choose significant interactions, and be prepared to interpret them with as broad a palette of rhetorical exegesis as is appropriate.

If our ambitions are scaled down a notch, formal analysis does offer the security of at least the beginnings of argument assessment to work with. It is not the end of the story – we saw how the informal logicians rejected the purely formal account of arguments – but it does give the analyst some starting point along a path towards describing what claims are at issue – which need not always, as we shall see, be rhetorically rich claims over topics, but sometimes more straightforwardly interactional claims about the procedure and manner of raising them. In the next chapter we shall stay with the spirit of argumentation with which Billig has moved us on from informal logic, but turn away from rhetorical persuasiveness and towards some more structured ways of reading the quarrels and claims that punctuate ordinary life.

9

Backing Claims in Quarrels

Ann:	The meat is dry
Mother:	No. I think it's delicious
Joyce:	It's not dry it's just [*inaudible*]
Mother:	Put some mushroom sauce on it
Joyce:	I didn't say it was–
Ann:	It's not dry it's just hard
Joyce:	It's good enough
	(6.0)
Mother:	[*to Father*] Uh Duane hollered at me today (2.1) That man's name is Virgil Long

(Vuchinich, 1990: 128)

The North American family above are quarrelling in much the same way as were the British family we saw at the end of the last chapter. Here though, the issues are more homely, and the claims that are at stake (whether or not the meat is dry, and what to do about it) are perhaps less amenable to a rhetorical treatment than quarrels about the British royal family. Might there be a way of modelling, fairly formally, and with close attention to conversational organization, the pattern of their exchange? Is there something regular about claims (*the meat is dry*), counter-claims and backings (*no. I think it's delicious*) and the way they're managed (six seconds pass and Mother changes the subject)? That is the question we shall be considering here in this chapter.

I shall work down from the abstract to the concrete. In the first half of the chapter I shall take a selective look at argumentation theory, which tries to model claims and backings as if they were speech acts. After a quick inspection of a classic version of argumentation theory, I move to a version which applies its speech-act analysis to real talk. In the middle of the chapter this gives way to models of claim-backing that add more organizational mechanisms into the analytical mix, ending up with a tentative stripping-down of argumentative backings to a three-part sequence. At the end of the chapter we broaden out again to colour the stricter conversation-analytic reading with an appreciation of (at least some of) quarrelling's cultural conventions.

Argumentation theory

The objective of argumentation theory is, like informal logic and rhetoric, to describe sound and unsound argument without dependency on deductive logical validity. Where it parts company with informal logic is in its refusal to stay within the confines of the structure of argument in its assessment of soundness. It sees argument as a social interaction between at least two people, one or both of whom want to defend a certain opinion and who will have counter-arguments of their own. So far it is consistent with rhetoric, but it resists rhetoric's seductive flexibility; it insists that one can make a stab at finding generalizable rules that describe the sequence of any such argumentative interaction.

We should beware the phrase 'argumentation theory', since, as van Eemeren (1988) observes, it is no guarantee that there is just one theory of argumentation (an echo of the situation we saw with attribution theory in social psychology in Chapter 2). If we stick to that part of the theoretical scene that is about argumentative dialogues, certain fundamentals of the idealized scheme are agreed: that interlocutors are competent speakers of the same language; that they are serious and mean what they say; that the listener is listening; that anything relevant can be said; that the proponent doesn't know in advance whether the audience already agrees with him or her; that the defender is prepared to defend what he or she says; and that anyone can dispute anything.

Speech acts in idealized argumentation

Let us press on with one clear and historically well-grounded statement of argumentation theory which proceeds down this line. Our point of departure is van Eemeren and Grootendorst's (1982, 1984) theory of speech acts in argumentative discourse. It starts from the rhetorical truism that an argument happens in an argumentative discussion – that it is an exchange of views over a difference of opinion; that the arguer means to defend a standpoint and the audience to attack it; and that they both want to resolve the dispute. The argument is a 'critical discussion . . . the purpose . . . being to establish whether the protagonist's standpoint is defensible against the critical reactions of the antagonist' (1984: 170), and the theory promises rules for the conduct of such discussions.

Rules of language use had been implicit in all the models of claims and backing we have mentioned so far, but van Eemeren and Grootendorst take the critical step of treating 'arguing' as a linguistic unit and weaving it into the fabric of 'speech acts' (which we came across in Chapter 4). Recall that utterances could be conceived of as things which were in their own right substantial acts: promising, forgiving, refusing and so on. To this list van Eemeren and Grootendorst intended to add 'arguing'.

Arguing as a speech act

We have already seen something of speech-act theory (pp. 53–6), so I won't go over it in detail here. Originally, it had been thought that speech acts might be captured by verbs, and Austin had indeed allowed the verb 'to argue' to stand for a speech act (distinct from 'to say', 'to observe', and so on). Moreover, later speech-act theory had extended the range of the theory beyond the class of verbs as such (a verbless statement like *whoah!* would warn), so it would seem that there would be no obstacle to calling arguing a speech act, even if the verb itself didn't appear. The difficulty is one of scale. Speech acts had always been considered as small-scale linguistic events – words, phrases or sentences. That might capture short, one-utterance arguments within its net, but it would miss all the more extended ones, and van Eemeren and Grootendorst want to define argument as dialectic, necessarily involving more than one utterance. Argument was too big, and it also required more than one person. How could this be reconciled?

One possibility is to admit argument into the fold as an 'indirect speech act'; that is to say, one that achieves its ends not by a literal understanding of what is said, but by some degree of interpretation and guesswork, possibly via a chain of statements. For example, to return to warnings: I might say, as you were about to sit down: *ah, that chair . . . I was meaning to have a look at it this afternoon.* If you assume that what I am saying is pertinent to what's going on, and is somehow informative, you will draw the inference that the chair needs attention and is possibly insecure; you will find another. But all this is indirect and unstated and, according to van Eemeren and Grootendorst, misses the essential feature of argument. An indirect speech act (like that warning) can be misconstrued, but argument can't – you know when you're arguing, or being argued with.

To bring argumentation into the realm of speech acts proper, van Eemeren and Grootendorst's strategy is simply to expand the definition of a speech act until it fits argumentation. They make a distinction between illocution at the sentence level and at a 'higher' level. The former they will call 'elementary illocutions' and the latter 'compound illocutions' or 'illocutionary act complexes'. Argumentation is such a 'complex'. In other words, van Eemeren and Grootendorst simply give themselves the permission to say that a speech act can, indeed, be made up of more than one linked statement.

This seems rather bare-faced, but there are several things to be said in its favour. It sounds intuitively plausible: if arguing in one go, as it were, fits perfectly within the speech-act scheme then more extended arguing stands a fighting chance of doing so, and speech-act theory does not explicitly disallow it. A number of other writers want to say the same kind of thing about argument (that it is a coherent linguistic device) as we shall see in a moment. But, leaving aside precedent, perhaps the best next step is to see how useful and enlightening it is when arguments are allowed to behave like speech acts.

If arguments are like speech acts, then speech-act theory should, according to van Eemeren and Grootendorst, now tell us: what the relation is between arguing and convincing or persuading; which speech acts are essential, permissible and impermissible in argument; and how to bring out unexpressed bits of an argument. If speech-act theory does do that then van Eemeren and Grootendorst will have proved their point.

Arguing, convincing and persuading

First, then, convincing and persuading. For van Eemeren and Grootendorst these need not be kept distinct: both require that the other's opinion be changed. Persuading goes further in implying that the person's behaviour is also altered, but van Eemeren and Grootendorst prefer keeping to the common ground so as to treat both together.

If the arguing is the illocutionary act – the communicative side of argumentation – then convincing is the perlocutionary outcome, or the interactional goal. This is the interactional guarantee that they were looking for in a theory of argumentation, and that was so lacking in logic. The virtue of speech-act theory is that the perlocution is necessarily (if not sufficiently) brought about by the illocution; there is no space between them that would otherwise have to be bridged (in van Eemeren and Grootendorst's eyes unsatisfactorily) in the theories of Toulmin and Perelman and Olbrechts-Tyteca. Illocution and perlocution, if they happen, happen by virtue of the same event. The perlocution of convincing is the sum of all of the felicity conditions of argument being met (all the preconditions that allow the utterance to be uttered *as* an argument – that there be a contradiction, that the arguer be sincere about it, and so on) plus the extra condition of the listener being satisfied.

All language users of a given linguistic community must know the conventions by which this is done; otherwise there would never be successful arguments or convincing accounts. There has to be some regularity in the forms, or schemas, of argumentation, and this is where the catalogues of Perelman and Olbrechts-Tyteca would fit comfortably, as would the argument forms identified by the informal logicians.

Which speech acts and when?

Arguing is the high-level interpretation of what is going on, and below and around it are a collection of subunits which (at the same time) are doing other speech acts. Chronologically, this is how claims and backings would appear in an idealized argument set off by disagreement about an opinion O. The speech acts are underlined, and I have invented some dialogue to flesh out the skeleton.

The confrontation stage

Person A <u>asserts</u> an opinion	*A*: It's not worth bothering to vote in this constituency
Person B <u>casts doubt</u> on what A said	*B*: Oh, I think it definitely is

The opening stage

B <u>challenges</u> A to defend her point of view	*B*: How can you say that?

A <u>accepts the challenge</u>	*A*: Look, it's quite simple – I'll lay it out for you
A and B <u>decide</u> to discuss the issue, and <u>agree</u> how they will proceed	*B*: All right, let's see. You show me just why you think it's not worth voting, and I'll see if I can spot holes in what you say
	A: Fair enough
The argumentation stage A makes <u>assertions</u> which together count as <u>arguing</u>	*A*: Our MP always gets elected with a majority of over 20,000. There's only one other runner in the race, and they'll never get any more than 5,000 votes, maximum. Whichever one I felt happier with, my one vote would make virtually no difference
B <u>accepts</u> (or not)	*B*: Yes, I see what you mean
The concluding stage A <u>upholds</u> (or <u>retracts</u>) her asserted opinion	*A*: So there's really not much point voting
B <u>retracts</u> (or <u>upholds</u>) her objection	*B*: All right, I guess I was wrong
They jointly <u>observe</u> that the dispute has been resolved	*A*: Well, I think that's settled that – shall we see what's on the television?
	B: Yes, all right

(simplified, and with fictional examples added, from van Eemeren and Grooten-dorst, 1984: 99–100)

You can see, in this highly idealized fiction, that the kernel of claim and backing is embedded in a complex social interaction of speech acts: asserting, casting doubt, challenging, and so on. The argumentation complex itself, the nucleus at the centre of the interaction, is made up of 'assertives' of various kinds, and is bounded by 'directives' (like B challenging A) and 'commissives' (like A and B deciding, or committing themselves, to thrash the matter out).

Validity and rationality

Van Eemeren and Grootendorst had objected that neither Toulmin's model, nor a more explicitly rhetorical model, was sufficiently fastidious about validity – that the models allowed the validity of an argument to be decided 'anthropologically' by local experts. They wanted a test of validity that a disinterested assessor could apply. Speech-act theory was introduced in part because of its express recognition of context, and in part because it offered a way of assessing an utterance's validity, with the extra attraction that this validity was independent of truth and falsity in the logical sense.

There is, though, a hint that the theory would indeed like to make arguments stand a test of validity. The proposal works like this: the interaction is a chain of speech acts, and each speech act has to be properly authorized by meeting the appropriate felicity conditions. One of these conditions is that the listener makes the best possible sense of the argument that the arguer has put forward, even if that means recreating any missing premises in her or his argument. So to utter something felicitous, the listener must (at least) make the arguer's argument good; in other words, valid: hence the validity of the argument is assured.

However, this extreme conclusion is drawn at some cost of implausibility from the cooperative and pragmatic features of the idealized model, and it is probably simpler to think of speech-act theory as being just silent on the question of validity of arguments, which it leaves to informal logic. The theory is more concerned to supplement standard tests of argument validity with the more general requirement that the interlocutors act in concert with the rules of the idealized model: in other words, that they be reasonable and rational users of the language.

Is the model too idealized?

Speech-act theory was not introduced to solve problems of the validity of argument. It was introduced to give power to the other insight that van Eemeren and Grootendorst pulled from their predecessors: that argument was given in a context, and that to argue was in an essential sense a social action. Speech-act theory allowed them to formalize that insight, and to bring out the pragmatically necessary preparations and obligations that went into a successful argument-interaction.

The great advance is to break the boundaries around argument which its logical treatment had imposed, and that, to a very large extent, had been uncritically inherited by the informal logicians. Now argument can be seen as a statement given in the right conditions; as van Eemeren puts it:

> Utterances which are argumentation in a situation of disagreement, when occurring in the context of a standpoint, may function as an explanation or simply as statements or as something else when the circumstances are different. Rather than *being* certain illocutionary acts, under certain conditions, utterances *serve* as these speech acts. (van Eemeren et al., 1987a: 205)

This passes the responsibility over to the observer who must spot when it is that the circumstances favour the interpretation of the utterances as argument or explanation. By itself, without that extra observer, the model is highly stage-managed, and its idealization runs a risk of making it difficult to apply.

The job of the observer is to find occasions when the model's conditions are met: when an initial explicit disagreement sets off two infinitely articulate and cooperative parties on a strictly paced, and pedantically complete, exposition and resolution. Intuitively, we might feel that ordinary argument deviates from every point along that line, just as real life departs drastically from a theatrical script. Van Eemeren and Grootendorst's response is that their model is 'prescriptive', not descriptive, so it would not in any way disturb the model to find that people didn't act that way; on the contrary, if they acted in such a rational way already, they wouldn't need training. Nevertheless, our doubts persist. After all, Toulmin's model was proposed in part prescriptively too; and van Eemeren and Grootendorst themselves were very critical of the applicability of Toulmin's model to real arguments. It seems that the same will be true for theirs. It will be hard to identify – as speech acts – the opening, confrontation, argument and concluding stages of argumentation theory, just as it is hard to identify Toulmin's special premises and Perelman and Olbrechts-Tyteca's various types of argument (see p. 155).

Moreover, the claims that the model recognizes seem rather bloodless; both parties are interested only in seeing whether the opinion that one of them expressed is reasonable or not. This is convenient for the theory, which, being normative, is much more interested in rational procedure than in point-scoring. But that puts the wrong sort of gloss on what may seem to be factual argument; as we saw in the last chapter, arguments about the 'facts' of the British royal family might be serving other ends, and will not necessarily be offered or assessed always in a rational spirit. Moreover, it is not only a factual proposition that can spark a quarrel, as we shall soon see.

We emerge from the formal school trained now to see claim-backing in a certain way: as being recognizable as part of a conflict between inter-locutors, as being directed to some kind of resolution, and as being regulated by some linguistic mechanism. Our doubts are about its idealizations. Ordinary arguing and claim-backing is unlikely to be as explicit or complete as the model demands, and the abstraction of speech acts may hinder application. We turn now to a more conversationally orientated version of argumentation theory to try to resolve these doubts.

Speech acts in conversational argument

We saw above how van Eemeren and Grootendorst broadened the context of the claims and backing to include the context in which the argument was an illocutionary act, surrounded by other speech acts, all liable to tests of felicity. More or less independently, the North Americans Sally Jackson and Scott Jacobs (Jackson and Jacobs, 1980; Jacobs, 1986, 1987; Jackson, 1987) were working on a speech-act account of argumentation in the predomi-nantly North American tradition of communication studies, a much more empirical and interdisciplinary field. Rather than worry about how people arrived at the truth as the conclusion to an argument, Jackson and Jacobs' concern was the question 'how do people *manage disagreement*?', and this meant that they had to get involved in the regulation of real talk.

The argumentative adjacency pair

One of the most basic regularities Jackson and Jacobs work with is the 'adjacency pair'. You may remember from Chapter 5 that this is a conversational coupling between two utterances, usually given by different speakers, and which usually occur one after another, like a question and answer pair, or an offer and its acceptance. This first part is usually followed by a certain kind of utterance which works to complete the pair: an assessment by an appreciation, or a request by a compliance, for example. When it is not, then the interactants have a problem on their hands, and the subsequent talk is designed to cope with it (there is more in Chapter 5 on the conversation analysis story of which this is an extract).

Jackson and Jacobs' double insight was that, first, quarrelling and argument fit nicely into this pattern: person A says something that requires an agreement before the conversation can proceed; if that expressed argument isn't forthcoming, then person A has to defend themselves with an argument, and the whole interaction has become a quarrel. Up to this point, leaving aside the paraphernalia of first-pair parts and preferred second-pair parts, this is quite similar to van Eemeren and Grootendorst's normative pragmatics account. Where Jackson and Jacobs differ is in what they allow to provoke the disagreement: their second insight was to see that disagreement could be sparked off by *any* infelicity in *anything* person A said; not just, as van Eemeren and Grootendorst had it, by a straight disagreement about the proposition that A asserted.

Another way of thinking about these felicity conditions is as what Habermas (1984) calls 'validity claims': the kinds of pragmatic claims to which utterances necessarily commit the speaker, as a rational social agent. Habermas' point is that any utterance carries with it a suite of claims which, if accepted, give the utterance legitimacy, and that even what seem to be bald reports will necessarily carry a weight of validity claims without which the speaker would make no sense. Now we can read objections and disputes as wanting the speakers to argue for the validity of the claims implicit in their uttering of the proposition. If I say *the United Nations should never have got involved in Bosnia* you might dispute its surface propositional content or any of the validity claims that make it a sensible thing to say – the implied claim that they *did* in fact get involved, that I am competent to pass any judgement on their right to do so, or that the topic fits properly into the conversation we are having, and so on – the widest possible context of conversation. On reading this it makes sense for you to answer with something like *who are you to speak? you were the one who wanted the UN to invade Iraq*, or *well, just look at what time it is*, and so on. These only make sense if they are meant to orientate to the communicative force of the utterance – where what is at issue is not a state of affairs external to the conversation but rather the arguers' status as socially rational agents within it.

Failing felicity conditions

The point that Jackson and Jacobs stress is that any speech act you perform might fail somewhere in the battery of felicity-condition (or validity-claim) tests it has to pass, and your hearer would then legitimately refuse to give the proper, preferred second-pair part, and the whole conversation would have to detour until it was resolved. Take requests (the speech act that Jackson and Jacobs have worked on most energetically): at their most general, they require of the speaker (S) and the hearer (H) that:

(a) Speaker (S) wants hearer (H) to do an action (A)
(b) S has the authority to ask H to do A
(c) Time, place etc. of A are agreeable to both people
(d) H can do A
(e) H is willing or obligated to do A
(f) H wouldn't have done it anyway
(g) A needs to be done

So there are at least seven points to which the hearer can take objection (leaving aside all the special ones contingent on particular kinds of request). Suppose I ask you to defrost the fridge this evening. The second-pair part to that request – that is, the one which would allow the conversation to move on immediately – would, of course, be a signal of compliance. But, knowing the above list of felicity conditions, you might object that:

(a) I don't really mean it
(b) I have no right to ask you to do that
(c) It's not possible this evening as we're both going out
(d) You don't know how to
(e) You don't want to
(f) You were going to do it anyway
(g) It doesn't need defrosting

Any one of these would give you the right not to agree, and the quarrel would have started. Let's suppose that, in fact, it was the felicity condition (f) that I failed. The quarrel would be easy to solve (that is to say, in Jackson and Jacobs' conversation-analytic terms, that the conversation could be quickly repaired, and go on to other things) by my simply apologizing: *oh, sorry, I didn't realize. Thanks.* But if I failed on condition (b), that is, if my authority in asking you was insufficient, then the quarrel would take longer, and I would have to argue my case (for example, I could say: *well, I did it last time, and the time before that, so it really is your turn this time*).

These are invented examples and it would be a shame not to make use of the real-life examples that are one of the strengths of Jackson and Jacobs' work. Here is one where B objects to the implication that he or she can do what is asked in the time available:

> *A:* If you have time, why don't you get the car washed too when you get the gas?
> *B:* But I gotta go to the grocery store and I gotta do laundry and I got . . . classes
> *A:* Yeah, but it'll only take about five minutes to do that
> *B:* Ohh okay

> A: It's not really that much time
> B: Okay
> A: It's awfully dirty
> B: Okay! I'll do it when I get the gas
> (Jackson and Jacobs, 1980: 261; transcription somewhat simplified)

The quarrel, then, is stimulated not by an assertion, but by the felicity condition failure of an indirect request. It forces B to give an objection (which is, in fact, an argument: they can't do it because . . .) and it forces A to make the argumentative case that the request was indeed for a feasible action: that getting the car washed wouldn't take an unreasonably or impossibly long time in the circumstances. (Moreover, just to be on the safe side, A adds extra information (*it's awfully dirty*) to protect her/himself against any objection about another felicity condition: that the job must require doing.) The whole thing is resolved when B shows that A has made her/his point – if anything, too strongly (*okay!*).

The identification of felicity conditions as things which can trigger a dispute also nicely handles the run of the mill, single-utterance claim-backings which are very common in ordinary speech (Antaki and Leudar, 1992). These are occasions where, as Jackson (1987) says, the speaker is foreseeing that she or he may be called to account for the manner or timing of their utterance, rather than any question of the truth or persuasiveness of its content. For example:

> A: m Thank you very much indeed – do you know anywhere which does . . .
> sort of . . . service flats for people 'cos I've got, I ·. . think I shall
> probably have to come up to town . . . and stay for a few weeks in . . . in
> October
> (LL, reproduced in Antaki and Leudar, 1992: 191)

What is being 'explained' is the conversational move of rhetorically asking *do you know anywhere which does service flats?*, and the 'explanation' reveals the propriety of raising the issue at all: a defence against a potential accusation of impertinence or, more technically, a failure to work to the cooperative injunction to be relevant. Another example, this time in dialogue:

> A: I would like to come back in the afternoon if I may
> B: I'll give you a key in any case
> A: And borrow your telephone if I could
> B: Yes, of course
> → A: Because I want to go and see . . . BBC film people and I must make an
> appointment to go and see them
> (Antaki and Leudar, 1992: 191)

Speaker A's arrowed turn warrants her imposition of making use of her interlocutor's telephone, a conversational move whose 'explanation' must be an account uncovering the reasons why it was a legitimate thing to do.

Clearly, in cases like these two examples, what is at issue is not merely the content of the utterance, but the interactional implications of raising it in a certain way. In other words, it is a particularly clear example of the case where the speaker has in mind not a factual, propositional case (that is to say, not something to do with a rival state of affairs in the world) but very obviously with something that is squarely located in the interaction itself. In the second example the speaker could have found some formulation which did not project the speaker as having to perform a favour (lending the speaker the use of their telephone), and in the first one the speaker could have found some way not to raise a question which conversationally obliges the other interactant to give an answer.

Speech acts and conversation analysis

Jackson and Jacobs agree with van Eemeren and Grootendorst that argument is a series of speech acts: an 'illocutionary act complex' or, as they would put it, an 'expanded speech act sequence' (Jackson and Jacobs, 1983). Their contribution is to signal that what originates the series of individual speech acts is the failure of one or more felicity conditions for any speech act (the preconditions which authorize it) – not just, as in van Eemeren and Grootendorst's model, the actual proposition asserted by person A. The benefits of this liberalization are enormous. Intuition tells us, and Jackson and Jacobs' data confirm (Jackson, 1987), that ordinary arguments are not limited to disagreements over assertions; it would be hard to make van Eemeren and Grootendorst's model apply to as broad a range of everyday arguments as Jackson and Jacobs'.

The invocation of conversation analysis does show up the sharp difference between a model of argument as a managed interaction and as an idealized debate. Jackson and Jacobs see the arguers as motivated to unblock the conversation; van Eemeren and Grootendorst see them as motivated to reach a resolution of a difference of opinion. Perhaps the difference comes down to their model of people: in one case, as social interactants who are keen above all else to keep their lines clear and open; and, in the other, rational beings who value truth over social tolerance.

Supplementing speech-act theory

Although it is still recognizably a speech-act model, Jackson and Jacobs' model does import the conversation-analytic maxim that the spirit of the interaction is disagreement management (rather than the achievement of a truthful resolution), and that the quarrel is constructed through the second speaker's orientation to something latent, though not necessarily visible, in the first speaker's utterance.

We might want to help the applicability of their model to everyday talk by reaching one level down to spot 'markers' of claim and backing, as is done in Schiffrin's (1987) model of how speakers make their talk cohere. Her model grants quite a significant role to argument, and, in broad outline, shares enough ground with a speech-act model to promise easy transfer: the explainer puts forward a position, or claim, and some disputable aspect of that claim is then supported. Within this broad outline, the model is also consistent with the notion that the disputable aspect of the claim need not be its surface proposition – it can be, as Schiffrin puts it in a nod towards Goffman and speakers' concern for the moral order, things like 'the speaker's stance vis-à-vis the facts', including the 'personal or moral implications' of what the speaker says, 'the kind of person the speaker is revealed to be' (1987: 18). Where the model diverges is that it insists that the claim and backing are (at least sometimes) identifiable through linguistic marking.

The principal markers that Schiffrin identifies are *y'know*, *because* and *so* (though see Altenberg, 1984, for a fuller list of potential argument connectives), which are all illustrated in the following extract (from one speaker's talk):

1	[Claim marked by *y'know*]	I believe in that. Whatever's gonna happen is gonna happen. I believe . . . that . . . y'know it's fate. It really is
2	[Backing marked by *because*]	Because eh my husband has a brother, that was killed in an automobile accident, and at the same time there was another fellow, in there, that walked away with not even a *scratch* on him. And I really fee– I don't feel y'can push fate, and I think a lot of people *do*. But I feel that you were put here for so many, years or whatever the case is, and that's how it was meant to be. Because like when *we* got married, we were supposed t'get married uh: like abut five months later. My husband got notice t'go into the service and we moved it up. And my father dies the week . . . after we got married. While we were on our honeymoon. And I just felt, that *move* was meant to be, because if not, he wouldn't have been there
3	[Conclusion marked by *so*]	So eh y'know it just s– seems that's how things work

(after Schiffrin, 1987: 49–50; but labelled and broken up differently)

Y'know marks the position to which the speaker is committed (*y'know, it's fate*); *because* marks the evidence which backs it (two stories about predestination); and *so* marks its confident restatement (*so eh y'know it just s– seems that's how things work*).

The difficulty about markers is that, as Schiffrin herself admits, they can also do other work. *Because* and *so* also have obvious employment as signals of straightforward causation, and *y'know* occurs often enough in attention-getters of all kinds. It is impossible to yoke them to particular speech functions. Moreover, she observes, listeners and analysts can spot something as being an argument without help from the explicit use of any markers at all.

This is at first sight disappointing news for us, but turns out in fact to be a positive and essential feature of her model, which holds that no stretch of talk can be understood by appeal only to devices like markers; it needs to be filled out with some attention to three other things. One of these is the exact context of the conversational exchange: the classic conversation-analytic claim, and the one we are looking to exploit. The other two, though, offer less comfort to conversation analysis. Schiffrin's model wants to disambiguate people's meaning (including, of special interest to us, their claims and backing) by appeal to the 'action structure' and the 'ideational structure' of what they are up to.

The 'action structure' is a description, one storey up, of what the conversation management is achieving (so a certain sequence of information-seeking and giving can be described as a 'clarification sequence'). This is probably compatible with conversation analysis, though purists would be puzzled as to what such abstraction might add to the understanding of the events going on at ground-floor level. They would be even more puzzled by the 'ideational level', since this seems to be a matter of the semantics of the various words used in the exchange (*so* and *because* mark what a semantic analysis would allegedly recognize as 'main' and 'subordinate' segments of argument).

Schiffrin's model seemed at the outset to be a path towards greater specification of the conversational mechanisms of claim-backing. But its ambition to mesh together different 'levels' of talk necessarily turns it towards greater reliance on abstraction and content. A more sternly conversation-analytic treatment would keep its head down and its eyes fixed more resolutely on the specifics.

This is perhaps an appropriate place to mention the very different French tradition of work on argumentative language (based around the work of Anscombre and Ducrot, 1983). They are in full agreement with van Eemeren and Grootendorst's view of argumentation as a social act, and would even lean towards Billig's insistence on its pervasiveness; their central notion, however, is that such argument can be done on a very small scale; indeed, that language even at its finest grain is, or can be, argumentative. There is a (large) class of words and expressions in the language – far larger than the markers identified by Schiffrin, or the connectives identified by Altenberg (1984) – that are, in themselves, infused with quasi-logical implications, and which drive the speaker and listener down a path towards a conclusion. Thus, for example, to use a word from the set that includes *nevertheless, in spite of* and *after all*, strongly implies that one is challenging the preceding material; to use the word *even* in a sentence like *they've even got a yacht* is to imply a claim that they have everything up to that luxury; words like *nearly* can be used to imply the virtual opposite of their face value (as in the implied argument that if someone *nearly won the election*, they did quite well, even though, literally, they lost); and so on. In short, any utterance that tries to limit the field of sensible subsequent ones has a dictionary's worth of devices to help it do so. As Anscombre and Ducrot put it:

> It is a constitutive feature of many utterances that they can't be used without attempting to orient the audience towards a certain type of conclusion . . . one ought, when one describes such an utterance, to say what orientation it bears, or . . . in favour of what argument it might be offered. (1989: 30; author's translation)

Their recommendation to analysts is that they look to the internal disposition of utterances to see how they lead the speaker and hearer towards this or that type of conclusion – an orientation not deducible merely from the informational content, but implied through the use of markers like the ones we saw above, independently of strict logic. This is partly understandable as a cognitive programme (which would help such enter-prises as the conversation model of attribution theory, as we saw in Chapter 3; indeed, some of its recent projects – for example, Kahneman and Varey, 1990 – come close to this pragmatic mapping, albeit as a matter of mental reasoning). It is, perhaps, more readily understandable as a pragmatic programme whose aim is to bring to the surface that class of implication which has the peculiar flavour (as not all implications have) of pushing on towards a conclusion. Some of these implications (coming from traditionally argumentative signals like *because, since, although, but*, and so on) can be handled by informal logic (as we saw in Chapter 8) but some escape them, and must be caught with a linguistic net.

The strength of the French work is its teasing out of the hidden force of certain words and expressions, enriching the flatter notion of argument 'markers'. However, like classic argumentation theory, its roots in tra-ditional pragmatics confine it to a test-bed of invented examples, the arbitration of which is in the hands of the analysts, rather than speakers and listeners. In that sense it is liable to the same objection with which we left Schiffrin's call to interpret the use of argument markers at an abstract level.

To keep hold of this objection while doubling back for a moment to the implications of Jackson and Jacobs' speech-act model: if we as analysts can spot the work that speakers are doing as a matter of management and sequencing, we can (as we did with exonerations in Chapter 5) leave off too much concern for classifying the steps in their arguments as being one or other identifiable linguistic act. Jackson and Jacobs' notion of the disputabi-lity of felicity conditions is, as we saw above, very useful for recognizing that argument can be started even where the facts of the matter aren't in dispute; but that can be decoupled from the notion that what the felicity conditions authorized were necessarily speech acts as such. We bear in mind Schiffrin's identification of the (occasional) markers *y'know, because* and *since*, and Anscombre and Ducrot's identification of the argumentative implications of a larger range of words and phrases, and move on to consider claim-backing much closer to the ground of interactive talk.

Claims in quarrels

The ground we want to cover takes us into more empirical territory. There is some very suggestive further work on arguments in the sense of quarrels which (usually implicitly) recognizes Jackson and Jacobs' point that disputes can be over felicity conditions as much as over propositions, and pushes towards a conversation-analytic account of what happens thereafter. Much of it is done in an ethnographic spirit, often (but not exclusively) taking as its data children's arguments. It stays one step back from pure conversation analysis in wanting, still, to describe what happens *functionally* (for example, for the consequences in maintaining children's friendships or staking out literal or metaphorical territory) and in describing the interactions above the level of the structure.

The general style is empirical, collecting episodes of argument from naturalistic observation (usually recorded on videotape, taking advantage of the possibilities of the controlled environments that kindergartens and junior schools offer). The definition of argument is a wide one, ranging from pure contradiction through disagreements to 'status disputes' and on to still less behaviourally specifiable 'adversative episodes'. Some of these require too much interpretation to fit happily into our ideal of participant-marked dispute, so we shan't be talking about rough-houses and other wrangles which aren't linguistically marked in some way.

Any event, according to the model we have brought with us from argumentation theory, can be the stimulus for an argument, and it is the *subsequent turns* that make what is said into a disputable position or not. A given turn admits of many readings, both of the proposition it expresses, and of the felicity conditions or validity claims it presupposes, and if the next speaker chooses to orientate to an 'arguable' one, then that is what it will be constituted as – until the original speaker's next turn, which could defuse the original implicit accusation, in which case the 'argument' will never have actually happened. Here is a prototypical example of a child choosing to construct the first speaker as making a point of factual dispute, and the first speaker then confirming it, and so on:

(US first-grade children, i.e. 4–6 years old)
B: This is my crayon right here
A: It is not
B: It is
A: It is not
B: It is too
A: It is not
B: Yes it is, yes it is, yes it is
(Maynard, 1985: 3)

Here, on the other hand, is an example where the argument stays potential:

(Ralph and Barb are at the drawing table)
Ralph: That doesn't look like a duck
             (1.6)
             Duck's supposed to have a beak
             (2.0)
Barb: [*shrugs*] Well, I could make a beak
(Maynard, 1985: 5)

Ralph's utterance constructs Barb as having claimed that her drawing was a duck. He gives her time to acknowledge the complaint and accept it; her silence (which, as we know, is a dispreferred response) gives him licence to take the floor again. His second utterance does three things at once: (a) it repeats his accusation; (b) it bolsters his own claim (by showing *how* it doesn't look like a duck); and (c) it offers a way in which the interaction can be repaired (by showing how the drawing could be rectified).

This is the point at which Barb can turn the interaction into a public quarrel or not (in just the same way Carol, in the ice-cream episode we looked at in Chapter 5, could turn Sherri's 'noticing' into the trigger for a public inquiry). Her turn is crucial. If she says something like *it* is *a duck* she will have unambiguously confirmed Ralph as making a proposition incompatible with her own claim, and the argument will be on; equally she might challenge the felicity conditions of what he says; for example, his authority in passing such a judgement (she might say *what do* you *know?*), and that, too, would confirm the argument as live. In fact, she chooses neither of these. The response she actually gives pacifically acknowledges the complaint's justification (by hedging her utterance with *well*) and resolves the situation by indicating that she will change the drawing, neatly constructing Ralph's utterance as an instruction to repair and, at the same time, carrying it out.

Three-part sequences in quarrels

There is something about the examples above that suggests a paring down of what is left of the speech-act model (which we saw at its most elaborate in van Eemeren and Grootendorst's model, but is still committed to an exchange of a multitude of speech acts in others') to a barer skeleton. What is common to all the versions we have seen so far is that the setting up of the argumentative interaction seems to involve three moves: speaker A makes some utterance; B orientates to a disputable meaning of that utterance; and A confirms that disputable meaning. If the second move isn't made, the argument stays potential, as we saw in the interaction between Ralph and Barb alone. A speech-act account would be that each of these moves is in itself recognizable by virtue of its content or its marking by some small set of indices (*y'know* and so on), and that what is at issue, if it is not the propositional content of the first utterance, is its stumbling over one or other of its conditions (felicity conditions or validity claims) that would authorize it.

The alternative now is to do away with a reliance on content and implied conditions as much as possible, and look only to visible structure and preference organization – to attack the problem with a conversation-analytic broadside. Coulter (1990) sets us off with an analysis of quarrels which are marked by assertion and counter-assertion, like this one:

A: Well, he had all the chances and didn't make much of 'em
B: That's not really true
A: Oh? Why not?

B: For a start, y'c'd hardly blame im for iz wife's illness and that's when the
      rot started (. . .)
(Coulter, 1990: 187)

Coulter whittles down the basic exchange to a regular structure of declarative assertion, followed by either a preferred agreement (in which no argument ensues) or a disagreement token or counter-assertion. If either of these latter two, then a third part is prefigured, which has to be either a backdown (which finishes the episode off), or a reassertion or next assertion (which prolongs it). Going back to the crayon example above:

B: This is my crayon right here   [*assertion*]
A: It is not   [*disagreement*]
B: It is   [*reassertion*]
A: It is not
B: It is too
A: It is not
B: Yes it is, yes it is, yes it is
(Maynard, 1985: 3; in this and the following examples, labels have been added)

A speech-act account would have it that, in turn 2, A is disputing some or other felicity condition authorizing B's turn 1. The more cautious conversation-analytic account would be that A is signalling that he or she has chosen to hear turn 1 as disputable (without going into the whys and wherefores). In so doing, turn 2 'constructs' turn 1 as disputable. That relieves the analyst from having to go to the theoretical trouble of trying to decide on B's (invisible) failures; it hands over to the participants themselves the arbitration as to whether or not the utterance is faulty. Treating the utterances as pairs which march with, or deviate from, simple statistical regularity excuses the analyst from sitting in judgement.

A conversation analysis could, as Coulter's (1990) does, stick only to straight disputes like this one, where what the second speaker disputes is a reading of the overt assertion in the previous turn; but, as we have seen, there is much else that can be disputable. We can drop the restriction on assertion and counter-assertion at this point, in recognition of the fact that the first utterance is only latent with argumentative meaning until the second utterance comes along and decides the issue one way or another. So to keep it at its most general, we might say that the sequence starts with A's pregnant utterance, which is then taken up by B's choice of dispute meaning and then prolonged by A's confirmation of dispute.

In the following example, we see that what turn 3 does is not to react to the overt assertion that Judy has or has not scribbled on Mary's paper (which she all too patently has) but reacts rather to its status as a 'noticing' flavoured with the sing-song intonational marker of teasing. The quarrel is set up, but is avoided at the last gasp, as it were, by the third part not being taken up:

(Judy and Mary are drawing together; Judy scribbles on Mary's paper;
Mary pushes part of her paper over part of Judy's)
1   J: [*shoulders slump*] Thank you
          [*Judy draws on her paper but the marks cross onto Mary's overlapping
          sheet*]

>   (2.0) [*M coughs twice*]
>   2   J: [*singsong*] I wrote on your paper   [*utterance*]
> → 3   M: [*mimics the same singsong*] I don't care   [*chooses disputable meaning*]
>   (4.8)   [*does not confirm disputable meaning*]
>   .4 M: What is that
>   5   J: A house
>   (Maynard, 1985: 12; paraphrases reworded)

Mary's arrowed turn can be read as turn 2 in the quarrel sequence. What happens thereafter will confirm it, but in fact there is quite a long period of silence which shows that Judy, whose turn it is, is backing down, or choosing not to take up its argumentative meaning. Mary confirms the non-argumentative reading by offering a cooperative change of topic after time for Judy's potential turn is up. Another example, this time in a sequence which Maynard insists (as ethnographers often do) can only be understood by appreciating the extra-conversational status of the particular participants:

>   (Gary, Andrea and Vicky at a table. Gary has already asked Andrea two 'what's that?' questions about parts of her drawing)
>   G: [*pointing to a third place*] What's that?
>   1   A: [*pointing to same area*] What does it say there?
>   G: [*nods*]
>   A: [*indecipherable*]
>   2   G: What? [*Vicky looks up from work and gazes at Gary*]
>   A: [*whisper indecipherable*] [*Vicky gets up from chair, stands next to Andrea, continues to gaze at Gary*]
>   3   V: None of your business!
>   (2.1) [*Gary moves from semi-slumped position in chair to straight-backed, neck-extended position. His gaze is directed up to Vicky*]
>   4   G: Jus' screw you
>   (3.5) [*Vicky's mouth drops open; Gary looks down and returns to his work in his reading book*]
> → 5   V: You're only five
>   [*Gary continues working, while Vicky repeats, several times, that he's 'only five'. She and Gary exchange a number of assertion/denial turns before someone makes a 'shh' sound*]
>   (Maynard, 1985: 16; comments paraphrased, and otherwise slightly simplified)

How to make sense of the arrowed insult? Maynard draws our attention away from the sequence itself and asks that we shouldn't interpret it as a literal argument about Gary's age, but we should see it as a continuation of the verbal and non-verbal interaction that went before. He infers a 'deep' level of interaction which makes sense of its surface content. A structural reading, however, wouldn't need 'depth' to see *you're only five* for what it is.

A three-part sequence reading of the interaction would go along these lines: Andrea has signalled a potential dispute by her combative reaction at (1) to Gary's question. Gary seems to be keeping the issue live at (2), at which Andrea makes an indecipherable utterance and Vicky intervenes, literally siding with Andrea and looking directly at Gary. This is the beginning of the sequence proper, as her utterance at (3) is easily interpretable as a verbalized dispute trigger, and Gary indeed chooses to reply to it in those terms at (4) with a sit-up posture and an insult formula. Vicky registers 'shock' and her utterance at (5) uses a 'noticing' to confirm that the dispute is on. We know by analogy with Schegloff's account of the ice-cream episode (see pp. 71–4) that by choosing to 'notice' Gary's age Andrea makes it relevant and accountable (in the way that we saw Sherri make Carol's not having the ice-cream relevant and accountable).

Although it is never developed in the rest of the interaction (not reported here), we (and Gary) will read Vicky's third part as energizing what was always latent in the interaction: Gary's 'moral status', specifically his right intrusively to interrogate people older than himself. This is sketchy, but it does show the possibility of doing all the analysis on one 'level' and not having to go down the dangerous road of separating 'deep' from 'surface' phenomena.

Nevertheless, some analysts would insist that there are 'deep' things that just can't be dealt with by insistently flat analysis. Emihovich (1986), for example, argues that you have to know the status hierarchy among a group of children before you can properly understand what's going on in their dispute. The worry of a conversation analyst is that there is no such thing as pre-existing 'status' (in the same way as there is no pre-existing 'blame-worthiness', or 'friendship' or other analytic category): there is only the practice of the moment, in which the participants construct themselves as having status or not (or being blameworthy or not, or being friends or enemies, and so on) by the way they organize their talk (for an eloquent account of the general version of this position, see Schegloff, 1992). 'Status' is just a short-hand for a certain combination of verbal practices (not being interrupted, taking long turns, not responding to others' first-pair parts, and so on). Anyone can try those practices out, and it will be up to the co-participants to ratify them or not. So to speak of the children coming into the interaction with pre-existing statuses is wrong, since status is always being constructed. When researchers talk of 'status hierarchies' they forget that these are always changing, and this leads them to the mistaken idea that the hierarchies somehow exist outside or 'before' the social interaction. This is a powerful reminder of conversation analysis' uncompromising but theoretically coherent position: that the social phenomenon exists at the moment of its being 'done' by the participants.

Claim-backing conventions

The section above pursued a structural analysis of claim-backing, but we need now perhaps to finish off by standing away from arguments with which we are wholly culturally familiar and in which the participants expertly managed their disagreements (quarrelsome though these might have been) by appeal to the same conversational conventions. Such harmony disguises the effect of certain features of the conversation which, when they go awry, perturb the smooth working of the argumentative exchange. If both parties are marching in step then we might be misled into thinking that the beat can safely be ignored as a variable for analysis. (The danger is indeed written into any idealized model of argument which, like abstract argumentation theory, is predicted on the optimistic notion that every combination of speaker and listener is equally competent in the language.)

It is worth, then, ending this chapter on claims and their backings by looking at occasions when the participants themselves seem to be having trouble understanding each other's arguments. From the resulting misunderstanding we shall hear the beat more plainly and realize that it runs at different rates for different people.

One such background convention, Gumperz (1992) shows, is the physical colouring of the talk – its intonation and other markings. This can be overlooked by the analyst because it is dealt with so smoothly by people who share the same conventions in its use. In an encounter between people who play to different conventions, though, it will produce misunderstandings grave enough to cause a dispute and unchain a series of claims and explanations which will, in their turn, fail to mesh together, and so prolong the problem.

The transcript below is part of a longer piece reported in Gumperz (1992). For the sake of clarity, I will pre-judge the reading of the extract by giving my paraphrase of what is going on. The setting is the office of Lee, a female native English speaker who is a lecturer at an adult education centre. Don is a male Indian student who, although he has lived in Britain since the 1960s, is currently on a course (referred to in the transcript as the 'twilight course') to improve English language communication skills. Don, who already holds a university degree from India, wants to attend a new and more vocational course. At the start of the encounter (which the transcript misses) Don says something which is heard by the lecturer as an accusation that she intentionally failed to send him the application forms for this new course. Two quarrels ensue. The first is whether or not Lee failed to send Don the forms. The second is whether Don is in any case eligible to be considered for the course.

We join the conversation at the point where Lee gives an explanation in reply to Don's apparent accusation of secrecy. The talk has been set out on separate lines to help the analysis.

Lee: 1 I haven't *said* it's a secret//
    2 <I didn't say it was a secret> what I *said* was/
    3 (.) that it was *not* a suitable course/
    4 (.) for you to *apply* for//
    5 because it is [*unintelligible*]//
    6 (.) [*lower pitch*] now if you *want* to apply for it/
    7 [*higher pitch*] of *course* you can do what you *want*//
    8 but/ [*higher pitch*] if you are *doing* the twilight course at the *moment*/(.)
    9 [*lower pitch*] it was *not* something which– (.)
    10 Mrs N and Mr G *thought/ originally/*

11   that it was a course to carry *on*/ *with* the twilight course/
12   [*higher pitch*] but that is NOT the case//

(Gumperz, 1992: 236; transcription slightly simplified. Material between < and
> is spoken faster. Double slashes indicate a final fall in intonation; single slashes
a slight fall 'indicating more is to come' (1992: 247))

Lee, the lecturer, uses a variety of stylistic devices common in her register
of native British speech to make her account cohere and to mark off its
various parts. She varies her intonation, finishing off five phrases (in lines 1,
4, 5, 7 and 12) with a clear final fall, giving what she says an air of
definiteness. She sets up the first part of a contrast in line 2 (*I didn't say it was
a secret what I* said *was*) which she completes immediately (*that it was* not *a
suitable course/ (.) for you to* apply *for*//) and again, binding the whole turn
together, right at the end (*but this is NOT the case*). She shifts pitch in a
regular way to signal which voice, or position, she is momentarily taking for
the purposes of her explanation: low pitch signals her own voice (*now if you
want to apply for it*), while high pitch signals (what she casts as) Don's
position (*if you are* doing *the twilight course at the* moment/). It all reads quite
clearly to a fellow native British speaker, familiar with her conventions: Lee
can be heard to be denying the accusation of keeping the course secret; as
clarifying that she did not, and does not, think that Don is suitable for it; and
(though this is less easy to interpret) as conceding that two other people may
have thought the new course was a continuation of the current one, but that
they were wrong.

Don, however, is working to different conventions. His response, which
comes immediately after Lee's *but that is NOT the case* is as follows:

Don: 1   No// what you – you take *one thing at a time*//
         2   this case// that whatever *they know*//
         3   I get even . . . hmm// for a Don . . . *me*//
         4   [*lower pitch*] and I am *student in E College*//
         5   and Mr W *knows me*// he// (.) I am student in the *same school*//
         6   he knows *my qualifications*// and what– whether I'm suitable *or not*//
         7   ⌈but
Lee: 1   ⌊This has nothing to DO with qualifications

(Gumperz, 1992: 238; transcription slightly simplified)

Two things stand out as general differences between Don's style and
Lee's. Don discriminates less between strong and neutral final falls, and his
contrast markings tend to fall on a group of syllables, rather than just one.
Both of these mean that the turn is less differentiated, or at least
differentiated in a way different from Lee's. Native British speakers would
have difficulty parcelling up Don's explanation in a way they wouldn't with
Lee's.

How can Don's account be glossed? By the initial *no* in line 1 he sets up an
explanation slot for himself (as we described it in Chapter 5) and seems to be
constructing Lee's previous utterance as being arguable. The next two words
(*what you–*) are choked off so the account seems to be subsequent *you take
one thing at a time*//, which ideally should be understandable as a specification
of exactly what is arguable about Lee's turn. It may not be so, partly since

the accenting pattern loads weight on an entire phrase (*one thing at a time*, where a native speaker might have only accented the last word), and partly because the construction could mean you *do* or you, or one, *ought to* take one thing at a time. The subsequent expansion, though, does not adequately disambiguate which of these claims he is making, again partly because of intonation: each segment is terminated with equal weight, unlike Lee's practice of selecting some, but not other, segments for highlighting. So Lee can't use the terminations to pick among Don's various possible expansions in lines 2, 3 and 4.

Moreover, his accenting conventions are different from Lee's: in line 4, he emphasizes the phrase *student in E College* at the expense of the rest of the phrase, which is spoken in low pitch; yet, on enquiry afterwards, Don tells Gumperz that he meant to inform the lecturer that he himself was already enrolled at the College which taught the new course – and so might be expected to know what he was talking about. His claims and their backings, then, don't come off, and what is responsible is the distance between his and his audience's intonation conventions. The upshot is that Lee reacts not to the issue of Don's knowledge of the course and the College which is offering it (an issue backing his claim that she withheld information about the course), but rather to the word 'qualifications' in his last utterance (she interrupts: *this has nothing to DO with qualifications*). By taking that word as the key she fuels the flames of a different quarrel and complicates the quarrel still further.

Were we to stop at this level of analysis I think we would already have learnt the useful lesson that an apparently routine channel of speech (in this case, intonation) carries a certain cargo of information which significantly affects the orderly progression through the standard three-part argument sequence. Gumperz does, however, go a little further, and we can link up what he says to the notion of 'genre' we came across in Chapter 7 on discourse analysis and the note on context we made earlier in this chapter.

The larger claim that Gumperz makes (see also Gumperz, 1982) is that background features (like intonation and so forth) have their effects by telling the listener what 'context' is in operation. He thinks of them as being subtle ways of instructing the listener to interpret what the speaker is saying as it (say) it took place in a courtroom or in a confessional, and so forth, That is, he is proposing that there is some set of devices in the talk without which a candidate utterance couldn't be heard as a proper 'claim' or 'backing'.

As an example of conflict between Don and Lee at that level of genre, consider this extract from further on in the conversation.

Lee: 1 I mean two things [*lower pitch*] I said/
2 <I said to you/> you can– you– I'll send you the things
3 when they *come*/ I've only just *received* them//
4 and *then* I said to you/ that I *didn't* think you were suitable/
5 OK/ *nothing* ⌈more
Don: 1   ⌊I didn't need it for myself//
2 because I came to *this course*//
3 uh heh heh/ and that eh– and that's *why it happened*

4   hmm I'm not *insulting you*// I just hm
5   feeling sorry for myself
(Gumperz, 1992: 249; transcription and numbering of lines simplified)

Don's non-take up of Lee's outlining and separation of the two quarrels (over the sending of the forms and her judgement of Don's suitability) may seem merely to be a sign of perversity or uncooperativeness, but what he says gives us a clue that he is indeed orientating to what she is saying, but is doing so according to a different 'genre'. Gumperz's Indian informants identified Don's use of *feeling sorry for myself* as coming from a different kind of encounter, in which the plaintiff assumes an explicitly inferior position to the figure in authority. (An example of this is an Indian claimant introducing a complaint about the non-payment of his unemployment cheque with the self-deprecation *I'm in terrible trouble*.) Don, then, is actually showing very clearly that he understands that Lee is describing disputes, but his manner of doing so comes from a genre which Lee (and the unprepared reader with different conventions) does not recognize.

This is not just a matter of claims or backing coming from different domains of knowledge, or being proper or improper in their content; it is a matter of their success or failure to mobilize something deeper and more fundamental about the communicative context in which the speakers find themselves.

Explanations, quarrels and conversational organization

We started this chapter by running through an idealized speech-act account of the way people back their claims, turning away (as we have done before in this book) from a strict speech-act path and approaching claim-backing instead as a part of some structured quarrel. We had reason, though, to query whether ordinary interlocutors would, as an idealized quarrel model might require, generally be driving towards rational agreement. Jackson and Jacobs' model seemed to square better with ordinary experience by allowing people the more achievable ambition merely of managing disagreement.

An important advance in their model is to recognize that interactants don't just argue about the face value of what they say. Quite how to deal with these covert aspects is a theoretical worry, though, and to avoid the difficulties in cataloguing (as a speech-act theorist would) the forests of potential felicity conditions through which speakers must navigate, one can (as a conversation analyst might) keep one's eye on the speakers themselves and see, by virtue of the twists and turns they take, how they are marking out the argumentative terrain.

That conversation-analytic approach seems to show interactants using a three-part sequence of claim and counter-claim as a ladder for the argumentative exchange, each step depending on the previous one and constructing it either as another rung up the dispute or as an opportunity to jump off. The speakers, by continually arbitrating on the acceptability of each other's claims, mark out the direction and the scale of the quarrel.

We have remarked that smoothly meshed performance can hide conventions which are nevertheless important in bringing the argument off. There is, of course, a large variety of potential ways in which an explanation might fail to warrant a speaker's claims, and the last section of this chapter has focused on one example of how incommensurate conventions can ruin participants' appreciation of where they are in the argument, prolonging the quarrel and perhaps making its claims and warrants unresolvable.

This chapter, like the one before it, has concentrated on explanation understood as 'making plain' in argument and quarrel. This has, of course, a family resemblance to all the other readings of explanation elsewhere in the book, and just as it would be possible to look back and see flashes of argumentation and dispute in virtually all of the previous chapters, one could equally find traces of exoneration, warranting and accounting in the material here.

Perhaps the last note to strike is the key of the theme that unites the treatment of explanation throughout the book. Explanations in argumentation, as in other domains, are part of the way in which people prosecute their interactional business. They do so by the language they use – at work, in court, at the doctor's, on a bus – and our job as analysts has been to look on and chart how explanations qualify as that kind of business-like talk. When participants argue and explain, they set up different versions of what is the case in the world, and deal with each other's proposals for how those different versions might be resolved: it is those accounts, and the way they deploy them, that keeps people on this side of the boundary of the moral order.

10

Conclusion: Explaining and Arguing in Participants' Own Words

The spirit of the book has been to look to *speakers' own practices* as the grounds for things that analysts might want to say about explaining and arguing. At the risk of repeating some of the things that have been weaving in and out of the chapters so far, it is perhaps worth just drawing the threads together so as to see what is at stake in taking this line of social scientific reasoning.

The strong form of the conversation analysis project – of which this book's account of explaining and arguing has been a rather dilute example – is very clear. It is only in the participants' own ways of organizing themselves, the conversation analysis argument runs, that we shall find solid ground for our analytical claims. That seems, on the face of it, to outlaw very many things with which social scientists are comfortable. The move from analysts' to participants' orientation seems to challenge social scientists' skills as informed readers of the common mind, and professional testers of their theories about it. It may appear unsatisfactory to sociologists, anthropologists and ethnographers, used to making their own claims about what Malinowski calls the 'context of culture' and the 'context of situation'. It might be specially uncomfortable for experimentalists, used to conceiving of behaviour as open to manipulation and to being restricted to the channels set out in controlled scenarios. Many social scientists are used to saying things about people's behaviour which do not rely on being grounded in the orientations of the people themselves. Some may choose not to check whether there is such grounding or not, since the kind of categories they think are operative are of a kind too distant from behaviour to be visible: the halo of class, the unconscious urges of psycho-dynamic forces, and so on. The domain of explanation and argument is not out of the reach of this general epistemological wrestling. Some social scientists will want to hang on, come what may, to the notion that there are things about explaining and arguing which are worth saying on their, as opposed to their subjects', analytical grounds.

This is what is at stake in the fighting over such apparently different claims as those of the cognitivists of Chapters 2 and 3, the social constructionists of Chapters 6 and 7 and the argumentation theorists of Chapter 9. All, in their various ways, wanted to keep the right to make analytic claims not grounded in the conduct of the people from whom they harvested their data. The cognitivist social psychologist might want to say about such-and-such a pattern of explaining that it demonstrated the inner workings of a mental process that had a bias towards attributing events to personal causes. The constructionist might want to say that this or that pattern of arguing demonstrated institutional discourses of sexism. The argument theorists might want to say that one child's dispute with another was a matter of status hierarchy and a metaphor for territorial claims. And so on. In all those kinds of cases – of which we have seen an abundance in this book – appeal is made to analytic categories and concepts (mental process, sexism, status) that might (as a matter of principle, or just by empirical chance) not actually appear in the overt orientations of the participants themselves.

The attraction of such reasoning is that it proceeds from categories that are well-established in theory and have a significance in either lay or social scientific talk, or in both: it would be an unfamiliar discipline to give up speaking of memory or stereotyping, or of gender, race and class, on the grounds that these did not feature visibly in the way that participants themselves conceived of what was going on in a given interaction. And yet this is what conversation analysis seems to be advocating.

Nevertheless, analytical categories have popped up insistently throughout this book, and context has often been provided to make sense of extracts of explaining and arguing (with such introductions as 'friends talking about jobs', or 'a counselling session', and so on); the habit of using familiar categories, and seeing them as somehow explanatory, is not easily lost. We see the same thing happening in Buttny's (1993) eloquent demonstration of the social construction of accounts. It is thick with appeal to participants' conversational organization and is a powerful argument in favour of dispensing with pre-given analytical categories. He carries off a story about a range of account-giving practices by appeal only (or very largely) to what the participants show him they are up to. Nevertheless he too has reason, on occasion, to tell us rather more about his participants' situation than is, strictly speaking, revealed through their talk: he needs to tell us that this talk comes from a television interview, that extract from a Zen tutorial, or from a couple-therapy session and so on. Indeed, his motivation to show how 'the consequences of accounts talk in interpersonal relations can affect one's claims to good character or alignments with others, and in institutional contexts can affect one's success or competencies' (Buttny, 1993: 170) is couched in terms of analytic categories familiar to the social scientist but, strictly speaking, nearer the social constructionist traditions of interpretation than to conversation analysis' blanker, more insistently local language. To that extent it keeps the door open to the analyst's interpretation of what counts as the proper context for interpretation. In this book too there have been occasions where it has been hard to resist interpretation. Certainly it seemed necessary, in the account of exonerations at least (Chapters 4 and 5), to have recourse to a culturally pre-given vocabulary of excuse and justification.

The attraction of giving an analytic context and offering one's own diagnosis of what is going on seems too strong to resist. Even Schegloff (1992), in perhaps the most steadfast argument in favour of conversation analysis' strong claim that everything is to be sought in the participants' own version of what counts as context, is not so dogmatic as to deny that extra information may on occasion be necessary. Rather such information is at best equivocal, and always less significant than the primary evidence of the participants' more explicit behaviour.

Finding participants' orientation in the wider context

What is this direct evidence that is open to us? Schegloff (1992) advises that if we think there are other things happening – if we believe that there is something in the wider context which is silently informing what is going on – then we should start looking for evidence of it in the territory immediately round about, and broaden our search only if the closest trawl reveals nothing. This sort of search will reveal things more or less close at hand which give the participants' context for, and so the sense of, the troublesome event. We saw an example of this sort of searching in the account of Dai's sherry party leave-taking episode on p. 89. We discovered Dai uttering what seemed, even in the local context, to be an absurd and pointless statement (*I can't offer you any of Malcolm's sherry because he hasn't got any*). But on looking back to the beginning of the interaction we saw that the participants themselves had given a context where this made perfect sense. Dai had initially been welcomed into the sherry party with the host's self-deprecating mention of the lack of drinks, marking it as an opening bracket ready, eventually, for Dai to close off. By doing so, Dai freed himself from his and the others' obligation to continue responding to each other's turns at talk, and allowed himself to take his leave. There, as Schegloff had advised, our puzzlement over what seemed a peculiar utterance (or, more precisely, an utterance that seemed not to attract the reaction that its outward peculiarity seemed to warrant) was dissolved once we had widened the focus and looked to another, earlier, part of the scene.

What social scientists may nevertheless find frustrating is this insistence on still looking for grounds within the talk, and not outside it. What has changed, they would object, is not the level of analysis, but only its extension in time. They can point, at the very least, to practical objections: researchers, they may complain, may have only limited chunks of data to work on, and might be unable to command extra access to the surrounding context. Moreover, they can go further and say that it is perverse to go to all that trouble when one could more easily invoke such obvious analytical concepts as personal motivation or social process. Why not just say, in this particular case: *Dai wanted to go*, or make an economical interpretative gloss: *Dai was being polite*? The reason, as conversation analysis is at pains to point out (as we saw in Chapter 5), is that these turn out, respectively, to be grounded in untestable guesswork (and in that sense conversation analysis shares behaviourists' suspicion of assertions about internal states) or unhelpful redescriptions that fail to explain just what is going on. In both cases, the landscape of what people actually do – even if we have to extend it outwards either side of the puzzling feature – is a more satisfying source of evidence.

Analytical categories

The unsatisfied analyst might press further. We may do away with internal states and descriptive glosses, but how can we do away with broad analytical categories like race, gender and occupation, or narrower ones like 'job interview', 'counselling session', 'medical examination' and so on? We have certainly had recourse to categories like these at various times in the book, even if only to set a scene (introducing a snatch of talk as coming from a counsellor or a caller, or a judge or a witness, for example). Categories like these figure very heavily in the traditional social scientist's (and the lay person's) analytic explanation of what is going on, and it is hard to give them up even if they fail to appear explictly in the narrower or wider landscape of the participants' visible interaction.

Take the following example. We have a set of observations about the explanations solicited, offered and evaluated as they come up in a series of selection interviews. As it happens, we are interested in the interviewers' treatment of candidates who differ on our social-scientific analytical category of *ethnic status*. We know that this status is available to the interviewers because of various signals in the physical set-up of the occasion: it is, we assert, there in the candidates' names on the application forms in front of the interviewers, and in the candidates' appearance, and so on.

Suppose now we trawl through the transcripts and find that the interviewers never display any explicit spoken orientation to the candidates' ethnic status (or, if you like, no orientation of any kind; there is no indexing of ethnic identity via body posture, facial expression and so on). On that score – on the grounds of participants' visible understandings – we have, apparently, no reason whatever to compare the behaviour of the interviewers (who we might know to be white) towards white and Asian candidates. Yet we proceed to do so, on a hunch that there might be something in them, and we find some significant pattern of results: that the Asians are routinely asked to account for themselves more often than the whites, for example, or that their accounts are less often ratified as acceptable, and so on.

There are, I think, three reactions that might count as conversation analysis responses to this state of affairs. The first, and most principled, is simply not to get involved, pleading that the situation is hypothetical, and refusing to concede that in such a case there would be no visible markers in the participants' orientations. This is a legitimate response, since the concession that there is indeed no identifiable marking of the candidates' ethnicity in the talk is a very large one. But let the conversation analyst grant the point, just to cover those cases where there does turn out to be no such marking, and so that we can go on to make the argument general.

The second response is to agree to enter into the debate, but once again to take up Schegloff's (1992) claim, and say that there might indeed be a proper reason to take ethnicity as the distinguishing factor in the treatment of the two groups of interviewees – were such grounds to appear in the talk immediately surrounding the interaction. The principle here would be that to take the beginning and end of each interview as the boundary of the interaction was to foreclose too early on what participants made of what was going on; there is no reason to suppose that the participants held off reflecting on the interviews before the interviewees came in or after the door had closed behind them. Were we to have access to the pre- and post-interview talk we might find that the interviewers commented on, paused at, left attributably unsaid, or in some other way marked the ethnic identity of the candidates they were about to see or had just seen. This would give us our warrant for claiming that ethnic identity was a factor in the interaction.

As a response to the accusation that familiar analytical categories are being missed, this insistence that we broaden the scope of context to incorporate more talk is an impeccably proper conversation-analytic reply, just as it was for dispensing with personal motivation, inner states and descriptive glosses. But many analysts (and certainly many of the discourse analysts we acquainted ourselves with in Chapter 7) may still express themselves unhappy. Rather than subject themselves to what they will see as laborious and roundabout empiricism, they will, on the contrary, press directly on to use what they see as the significant analytical category. Certainly those discourse analysts who insist on a politically committed engagement with the phenomena they study will be loath to give up such significant categories as class, race and gender, and will be puzzled at the requirement that, in our example, we search in the surrounding text before admitting that the ethnic identity of the candidates was the distinguishing factor in the interviewers' behaviour. If Asian interview candidates were called to account more often than whites, it would, a discourse analyst of this persuasion might argue, be intellectually perverse not to recognize the glaring fact that race was operative as a factor in the interaction, even if no participant made it an explicit issue there or in the surrounding text.

One can understand that kind of impatience in two ways. On the one hand, the analyst may be insisting that a certain social category is a factor in the phenomenon at hand because of its persuasiveness in some different, more overarching social theory. On such grounds it might not even be necessary to have two groups of interviewees, but simply to record the behaviour of interviewers to one group of candidates, and explain the appearance of significant degrees of accountability talk that they are subjected to by appeal to an independently argued theory of institutional racism. On the other hand, the analyst may be appealing to the brute empirical difference between the two observed groups, and here it does matter that there are two groups to be compared. These are grounds that come from an older rhetoric of evidence: that there is something to say about the category at issue (in our example here, ethnic identity) *if that is the distinguishing feature between the two sets of observations*. That is to say, we shall be allowed to make guesses about our analytic-but-unobserved categories when we can demonstrate that, in two sets of discriminably different observations, only that category (here, ethnicity) is the sustainable difference. (Of course, this is not to say that ethnicity is the 'explanation' of the difference, but rather to say that its marking is a part of the complex of what is going on, at least in the behaviour of the interviewers.)

But these grounds are only safe if one can be satisfied that there really is nothing else that distinguishes the two sets of observations from each other, and in that respect at least, a conversation analyst would be wearing just the same sceptical expression as the most tough-minded empiricist. They would want to know that no other descriptions of the scene admit of the same distinguishing factor. In our example, it must not be the case that all the Asians in the sample were men, or all the whites were old; or that there was a confound between ethnicity and class, or time of day, or interview room, or anything else that might be held to have the observed effect on the exchange of explanations or any other aspect of the conduct of the interviews.

In fact, it turns out that the very strongest form of the conversation analytic position is unlikely to be satisfied on this criterion: in keeping with the ethnomethodological tradition, it is at pains to remind us that the list of descriptions of events is in principle endless, so a search for the single, defining difference is liable to go unrewarded. At that point we seem to reach something of an impasse: on the one side stands the interpretative analyst willing to accept at least the empiricist criterion (that the category at issue does seem to distinguish one set of observations from others); and on the other side stands the quizzical ethnomethodologist, never wholly convinced that even the most appealing distinguishing category is the one the participants are playing to – unless they reveal it themselves. There is nothing to be done about this disagreement: either one is willing to grant the analysts' grounds for identifying what is at issue, or (even when it is such an obvious and important thing as ethnicity, or, had we chosen another example, gender, class and so forth) one is not. One side of the argument privileges the analyst's judgement, the other, the participants'.

Orientation in the wider text

There is, however, a third discursive position that detours round the impasse and finds a way of reconciling the two apparently conflicting demands of analytical inspiration and visibility. It could always be said that a category (ethnicity, in our long-suffering example) *was* indeed explicitly a textual issue, and an issue of participants' orientation, but *in the texts and discourses of society at large, and a matter of many players' orientations*, rather than only in the talk and orientations of the particular participants, or even in their extended surroundings. This is the kind of rapprochment favoured by discourse analysts who are keen to keep the criterion of people's own displayed understandings, but who also want to say something about analytical categories they consider to be at work in the general atmosphere of society.

We have seen examples of the style of reasoning that this mixture produces in the work of the Anglophone tradition represented perhaps most clearly by Edwards and Potter's talk-based discourse analysis. There, the system of reasoning is either literally or by analogy conversation analytical: claims about the categories at stake are grounded in the participants' texts, but such texts are extended outside the stricter confines of the physically present participants to include other sources. These might be the same people at other places and times, or might be their representatives, or co-category members, or opponents; in any case, there will be some principled reason for taking these new participants' texts as being somehow on the same footing as the original speakers'.

Ideally, of course, the reason for admitting these new sources as legitimate speakers in the scene will itself be grounded in participants' orientation: that the interviewers, in their ordinary routines around the workplace, advert in such and such a way to racist jokes, or subscribe to this or that equal-opportunities policy; or that, in their social lives, they express this or that orientation to issues of ethnicity; or that their daily practices include this or that categorization of people into groups; and so on. Evidence like this will, on this reading, count as grounds for taking the analytic category as operative, even if, in the closed forum of the smaller data set – the recorded interviews – there is no direct evidence of the category being at work. If it does not appear in the original speakers' orientation, evidence for the relevance of an analytic category can appear in: the orientation of the institution that employs them; the social network that supports them; the culture that privileges them; and so on, as far as one's level of abstraction demands, and one's ability to make the case can reach. That kind of argument does, I think, skirt round the blockage of the simple theorists-versus-participants conflict, and promises a principled way of saying something about factors that might be operative but un-oriented-to in the local talk.

Nevertheless, putting the case for treating analytical categories as matters of orientation on a wide, rather than a local, stage is speculative, and ahead of a sustained argument. The favoured style of reasoning in the greater part of this book has been to try out the discipline of operating without analytical categories, so far as that was possible. Had I attended to them from the beginning, I might have used the rationale of taking wider sources of orientation than the local turns-at-talk which are the more obviously secure footholds available to the sceptical analyst, and the result might have been a different book. However, until we have a fully powered rationale for taking wider, societal players as participants on the same footing as the actual people engaged in the interplay of conversational regulation, it is perhaps safer to stay there, on the ground, and let the actors themselves show us what is going on.

References

Abraham, C. (1988) Seeing the connections in lay causal explanation: a return to Heider. In D. Hilton (ed.), *Contemporary Science and Natural Explanation*. Brighton, England: Harvester

Altenberg, B. (1984) Causal linking in spoken and written English. *Studia Linguistica*, 38: 20–69

Anscombre, J.-C. and Ducrot, O. (1983) *L'argumentation dans la langue*. Liège: Margada

Antaki, C. (1988) Structures of belief and justification. In C. Antaki (ed.), *Analysing Everyday Explanation*. London: Sage

Antaki, C. and Leudar, I. (1992) Explanation in conversation: towards an argument model. *European Journal of Social Psychology*, 22: 181–94

Ashworth, P. D. (1979) *Social Interaction and Consciousness*. Chichester: Wiley

Atkinson, J. M. (1984) *Our Masters' Voices*. London: Routledge

Atkinson, J. M. and Drew, P. (1979) *Order in Court: The Organisation of Verbal Interaction in Judicial Settings*. London: Macmillan

Austin, J. L. (1961) A plea for excuses. In J. D. Urmson and G. Warnock (eds), *Philosophical Papers*. Oxford: Oxford University Press

Austin, J. L. (1962) *How to Do Things with Words*. Oxford: Clarendon Press

Backman, C. (1976) Explorations in psycho-ethics: the warranting of judgements. In R. Harré (ed.), *Life Sentences*. London: Wiley

Barthes, R. (1973) *Mythologies*. Selected and trans. from the French by Annette Lavers. London: Paladin

Beneke, T. (1982) *Men on Rape*. New York: St Martin's Press

Bennett, M. (1989) Children's understanding of the mitigating function of disclaimers. *Journal of Social Psychology*, 130: 29–37

Bergmann, J. R. (1992) Veiled moralities: notes on discretion in psychiatry. In P. Drew and J. Heritage (eds), *Talk at Work: Interaction in Institutional Settings*. Cambridge: Cambridge University Press

Billig, M. (1987) *Arguing and Thinking: A Rhetorical Approach to Social Psychology*. Cambridge: Cambridge University Press

Billig, M. (1989) The argumentative nature of holding strong views: a case study. *European Journal of Social Psychology*, 19: 203–23

Billig, M., Condor, S., Edwards, D., Gane, M., Middleton, D. and Radley, A. (1988) *Ideological Dilemmas*. London: Sage

Blair, J. A. (1987) Argumentation, inquiry and speech act theory. In F. H. van Eemeren, R. Grootendorst, J. A. Blair and C. A. Willard (eds), *Argumentation: Across the Lines of the Discipline*. Dordrecht: Foris

Blumstein, P. W., Carssow, K. G., Hall, J., Hawkins, B., Hoffman, R., Ishem, E., Maurer, C. P., Spens, D., Taylor, J. and Zimmerman, D. L. (1974) The honoring of accounts. *American Sociological Review*, 39: 551–66

Bourdieu, P. (1993) *The Field of Cultural Production: Essays on Art and Literature*. Cambridge: Polity Press

Britton, B. K. and Pellegrini, A. D. (eds) (1990) *Narrative Thought and Narrative Language*. Hillsdale, NJ: Erlbaum

Brown, R. and Fish, D. (1983) The psychological causality implicit in language. *Cognition*, 14: 237–73

Burke, K. (1945/69) *A Grammar of Motives*. Berkeley: University of California Press

Burman, E. and Parker, I. (eds) (1993) *Discourse Analytic Research*. London: Routledge

Burnett, R., McGhee, P. and Clarke, D. (eds) (1987) *Accounting for Relationships*. London: Methuen

Buttny, R. (1993) *Social Accountability in Communication*. London: Sage

Button, G. (1987) Moving out of closings. In G. Button and J. R. Lee (eds), *Talk and Social Organisation*. Clevedon: Multilingual Matters

Button, G. and Casey, N. (1984) Generating topic: the use of initial topic indicators. In J. M. Atkinson and J. Heritage (eds), *Structures of Social Action: Studies in Conversation Analysis*. Cambridge: Cambridge University Press

Button, G. and Casey, N. (1985) Topic nomination and topic pursuit. *Human Studies*, 8: 3–55

Cockcroft, R. and Cockcroft, S. M. (1992) *Persuading People: An Introduction to Rhetoric*. London: Macmillan

Cody, M. J. and McLaughlin, M. L. (1985) Models for the sequential construction of accounting episodes. In M. L. Knapp and G. R. Miller (eds), *Handbook of Interpersonal Communication*. Beverly Hills, CA: Sage

Cody, M. J. and McLaughlin, M. L. (1988) Accounts on trial: oral arguments in traffic court. In C. Antaki (ed.), *Analysing Everyday Explanation*. London: Sage

Cody, M. J. and McLaughlin, M. L. (1990) Interpersonal accounting. In H. Giles and W. P. Robinson (eds), *The Handbook of Language and Social Psychology*. Chichester: Wiley

Condor, S. (1990) The role of context in post-crisis social psychology. Paper presented to the 12th International Sociology Conference, Madrid

Conley, J. M. and O'Barr, W. M. (1990) Rules versus relationships in small claims disputes. In A. D. Grimshaw (ed.), *Conflict Talk*. Cambridge: Cambridge University Press

Coulter, J. (1979) Beliefs and practical understanding. In G. Psathas (ed.), *Everyday Language: Studies in Ethnomethodology*. New York: Irving

Coulter, J. (1990) Elementary properties of argument sequences. In G. Psathas (ed.), *Interaction Competence*. Washington, DC: University Press of America

Davidson, J. A. (1984) Subsequent versions of invitations, offers, requests and proposals, dealing with potential or actual rejection. In J. M. Atkinson and J. Heritage (eds), *Structures of Social Action*. Cambridge: Cambridge University Press

Deschamps, J.-C. (1983) Social attribution. In J. M. F. Jaspars, F. Fincham and M. Hewstone (eds), *Attribution Theory and Research: Conceptual, Developmental and Social Dimensions*. London: Academic Press

van Dijk, T. A. (ed.) (1985) *Handbook of Discourse Analysis*, 4 vols. London: Academic Press

van Dijk, T. A. (1992) Discourse and the denial of racism. *Discourse and Society*, 3: 87–118

Draper, S. (1988) What's going on in everyday explanation? In C. Antaki (ed.), *Analysing Everyday Explanation*. London: Sage

Edwards, D. and Potter, J. (1990) Nigel Lawson's tent: discourse analysis, attribution theory and the social psychology of a fact. *European Journal of Social Psychology*, 20: 24–40

Edwards, D. and Potter, J. (1992) *Discursive Psychology*. London: Sage

van Eemeren, F. (1986) The normative reconstruction of argumentative discourse. In T. Ensink, A. van Essen and T. van der Geest (eds), *Discourse Analysis and Public Life*. Dordrecht: Foris

van Eemeren, F. (1988) Argumentation analysis: a Dutch counter-balance. In A. Fisher (ed.), *Critical Thinking*. Proceedings of the First British Conference on Informal Logic and Critical Thinking. Norwich: University of East Anglia Press

van Eemeren, F. (1990) The study of argumentation as normative pragmatics. *Text*, 10: 37–44

van Eemeren, F. H. and Grootendorst, R. (1982) The speech acts of arguing and convincing in externalised discussions. *Journal of Pragmatics*, 6: 1–24

van Eemeren, F. H. and Grootendorst, R. (1984) *Speech Acts in Argumentative Discussions: A Theoretical Model for the Analysis of Discussions Directed towards Solving Conflicts of Opinion*. Dordrecht: Foris

van Eemeren, F. H., Grootendorst, R., Blair, J. A. and Willard, C. A. (eds) (1987a) *Argumentation: Across the Lines of the Discipline*. Dordrecht: Foris.

van Eemeren, F. H., Grootendorst, R. and Kruiger, T. (eds) (1987b) *Handbook of Argumentation Theory*. Dordrecht: Foris

Emihovich, C. (1986) Argument as assertion: contextual variations in children's disputes. *Language in Society*, 15: 485–500

Fairclough, N. (1992) Discourse and text: linguistic and intertextual analysis within discourse analysis. *Discourse and Society*, 3: 193–217

Felson, R. B. and Ribner, S. A. (1981) An attributional approach to accounts and sanctions for criminal violence. *Social Psychology Quarterly*, 44: 137–42

Fisher, A. (1988a) *Critical Thinking*. Proceedings of the 1st British Conference on Informal Logic and Critical Thinking, University of East Anglia

Fisher, A. (1988b) *The Logic of Real Arguments*. Cambridge: Cambridge University Press

Fisher, S. (1991) A discourse of the social: medical talk/power talk/oppositional talk? *Discourse and Society*, 2: 157–82

Fisher, S. and Groce, S. (1990) Accounting practices in medical interviews. *Language in Society*, 20: 225–50

Frayn, M. (ed.) (1963) *The Best of Beachcomber*. Harmondsworth, Middlesex: Penguin

Gastil, J. (1992) Undemocratic discourse: a review of theory and research on political discourse. *Discourse and Society*, 3: 469–500

Gergen, K. J. (1985) The social constructionist movement in modern psychology. *American Psychologist*, 40: 266–75

Gergen, K. and Gergen, M. (1987) Narratives of friendship. In R. Burnett, P. McGhee and D. Clarke (eds), *Accounting for Relationships*. London: Methuen

Gilbert, G. N. and Mulkay, M. (1984) *Opening Pandora's Box: A Sociological Analysis of Scientists' Discourse*. Cambridge: Cambridge University Press

Gill, R. (1993) Justifying injustice: broadcasters' accounts of inequality in radio. In E. Burman and I. Parker (eds), *Discourse Analytic Research*. London: Routledge

Goffman, E. (1956) Embarrassment and social organisation. *American Journal of Sociology*, 62: 264–74

Goffman, E. (1959) *The Presentation of Self in Everyday Life*. New York: Doubleday

Goffman, E. (1971) *Relations in Public: Microstudies of the Public Order*. New York: Basic Books

Goodwin, C. (1984) Notes on story structure and the organisation of participation. In J. M. Atkinson and J. Heritage (eds), *Structures of Social Action*. Cambridge: Cambridge University Press

Govier, T. (1985) *A Practical Study of Argument*. Belmont: Wadsworth

Govier, T. (1988) Ways of teaching reasoning directly. In A. Fisher (ed.), *Critical Thinking*. Proceedings of the First British Conference on Informal Logic and Critical Thinking. Norwich: University of East Anglia Press

Grice, H. P. (1975) Logic and conversation. In P. Cole and J. L. Morgan (eds), *Syntax and Semantics 3: Speech Acts*. New York: Academic Press

Gross, E. and Stone, G. P. (1964) Embarrassment and the analysis of role requirements. *American Journal of Sociology*, 60: 1–15

Gumperz, J. J. (1982) *Discourse Strategies*. Cambridge: Cambridge University Press

Gumperz, J. J. (1992) Contextualisation and context. In A. Duranti and C. Goodwin (eds), *Rethinking Context: Language as an Interactive Phenomenon*. Cambridge: Cambridge University Press

Habermas, J. (1984) *The Theory of Communicative Action*. Vol. 1: *Reason and the Rationalization of Society*. London: Heinemann

Hacker, K., Coste, T. G., Kamm, D. F. and Bybee, C. R. (1991) Oppositional readings of network television news: viewer deconstruction. *Discourse and Society*, 2: 183–202

Hale, C. L. (1987) A comparison of accounts: when is a failure not a failure? *Journal of Language and Social Psychology*, 66: 117–32

Harré, R. (1979) *Social Being: A Theory for Social Psychology*. Oxford: Blackwell

Harré, R. (1981) Expressive aspects of descriptions of others. In C. Antaki (ed.), *The Psychology of Ordinary Explanations of Social Behaviour*. London: Academic Press

Harris, B. and Harvey, J. H. (1981) Attribution theory: from phenomenal causality to the intuitive social scientist and beyond. In C. Antaki (ed.), *The Psychology of Ordinary Explanations of Social Behaviour*. London: Academic Press

Harvey, J. H., Weber, A. L. and Orbuch, T. L. (1990) *Interpersonal Accounts: A Social Psychological Perspective*. Oxford: Blackwell

Heath, C. (1988) Embarrassment and interactional organisation. In P. Drew and A. Wootton (eds), *Erving Goffman: Exploring the Interaction Order*. Oxford: Polity Press

Heider, F. (1944) Social perception and phenomenal causality. *Psychological Review*, 51: 358–74

Heider, F. (1958) *The Psychology of Interpersonal Relations*. New York: Wiley

Henriques, J. W., Hollway, W., Urwin, C., Venn, C. and Walkerdine, V. (1986) *Changing the Subject*. London: Methuen

Heritage, J. (1984) A change of state token and aspects of its sequential placement. In J. M. Atkinson and J. Heritage (eds), *Structures of Social Action: Studies in Conversation Analysis*. Cambridge: Cambridge University Press

Heritage, J. (1988) Explanations as accounts: a conversation-analytic approach. In C. Antaki (ed.), *Analysing Everyday Explanation*. London: Sage

Heritage, J. and Greatbatch, D. (1991) On the institutional character of institutional talk: the case of news interviews. In D. Boden and D. Zimmerman (eds), *Talk and Social Structure*. Cambridge: Polity Press

Heritage, J. and Watson, R. (1979) Formulations as conversational objects. In G. Psathas (ed.), *Everyday Language: Studies in Ethnomethodology*. New York: Irvington

Herzfeld, M. (1985) *The Poetics of Manhood: Contest and Identity in a Cretan Mountain Village*. Princeton, NJ: Princeton University Press

Hewitt, J. P. and Stokes, R. (1975) Disclaimers. *American Sociological Review*, 40: 1–11

Hewstone, M. (1989) *Causal Attribution: From Cognitive Processes to Collective Beliefs*. Oxford: Blackwell

Hewstone, M. and Jaspars, J. M. F. (1982) Intergroup relations and attribution processes. In H. Tajfel (ed.) *Social Identity and Intergroup Relations*. Cambridge: Cambridge University Press

Hewstone, M., Jaspars, J. M. F. and Lalljee, M. (1982) Social representations, social attribution and social identity: the intergroup images of 'public' and 'comprehensive' schoolboys. *European Journal of Social Psychology*, 12: 241–69

Hewstone, M. and Ward, C. (1985) Ethnocentrism and attribution in Southeast Asia. *Journal of Personality and Social Psychology*, 43: 889–900

Hilton, D. (1988) *Contemporary Science and Natural Explanations*. Brighton: Harvester Press

Hilton, D. (1990) Conversational processes and causal explanation. *Psychological Bulletin*, 107: 65–81

Hilton, D. (1991) A conversational model of causal attribution. In W. Stroebe and M. Hewstone (eds), *European Review of Social Psychology*, Vol. 2. Chichester: Wiley

Hilton, D. and Knibbs, C. S. (1988) The knowledge-structure and inductivist strategies in causal attribution: a direct comparison. *European Journal of Social Psychology*, 18: 79–92

Hilton, D. and Slugoski, B. (1986) Knowledge-based causal attribution: the abnormal conditions model. *Psychological Review*, 93: 75–88

Holland, D. and Quinn, N. (1987) *Cultural Models in Language and Thought*. Cambridge: Cambridge University Press

Holtgraves, R. (1989) The form and function of remedial moves. *Journal of Language and Social Psychology*, 8: 1–16

Howard, J. A. and Leventhal, R. (1985) The overdue courtship of attribution and labelling. *Social Psychology Quarterly*, 48: 191–202

Hutchins, E. (1987) Myth and experience in the Trobriand Islands. In D. Holland and N. Quinn (eds), *Cultural Models in Language and Thought*. Cambridge: Cambridge University Press

Jackson, S. (1987) Rational and pragmatic aspects of argument. In F. H. van Eemeren, R. Grootendorst, J. A. Blair and C. A. Willard (eds), *Argumentation: Across the Lines of the Discipline*. Dordrecht: Foris

Jackson, S. and Jacobs, S. (1980) Structure of conversational argument: pragmatic bases for the enthymeme. *Quarterly Journal of Speech*, 66: 251–65

Jackson, S. and Jacobs, S. (1983) Speech act structures in conversation: rational aspects of pragmatic coherence. In R. T. Craig and K. Tracy (eds), *Conversational Coherence*. Beverly Hills, CA: Sage

Jacobs, S. (1986) How to make an argument from example in discourse analysis. In D. Ellis and W. A. Donahue (eds), *Contemporary Issues in Language and Discourse Processes*. Hillsdale, NJ: LEA

Jacobs, S. (1987) The management of disagreement in conversation. In F. H. van Eemeren, R. Grootendorst, J. A. Blair, and C. A. Willard (eds), *Argumentation: Across the Lines of the Discipline*. Dordrecht: Foris

Jefferson, G. (1978) Sequential aspects of storytelling in conversation. In J. Schenkein (ed.) *Studies in the Organisation of Conversational Interaction*. New York: Academic Press

Jefferson, G. (1991) List construction as a task and resource. In G. Psathas and R. Frankel (eds), *Interactional Competence*. Hillsdale, NJ: Erlbaum

Kahneman, D. and Varey, C. A. (1990) Propensities and counterfactuals. *Journal of Personality and Social Psychology*, 59: 1101–10

Kelley, H. H. (1967) Attribution theory in social psychology. In D. Levine (ed.), *Nebraska Symposium on Motivation*, Vol. 15. Lincoln: University of Nebraska Press

Kelley, H. H. (1973) The processes of causal attribution. *American Psychologist*, 28: 107–28

Kempton, W. (1987) Two theories of home heat control. In D. Holland and N. Quinn (eds), *Cultural Models in Language and Thought*. Cambridge: Cambridge University Press

Kendon, A. (1982) The organisation of behaviour in face-to-face interaction: observations on the development of a methodology. In K. R. Scherer and P. Ekman (eds), *Handbook of Methods in Nonverbal Behaviour Research*. Cambridge: Cambridge University Press

Krantz, S. E. and Rude, S. (1984) Depressive attributions – selection of different causes or assignment of dimensional meanings. *Journal of Personality and Social Psychology*, 47: 93–203

Kruglanski, A. (1975) The endogenous–exogenous partition in attribution theory. *Psychological Review*, 82: 387–406

Kruglanski, A. (1988) *Basic Processes in Social Cognition: A Theory of Lay Epistemology*. New York: Plenum Press

Labov, W. (1972) *Language in the Inner City*. Philadelphia: University of Pennsylvania Press

Lakoff, G. (1987) *Women, Fire and Dangerous Things*. Chicago: Chicago University Press

Lakoff, G. and Johnson, M. (1980) *Metaphors We Live By*. Chicago: Chicago University Press

Lakoff, G. and Johnson, M. (1987) The metaphorical logic of rape. *Metaphor and Symbolic Activity*, 2: 73–9

Lalljee, M. (1981) Attribution and explanation. In C. Antaki (ed.), *The Psychology of Ordinary Explanations of Social Behaviour*. London: Academic Press

Langer, E., Blank, A. and Chanowitz, B. (1978) The mindlessness of ostensibly thoughtful action: the role of 'placebic' information in interpersonal interaction. *Journal of Personality and Social Psychology*, 36: 635–42

Levinson, S. (1983) *Pragmatics*. Cambridge: Cambridge University Press

Levinson, S. (1988) Putting linguistics on a proper footing. In P. Drew and A. Wootton (eds), *Erving Goffman: Exploring the Interaction Order*. Oxford: Polity Press

Locke, D. and Pennington, D. (1982) Reasons and causes: their role in attribution processes. *Journal of Personality and Social Psychology*, 42: 212–23

Lutz, C. (1987) Goals, events and understanding in Ifaluk emotion theory. In D. Holland and N. Quinn (eds), *Cultural Models in Language and Thought*. Cambridge: Cambridge University Press

Maynard, C. (1985) How children start arguments. *Language in Society*, 14: 1–30

McHoul, A. (in press) Discourse. In *Encyclopaedia of Language and Linguistics*. Oxford: Pergamon/University of Aberdeen Press

McLaughlin, M. L. (1990) Explanatory discourse and causal attribution. *Text*, 10: 63–8

McLaughlin, M. L., Cody, M. J. and O'Hair, H. D. (1983) The management of failure events:

some contextual determinants of accounting behaviour. *Human Communication Research*, 9: 208–24

McNaghten, P. (1993) Discourses of nature: argumentation and power. In E. Burman and I. Parker (eds), *Discourse Analytic Research*. London: Routledge

Mehan, H. (1990) Oracular reasoning in a psychiatric exam: the resolution of conflict in language. In A. D. Grimshaw (ed.), *Conflict Talk: Sociolinguistic Investigations of Arguments in Conversations*. Cambridge: Cambridge University Press

Mehrabian, A. (1967) Substitute for apology: manipulations of cognitions to reduce negative attitude toward self. *Psychological Reports*, 20: 687–92

Michael, M. (1989) Attribution and ordinary explanation: cognitivist predilections and pragmatist alternatives. *New Ideas in Psychology*, 7: 231–43

Miller, F. D., Smith, E. R. and Ulleman, J. (1981) Measurement and interpretation of situational and dispositional attributions. *Journal of Experimental Social Psychology*, 17: 80–95

Miller, J. G. (1984) Culture and the development of everyday social explanation. *Journal of Personality and Social Psychology*, 46: 961–78

Miller, M. (1987) Culture and collective argumentation. *Argumentation*, 1: 127–54

Mills, C. W. (1940) Situated actions and the vocabularies of motive. *American Sociological Review*, 5: 904–13

Mishler, E. G. (1986) The analysis of interview narratives. In T. R. Sarbin (ed.), *Narrative Psychology: The Storied Nature of Human Conduct*. New York: Preager

Mishler, E. G. (1992) Work, identity and narrative: an artist-craftsman's story. In G. C. Rosenwald and R. L. Ochberg (eds), *Storied Lives: The Cultural Politics of Self-understanding*. New Haven: Yale University Press

Moerman, M. (1973) The use of precedent in natural conversation. *Semiotica*, 9: 193–218

Moerman, M. (1988) *Talking Culture: Ethnography and Conversation Analysis*. Philadelphia: Philadelphia University Press

Morris, M. (1981) *Saying and Meaning in Puerto Rico*. Oxford: Pergamon

Morton, A. (1988) Making arguments explicit: the theoretical interest of practical difficulties. In A. Fisher (ed.), *Critical Thinking*. Proceedings of the First British Conference on Informal Logic and Critical Thinking. Norwich: University of East Anglia Press

Murray, K. (1985) Life as fiction. *Journal for the Theory of Social Behaviour*, 15: 172–85

Myers, G. (1989) Persuasion, power and the conversational model. *Economy and Society*, 18: 221–44

Nichols, L. (1990) Reconceptualising social accounts: an agenda for theory building and empirical research. *Current Perspectives in Social Theory*, 10: 113–44

Ong, W. J. (1958/1983) *Ramus: Method and the Decay of Dialogue*. Harvard: Harvard University Press

Paprotte, W. and Dirven, R. (eds) (1985) *The Ubiquity of Metaphor: Metaphor in Language and Thought*. Amsterdam: John Benjamins

Parker, I. (1992) *Discourse Dynamics*. London: Routledge

Parker, I. and Burman, E. (1993) Against discursive imperialism, empiricism and constructionism: thirty-two problems with discourse analysis. In E. Burman and I. Parker (eds), *Discourse Analytic Research*. London: Routledge

Paul, R. W. (1987) Critical thinking in the strong and the role of argumentation. In F. H. van Eemeren, R. Grootendorst, J. A. Blair and C. A. Willard (eds), *Argumentation: Across the Lines of the Discipline*. Dordrecht: Foris

Pavel, T. G. (1986) *Fictional Worlds*. Harvard: Harvard University Press

Perelman, C. and Olbrechts-Tyteca, L. (1969) *The New Rhetoric: A Treatise on Argumentation*. London: University of Notre Dame Press

Pettigrew, T. F. (1979) The ultimate attribution error: extending Allport's analysis of prejudice. *Personality and Social Psychology Bulletin*, 5: 461–76

Philips, S. U. (1990) The judge as third party in American trial court conflict talk. In A. D. Grimshaw (ed.), *Conflict Talk: Sociolinguistic Investigations of Arguments in Conversations*. Cambridge: Cambridge University Press

Pollner, M. (1974) Mundane reasoning. *Philosophy of the Social Sciences*, 4: 35–54

Pollner, M. (1979) Explicative transactions: making and managing meaning in traffic courts. In G. Psathas (ed.), *Everyday Language: Studies in Ethnomethodology*. New York: Irving

Pollock, J. L. (1987) Defeasible reasoning. *Cognitive Science*, 11: 481–518

Pomerantz, A. (1978) Attributions of responsibility, blamings. *Sociology*, 12: 115–21

Pomerantz, A. (1980) Telling my side: 'limited access' as a 'fishing' device. *Sociological Inquiry*, 50: 186–98

Pomerantz, A. (1984a) Descriptions in legal settings. In G. Button and J. Lee (eds), *Talk and Social Organisation*. Clevedon: Multilingual Matters

Pomerantz, A. (1984b) Agreeing and disagreeing with assessments: some features of preferred/dispreferred turn shapes. In J. M. Atkinson and J. Heritage (eds), *Structures of Social Action: Studies in Conversation Analysis*. Cambridge: Cambridge University Press

Pomerantz, A. M. (1986) Extreme case formulations: a way of legitimizing claims. *Human Studies*, 9: 219–30

Pomerantz, A. and Atkinson, J. M. (1984) Ethnomethodology, conversation analysis and the study of courtroom interaction. In D. J. Muller, D. E. Blackman and A. J. Chapman (eds), *Topics in Psychology and the Law*. Chichester: Wiley

Potter, J. and Wetherell, M. (1987) *Discourse and Social Psychology: Beyond Attitudes and Behaviour*. London: Sage

Propp, V. (1968) *The Morphology of the Folktale*. Austin: University of Texas Press. (Original published in Russian, 1928)

Quinn, N. and Holland, D. (1987) Culture and cognition. In D. Holland and N. Quinn (eds), *Cultural Models in Language and Thought*. Cambridge: Cambridge University Press

Reddy, M. J. (1979) The conduit metaphor – a case of frame conflict in our language about language. In A. Ortony (ed.), *Metaphor and Thought*. Cambridge: Cambridge University Press

Riordan, C. A., Marlin, N. A. and Kellogg, R. T. (1983) The effectiveness of accounts following transgression. *Social Psychology Quarterly*, 46: 213–19

Rimmershaw, R. (1992) A discourse repertoire for negotiating explanations. In R. Moyse and M. T. Elson-Cook (eds), *Knowledge Negotiation*. London: Academic Press

Rosenwald, G. C. and Ochberg, R. L. (1992) *Storied Lives*. New Haven, Conn.: Yale University Press

Ross, M. and Fletcher, G. J. O. (1985) Attribution and social perception. In G. Lindzey and E. Aronson (eds), *Handbook of Social Psychology*, Vol. 2, 3rd edition. New York: Random House

Russell, D. (1982) The causal dimension scale: a measure of how individuals perceive causes. *Journal of Personality and Social Psychology*, 42: 1137–45

Sabini, J. and Silver, M. (1982) Baseball and hot sauce. *Journal for the Theory of Social Behaviour*, 10: 83–95

Sacks, H. (1972) On the analysability of stories by children. In J. J. Gumperz and D. Hymes (eds), *Directions in Sociolinguistics: The Ethnography of Communication*. New York: Holt, Rinehart and Winston

Sacks, H. (1974) An analysis of a joke's telling in conversation. In R. Bauman and J. Sherzer (eds), *Explorations in the Ethnography of Speaking*. Cambridge: Cambridge University Press

Sacks, H. (1984) On doing 'being ordinary'. Compiled by G. Jefferson, in J. M. Atkinson and J. Heritage (eds), *Structures of Social Action: Studies in Conversation Analysis*. Cambridge: Cambridge University Press

Sacks, H., Schegloff, E. A. and Jefferson, G. (1978) A simplest systematics for the organisation of turn-taking in conversation. In J. N. Schenkein (ed.), *Studies in the Organization of Conversational Interaction*. New York: Academic Press

Schegloff, E. A. (1988) Goffman and the analysis of conversation. In P. Drew and A. Wootton (eds), *Erving Goffman: Exploring the Interaction Order*. Cambridge: Polity Press

Schegloff, E. A. (1992) In another context. In A. Duranti and C. Goodwin (eds), *Rethinking Context: Language as an Interactive Phenomenon*. Cambridge: Cambridge University Press

Schenkein, J. N. (1978) Identity negotiation in conversation. In J. N. Schenkein (ed.), *Studies in the Organisation of Conversational Interaction*. New York: Academic Press
Schiffrin, D. (1984) Jewish argument as sociability. *Language in Society*, 13: 311–35
Schiffrin, D. (1985) Everyday argument: the organisation of diversity in talk. In T. van Dijk (ed.), *Handbook of Discourse Analysis*. New York: Academic Press
Schiffrin, D. (1987) *Discourse Markers*. Cambridge: Cambridge University Press
Schlenker, B. R. (1980) *Impression Management*. Monterey: Brooks/Cole
Schlenker, B. R. and Darby, B. W. (1981) The use of apologies in social predicaments. *Social Psychology Quarterly*, 44: 271–8
Schlenker, B. R. and Leary, M. R. (1982) Social anxiety and self-presentation: a conceptualisation and model. *Psychological Bulletin*, 92: 641–69
Schönbach, P. (1980) A category system for account phases. *European Journal of Social Psychology*, 10: 195–200
Schönbach, P. and Kleibaumhüter, P. (1989) Severity of reproach and defensiveness of accounts. In M. J. Cody and M. L. McLaughlin (eds), *The Psychology of Tactical Communications*. Clevedon: Multilingual Matters
Scott, M. B. and Lyman, S. M. (1968) Accounts. *American Sociological Review*, 33: 46–62
Scriven, M. (1976) *Reasoning*. New York: McGraw-Hill
Semin, G. R. (1980) A gloss on attribution theory. *British Journal of Social Psychology*, 19: 291–300
Semin, G. R. and Fiedler, K. (1988) The cognitive functions of linguistic categories in describing persons: social cognition and language. *Journal of Personality and Social Psychology*, 54: 558–68
Semin, G. R. and Manstead, A. S. R. (1983) *The Accountability of Conduct*. London: Academic Press
Shotter, J. (1981) Telling and reporting. In C. Antaki (ed.), *The Psychology of Ordinary Explanation of Social Behaviour*. London: Academic Press
Shotter, J. and Gergen, K. J. (1990) *Texts of Identity*. London: Sage
Shweder, R. A. and Miller, J. G. (1985) The social construction of the person: how is it possible? In K. J. Davis and K. Gergen (eds), *The Social Construction of the Person*. New York: Springer-Verlag
Snyder, C. R., Higgins, R. L. and Stucky, R. J. (1983) *Excuses: Masquerades in Search of Grace*. New York: Wiley
Svartvik, J. and Quirk, R. (1980) *A Corpus of Conversational English*. Lund, Sweden: Gleerup
Sykes, G. M. and Matza, D. (1957) Techniques of neutralisation: a theory of delinquency. *American Sociological Review*, 22: 664–70
Taylor, T. and Cameron, D. (1987) *Analysing Conversation: Rules and Units in the Structure of Talk*. Oxford: Pergamon
Tedeschi, J. and Reiss, M. (1981) Verbal strategies in impression management. In C. Antaki (ed.), *The Psychology of Ordinary Explanations of Social Behaviour*. London: Academic Press
Thomas, S. N. (1986) *Practical Reasoning in Natural Language*. Englewood Cliffs, NJ: Prentice Hall
Todorov, T. (1984) *Mikhail Bakhtin: The Dialogical Principle*. Manchester: Manchester University Press
Toulmin, S. (1958) *The Uses of Argument*. Cambridge: Cambridge University Press
Toulmin, S., Rieke, R. and Janik, A. (1979) *An Introduction to Reasoning*. New York: Macmillan
Turnbull, W. and Slugoski, B. (1988) Conversational and linguistic processes in causal attribution. In D. Hilton (ed.), *Contemporary Science and Natural Explanation*. Brighton, England: Harvester
Ungar, S. (1981) The effects of status and excuse on interpersonal reactions to deviant behaviour. *Social Psychology Quarterly*, 44: 260–3
Vickers, B. (1988) *In Defence of Rhetoric*. Oxford: Oxford University Press
Vuchinich, S. (1990) The sequential organisation of closing in verbal family conflict. In A. D.

Grimshaw (ed.), *Conflict Talk: Sociolinguistic Investigations of Arguments in Conversations*. Cambridge: Cambridge University Press

Wales, K. (1989) *A Dictionary of Stylistics*. London: Longman

Weiner, B. (1986) *An Attributional Theory of Motivation and Emotion*. New York: Springer-Verlag

Weiner, B., Amirkham, J., Folkes, V. S. and Verette, J. A. (1987) An attributional analysis of excuse giving: studies of a naive theory of emotion. *Journal of Personality and Social Psychology*, 52: 316–24

Wetherell, M. and Potter, J. (1988) Discourse analysis and the social psychology of racism. In C. Antaki (ed.), *Analysing Everyday Explanation: A Casebook of Methods*. London: Sage

Wetherell, M. and Potter, J. (1989) Narrative characters and accounting for violence. In J. Shotter and K. Gergen (eds), *Texts of Identity*. London: Sage

Wetherell, M. and Potter, J. (1992) *Mapping the Language of Racism: Discourse and the Legitimation of Exploitation*. Hemel Hempstead: Harvester Wheatsheaf

Whalen, M. R. and Zimmerman, D. H. (1990) Describing trouble: practical epistemology in citizen calls to the police. *Language in Society*, 19: 465–92

White, P. A. (1989) A theory of causal processing. *British Journal of Psychology*, 80: 431–54

White, P. A. (1990) Ideas about causation in philosophy and psychology. *Psychological Bulletin*, 108: 3–18

White, P. A. (1991) Ambiguity in the internal/external distinction in causal attribution. *Journal of Experimental Social Psychology*, 27: 259–70

Widdicombe, S. (1993) Autobiography and change: rhetoric and authenticity of 'Gothic' style. In E. Burman and I. Parker (eds), *Discourse Analytic Research*. London: Routledge

Wooffitt, R. (1992) *Telling Tales of the Unexpected: The Organisation of Factual Discourse*. Hemel Hempstead: Harvester Wheatsheaf

Zimmerman, D. H. (1992) The interactional organisation of calls for emergency assistance. In P. Drew and J. Heritage (eds), *Talk at Work: Interaction in Institutional Settings*. Cambridge: Cambridge University Press

Index

Abraham, C., 12
accountability, 40, 41, 42
accounts
  conversation analysis, 107–13
  explanatory, 113–14
  formal description of, 94
  for offences, self-presentation, 45–6
  prefacing, 108–9
  sequential organization, 65, 107–8
  towards a simpler conceptual structure of, 66–7
  and social constructionism, 92–101
  structure of, 94
  use of exonerations, 50–2
    organization of, 60–2
  as variable, interested and constructive, 117–19
  see also storied accounts
'accounts literature', 44–8
  model of language in the, 53–60
accusations, identifying in talk, 57–9
action
  explanation as, 39–41
  talk in, 119–20
  voluntary and involuntary, 18, 23
adjacency pairs, 69, 80–8
  argumentative, 169–70
Altenberg, B., 174, 175
analogy, arguments by, 145
analysis of variance, 14–15
analytical categories, 188, 190–2, 193
Anscombre, J.-C., 175
Antaki, C., 8, 87, 142, 172
anthropology, 57, 100–1, 118, 150
arbitration, 60
arguing
  convincing and persuading, 166
  over differences of opinion, 159–60
  in participant's own words, 187–94
  as social fabric, 156–60
  as a speech act, 164–6
argument, 139
  analysis, 140–51
  compared with quarrel, 140

argument, *cont.*
  defining and assessing an, 147–50
  as a dialectical process, 147
  different from explanation, 140–2
  discipline-based modelling, 146
  logic in understanding ordinary, 142–51
  mainstream modelling of natural, 147
  modelling as general critical thinking, 146–7
  and quarrelling, 156–7
  quasi-logical, 155
  and rhetoric, 152–5
  types, 153
  war metaphor, 102–3
argumentation, 148–50
  'collective', 150
argumentation theory, 163–4, 187, 188
  speech acts in idealized, 164–9
argumentative language, studies of, 175
argumentativeness, Billig's rhetoric and, 156–61
Ashworth, P. D., 50
assessment
  assessment and agreement pair, 81–4
  choices, 83
  evaluations, 82
  factual claims, 82
  formulations, 83
  initiated, 88
Atkinson J. M., 60–3, 66, 133
attribution
  of cause, 8–26
  conversation model of, 28–38
  see also discursive action model (Edwards and Potter)
attribution theory, 5, 9–15
  classic, 25–6
  contribution to the study of ordinary explanation, 25–6
  and group functions, 24–5
  Heider's, 9–15, 38
attributional reasoning paradigm, 15–16
attributions, functions of, 24–5
audience, in rhetoric, 154–5